EYEWITNESS TRAVEL

P9-DCM-443

TOP 10
NEW YORK CITY

ELEANOR BERMAN

DK | Penguin Random House

Top 10 New York Highlights

The Top 10 of Everything

CONTENTS

New York Area by Area

Within each Top 10 list in this book, no hierarchy of quality or popularity is implied. All 10 are, in the editor's opinion, of roughly equal merit.
  Throughout this book, floors are referred to in accordance with American usage; i.e., the "first floor" is at ground level.

Front cover and spine *New York's iconic yellow cabs*
Back cover *New York City skyline from Brooklyn Bridge*
Title page *Aerial view of the Manhattan skyline at night*

Streetsmart

Welcome to
New York

High-kicking Broadway show tunes. World-class museums. Shopping on Fifth Avenue. Some of the tallest skyscrapers on the planet. Superlative cuisine – and cocktails. It's no surprise that New York is one of the most visited cities in the world. With Eyewitness Top 10 New York, it's yours to explore.

New York, New York. As the saying goes, it's the city so nice, they named it twice. We agree: where else in the country can you cruise down the mighty **Hudson River**, climb to the crown of **Lady Liberty**, peruse phenomenal art and sculpture at the **Metropolitan Museum of Art**, stroll the shaded walkways of **Central Park**, and sip cocktails while gazing out at the most famous skyline in the world?

Few cities equal New York's marvelously diverse culinary offerings. It's not a question of finding a cuisine, but rather of choosing from the plethora of options, from boisterous Italian trattorias to old-world delis with towering pastrami sandwiches. The outstanding museums and iconic sights are equally varied, from the looming **Empire State Building** to the **Museum of Modern Art**, with one of the world's largest collections of contemporary art. The theater scene is also incomparable, from splashy Broadway shows with a cast of hundreds to tiny underground stages. Spend one evening on the buzzing streets of New York City and you will understand why it's called the city that never sleeps. Evenings start late, and go on even later, with bars and clubs in the Meatpacking District and the **Lower East Side** spilling over with revelers.

Whether you're coming for a weekend or a week, our Top 10 guide brings together the best of everything the city can offer, from trendy **TriBeCa** to the elegant **Upper East Side**. There are tips throughout, from seeking out what's free to finding the liveliest festivals, plus easy-to-follow itineraries, designed to tie together a slew of sights in a short space of time. Add inspiring photography and detailed maps, and you've got the essential pocket-sized travel companion. **Enjoy the book, and enjoy New York.**

Clockwise from top: **Fulton St subway, Lower Manhattan skyscrapers, Statue of Liberty, Grand Central Terminal, Times Square, Chrysler Building, Bethesda Terrace Arcade in Central Park**

Exploring New York

New York City is densely packed with sights and sounds. Whether you are visiting for a weekend or a week, it helps to strategize your sightseeing to maximize your time here. Here are ideas for two and four days of exploring the city.

Two Days in New York

Day ❶
MORNING

Enjoy the view from the Statue of Liberty (see pp20–21), then saunter through Lower Manhattan (see pp78–83), snapping photos of Brooklyn Bridge (see p85). Have lunch in South Street Seaport (see p89).

AFTERNOON

Stroll through Central Park (see pp32–3) before perusing the Metropolitan Museum of Art (see pp34–7).

Day ❷
MORNING

Enjoy panoramic skyline views from atop the Empire State Building (see pp12–13), followed by a walk up Fifth Avenue (see pp14–15), making stops at its famous department stores.

AFTERNOON

Tour the American Museum of Natural History (see pp40–43), before topping off your visit amid the flashing lights of Times Square and the Theater District (see pp28–31).

Four Days in New York

Day ❶
MORNING

Get the lay of the land from atop the Empire State Building (see pp12–13). Afterwards, window-shop along Fifth Avenue (see pp14–15). You'll pass the famous stone lions fronting the New York Public Library (see p128), then pop into Grand Central Terminal (see p127) before taking a twirl through Rockefeller Center (see pp16–19).

AFTERNOON

Explore the superlative collections of the Metropolitan Museum of Art (see pp34–7), followed by a relaxing walk through Central Park (see pp32–3).

Skyscrapers in Lower Manhattan tower over the streets below.

The nearby Guggenheim Museum (see pp38–9) also makes for an easy and fascinating stop-in.

Day ❷
MORNING

Take the ferry (book ahead) to greet the morning on Ellis Island (see pp22–5), followed by views from the crown of the Statue of Liberty (see pp20–21).

AFTERNOON

Upon returning to Manhattan, walk through Battery Park (see p81) to the National September 11 Memorial and Museum (see p80). Afterwards, head through Lower Manhattan, passing City Hall Park (see p87) and the Brooklyn Bridge (see p85). Hop on the subway or walk to the Lower East Side and East Village (see pp96–101) for dinner and cocktails.

Day ❸
MORNING

Arrive early at the American Museum of Natural History (see pp40–43) for a morning of exploration, plus a visit to the Rose Center for Earth and Space.

The facade of Grand Central Terminal is topped by a 13-ft- (4-m-) high clock.

City Hall Park is a peaceful spot next to City Hall and the Municipal Building.

AFTERNOON

Walk through the **Upper West Side** (see pp142–7) to the **Lincoln Center** (see p142), then head to **Times Square and the Theater District** (see pp28–31). Nab tickets to a Broadway show at the **TKTS booth** (see p73).

Day ❹
MORNING

Explore the elevated park, the **High Line** (see p121). Refuel at the **Chelsea Market** (see p122) with artisanal cheeses and fresh baked goods.

AFTERNOON

Explore **Greenwich Village** (see pp108–13), passing **Washington Square Park** (see pp108–9) on the way to **SoHo and TriBeCa** (see pp102–7) for local cuisine and cocktails.

Key

— Two-day itinerary
— Four-day itinerary

Top 10 New York Highlights

Manhattan skyline

TOP10 New York Highlights

With its skyscrapers, great museums, and bright Broadway lights, New York is a city of superlatives. There are countless sights that have to be seen, but a handful are truly definitive of the city. The following chapter illustrates the very best of these.

1 Empire State Building
This Art Deco skyscraper is one of the most widely recognized symbols of the city. It offers unforgettable panoramas (see pp12–13).

2 Fifth Avenue
Fashionable shops and world-class architecture define this avenue, one of New York's best-known addresses (see pp14–15).

3 Rockefeller Center
An urban wonder, with gardens, restaurants, stores, over 100 artworks, offices, and a skating rink (see pp16–19).

4 Statue of Liberty

The lady holding the torch is the symbol of freedom for millions seeking a new life in the US *(see pp20–21)*.

5 Ellis Island

Carefully restored buildings bring to life the experience of the immigrants who have poured into New York over the years *(see pp22–5)*.

6 Times Square and the Theater District

An explosion of neon illuminates Broadway and Times Square, where more than 40 famous theaters play host to a changing parade of hit shows *(see pp28–31)*.

7 Central Park

The swath of green gives respite from the city's concrete. It took 16 years and over 500,000 trees to complete *(see pp32–3)*.

8 Metropolitan Museum of Art

It would take weeks to see all the treasures of this museum. It houses one of the greatest collections of the Western world and spans 5,000 years of culture *(see pp34–7)*.

9 Solomon R. Guggenheim Museum

This Frank Lloyd Wright building is a work of art in itself, and a fitting frame for such a major collection of contemporary art *(see pp38–9)*.

10 American Museum of Natural History

Long famous for its dinosaurs, the museum moved into the space age with the dramatic Rose Center for Earth and Space *(see pp40–43)*.

0 kilometers 1
0 miles 1

SECOND AVENUE
FIRST AVENUE
ND ST
H ST
MERCY ARK
EAST 14TH STREET
SECOND AVENUE
FIRST AVENUE
EAST VILLAGE
EAST HOUSTON STREET
ALLEN STREET
DELANCEY STREET
LOWER EAST SIDE
East River

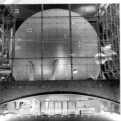

🔟 ⭐ Empire State Building

The Empire State Building is the most famous skyscraper in New York. More than 120 million visitors, including such luminaries as Queen Elizabeth II, have gazed down on the city from the observatories since it opened in 1931. Planned in the prosperous 1920s by the architectural firm of Shreve, Lamb, and Harmon, this Art Deco classic was completed during the Depression and was largely vacant for several years, giving rise to the nickname "Empty State Building." It has been featured in countless movies, most famously *King Kong*.

2 Lobby Mural
The main lobby houses a 36-ft (11-m) Art Deco relief that showcases the Empire State Building image in steel, aluminum, and gold leaf with dramatic impact **(left)**.

3 Elevators
Visitors can ride to the 86th floor in 45 seconds – 1,400 ft (427 m) per minute – in one of 73 Art Deco elevators. The last ride is at 1:15am.

4 86th Floor Observatory
Breathtaking views from the 86th floor's open-air observatory, 1,050 ft (320 m) above the city, attract more than 4 million visitors yearly.

1 The Building
A mooring mast for airships, now the base of a TV tower, was built to ensure the 102-story, 1,454-ft (443-m) building would be taller than the Chrysler Building.

5 102nd Floor Observatory
Visibility on a clear day from the 102nd-floor deck is up to 80 miles (130 km) **(below)**. Tickets are sold in advance online or upon arrival at the second-floor Visitors' Center ($20 extra).

NEED TO KNOW

MAP K3 ■ 350 5th Ave, at 34th St
■ www.esbnyc.com

Open 8am–2am daily

Main Deck: Adm: adults $32, seniors (62+) $29, children (6–12) $26, express ticket $65 for all; *Top Deck*: Adm: add $20; military in uniform and kids under 6 free; multimedia guide with all tickets

No bags over carry-on size allowed

■ There are a number of restaurants and shops on the ground level.

■ Visit at the end of the day to watch the city lights turn on.

9 New York Skyride

A virtual reality, big-screen simulation of a helicopter ride takes viewers over, under, and through the city's best-known landmarks.

6 Spire

The spire is lit to honor holidays, seasons, events, causes, and the many ethnic groups of New York: red, white, and blue for national holidays; green for St. Patrick's Day **(above)**; and blue and white for Hanukkah.

10 Fifth Avenue Gallery Windows

Four display windows in the marble-clad Fifth Avenue lobby exhibit art and memorabilia from the city's museums, galleries, and artists. Exhibits change regularly.

Empire State Building

7 Empire State Run-up

Each February, following a tradition dating to 1978, hundreds of runners race up the 1,576 steps from the lobby to the 86th floor **(above)**.

8 Valentine's Day

Weddings have been an Empire State Building tradition since 1994. Every year, 14 lucky couples are selected to get married on the one day that the ceremony is conducted here.

BUILDING THE EMPIRE STATE

William F. Lamb designed the building, following a brief to "make it big." It took only 410 days to build the 102-story, 365,000-ton limestone and granite skyscraper, with an average of four and a half stories added every week. However, in one outstanding ten-day period, the 3,500-strong construction team completed ten stories. Due to the building's relatively shallow foundations, 60,000 tons of steel beams were used to support the tower.

TOP10 ⭐ Fifth Avenue

Fifth Avenue is New York's best-known boulevard and home to three of its most famous buildings. In the late 1800s, it was lined with mansions belonging to prominent families, but as retailers moved north in the 1900s, society fled uptown. One remaining former mansion is the Cartier building, reputedly acquired from banker Morton F. Plant in 1917 in exchange for a string of pearls. Although commercial enterprises now share the avenue, it has remained a mecca for luxury goods.

1 Grand Army Plaza
This ornamented plaza is presided over by the 1907 Plaza Hotel and Augustus Saint-Gaudens' statue of General William T. Sherman. Hansom cab rides through Central Park can be boarded here.

2 Bergdorf Goodman
Founded in 1894 as a small ladies' tailoring and fur shop, New York's most elite department store **(left)** has been here since 1928. A separate shop for men was opened in 1990 across the road.

3 General Motors Building
Edward Durrell Stone's 1968 marble skyscraper is of interest not for its architecture but for the iconic glass-cube entrance to the Apple Store, which lurks below the sidewalk here.

4 Tiffany & Co.
Truman Capote's 1958 novella *Breakfast at Tiffany's* made this the most famous jewelry store in New York. The window displays are works of art, as are the items for sale within.

5 Trump Tower
A six-story open interior space, the Trump Tower Atrium is graced by hanging gardens and a spectacular 80-ft (24-m) water wall **(left)**.

6 St. Patrick's Cathedral
In 1878 James Renwick, Jr. designed New York's grandest church **(above)** in French Gothic style. Highlights include the bronze doors, the high altar, the Lady Chapel, and the rose window.

9 Cartier
Look up to admire what remains of the fine 1905 Beaux Arts mansion housing this famous luxury jeweler. At Christmas, the whole building is wrapped in a giant red ribbon **(left)**.

10 Saks Fifth Avenue
One of New York's most attractive stores, Saks is famous for the seasonal decor on the main floor of its 1924 building, and its exclusive fashions for men and women.

MILLIONNAIRE'S ROW

From its inception in the early 19th century, Fifth Avenue has been the territory of New York's well-heeled society, with homes costing as much as $20,000 after the Civil War. As retail and commercial ventures, albeit exclusive ones, encroached at the end of the 19th century, they moved their mansions further north. Mrs Astor set the trend by moving up to 65th Street after her nephew, William Waldorf Astor, built the Waldorf Hotel next to her former home.

7 New York Public Library
The epitome of Beaux Arts elegance, this 1911 landmark features vaulted marble halls and a paneled reading room that stretches for two blocks and glows with light from great arched windows **(above)**.

8 Lord & Taylor
Retailing on Fifth Avenue since 1914, Lord & Taylor **(left)** offers a mix of fashions for budgets low and high. The store is known for its elaborately animated Christmas windows.

NEED TO KNOW

MAP H3–K3 ■ New York Public Library: 212 930 0800 ■ www.nypl.org

Tourist Information: 212 484 1222

The heart of Fifth Avenue is from the Empire State Building *(see pp12–13)* on 34th St, to the Grand Army Plaza, 59th St, a walk of just over 1 mile (1.6 km)

■ **Free tours of the New York Public Library: 11am and 2pm Mon–Sat, and 2pm on Sun;** there's no need to book for groups of fewer than 10 people.

■ **St. Patrick's Cathedral is open to visitors 6:30am–8:45pm daily. Frequent services Mon–Sat; 7, 8, 9, 10:15am & noon, 1 & 5:30pm Sun**

TOP 10 ⭐ Rockefeller Center

Begun in the 1930s, this city within a city and National Historic Landmark was the first commercial project to integrate gardens, dining, and shopping with office space. Rockefeller Center is the hub of Midtown Manhattan, busy day and night. The number of buildings has grown to 19, though the newer buildings do not match the Art Deco elegance of the original 14 structures.

3 Comcast Building

The centerpiece of Rockefeller Center is a slim, 70-story limestone tower **(right)**. The building, with gradual setbacks as it rises, houses the studios of the NBC television network.

4 Sunken Garden

A skating rink in winter and outdoor café in summer, the Sunken Garden is always popular. It is surrounded by flags that represent the members of the UN.

1 Channel Gardens

Named after the English Channel because they separate the French and British buildings, the gardens **(above)** change with the calendar and are lined with glowing angels at Christmas.

2 Prometheus Statue

An 18-ft (5.5-m) gold-leafed bronze statue **(above)** by Paul Manship presides over the Sunken Garden. The pedestal represents Earth and the ring represents the heavens.

7 Atlas Statue

Sculpted by Lee Lawrie, this 14,000-lb (6,350-kg), 15-ft (4.5-m) figure is perched on a 9-ft (3-m) pedestal **(left)**. One of 15 works by Lawrie at the Rockefeller Center, Atlas stands at the entrance to the International Building.

JOHN D. ROCKEFELLER, JR.

Eminent philanthropist and multimillionaire John D. Rockefeller, Jr. (1874–1960) was son and heir to Ohio oil magnate John Davison Rockefeller's fortunes. John D., as Rockefeller, Jr. was known, strongly believed his inheritance should be used for the public good. Among his philanthropic donations were contributions to the building funds of the Cloisters (see p37) and the United Nations Headquarters (see p128).

5 Today Show Studio

This morning-TV show can be viewed live every weekday from the sidewalk. Outdoor concerts by well-known musicians often take place in the plaza.

8 NBC Studios

Backstage tours of the network's studios **(below)** are popular. Visitors can buy tickets online or by phone, or write ahead for shows; tickets are also available in the Comcast building.

6 Shopping Concourse

A variety of stores is found in the under ground concourse of the Comcast Building, including a branch of the Met Museum shop.

9 Radio City Music Hall

Tours of this Art Deco masterpiece and former movie palace offer a chance to admire the decor, the stage, and the Wurlitzer organ (see p63).

NEED TO KNOW

MAP J3 ■ Rockefeller Center extends from 5th to 6th Aves, between 48th & 51st Sts ■ www.rockefellercenter.com

NBC Studios: 30 Rockefeller Plaza; tours every 30 mins 8:30am–2pm Mon–Fri, 8:30am–5pm Sat & Sun; book on 212 664 3056 or at www.thetourat nbcstudios.com; Adm: adults $33, seniors (55+) and children (6–12) $29; reservations advised

Today Show: Rockefeller Plaza at 49th St; 7–11am Mon–Fri, 7–9am Sat, 8–9am Sun

Top of the Rock: 30 Rockefeller Plaza; 212 698 2000; 8am–midnight daily (last lift 11pm); www.topoftherocknyc.com; Adm: adults $32, seniors (62+) $30, kids (6–12) $26

■ From 5th Ave, walk via the Channel Gardens to the Sunken Garden.

■ Pick up a self-guided tour leaflet from the the Comcast Building lobby.

■ For 360-degree views, visit the 67th–70th-floor observation deck.

10 Top of the Rock

Visitors are treated to breathtaking, unob-structed views – and space to move about – on the observation deck's three levels **(below)**.

Rockefeller Center Artworks

1 American Progress
Jose Maria Sert's (1876–1945) mural depicts America's development over 300 years by uniting two forces, brain and brawn. Sert's *Time* mural adorns one of the ceilings.

2 Wisdom
The striking central figure of *Wisdom* by Lee Lawrie (1877–1963) grasps a compass pointing to light and sound waves and is carved on a screen made of 240 glass blocks.

3 Gaston Lachaise's panels
This two-panel work by the noted American sculptor (1882–1935) honors the contribution made by workmen to the Rockefeller Center's construction, depicting them at their labors.

4 News
This heroic sculpture by Isamu Noguchi (1904–88) is cast in stainless steel. The 10-ton panel illustrates the tools of the press, including camera, telephone, pad, and pencil.

5 Industries of the British Empire
Cast in bronze and finished in gold leaf, this panel by Carl Paul Jennewein (1890–1980) depicts nine major industries once crucial to the British Empire, including coal, fish, sugar cane, salt, and tobacco. A sun symbolizes the extent of the Empire.

Industries of the British Empire

6 Intelligence Awakening Mankind
Some one million tesserae (pieces of glass enamel) in more than 200 colors create Barry Faulkner's (1881–1966) mosaic representing spoken and written words.

Intelligence Awakening Mankind

7 Portals
Josef Albers' 1961 work of thin, highly polished, milky-white and ivory Carrara glass creates a surface of receding squares that gives the mural a sense of depth.

8 Winged Mercury
Lee Lawrie's stunning 1933 relief of Mercury, the Roman god of trade, profit, and commerce, celebrates the British Empire. The golden figure's helmet is a sign of protection.

Winged Mercury

9 The Story of Mankind
Another Lawrie piece is a bold 15-block history accented in gold, scarlet, and blue-green. History is topped with a clock, signifying the passage of time.

10 Wall Drawing 896
The Center's newest mural, a site-specific, geometric design created in 1999 by Sol Lewitt, covers four walls of the entrance to the headquarters of Christie's on 48th Street with brilliant color.

BUILDING THE ROCKEFELLER CENTER

When the Great Depression made John D. Rockefeller, Jr.'s original plan for a new opera house impractical, he instead developed a large, creative-commercial complex. The innovative Art Deco design, led by Raymond Hood (Rockefeller Plaza) and an underground concourse. The 14 buildings constructed in 1931–40 provided 225,000 jobs during the worst of the Depression. Artworks were an essential element; over 30 artists contributed work for foyers, facades, and gardens as part of the "New Frontiers" program.

TOP 10 STATISTICS

1 Tallest building: 850 ft (259 m), 70 floors

2 Elevators: 388

3 Passenger rides per day: more than 500,000

4 Fastest elevator speed: 1,400 ft (427 m) per minute (37 seconds non-stop to 65th floor)

5 Number working in the complex: 65,000

6 Telephones: 100,000

7 Office windows: 48,758

8 Restaurants: 45

9 Shops: 100

10 Daily visitors: 250,000

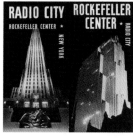
Radio City brochure

The Rockefeller Center under construction in 1932

🔟 ⭐ Statue of Liberty

New York's most famous statue, officially titled "Liberty Enlightening the World," has been a harbinger of freedom for millions since 1886. The statue, a gift from France to mark the US's 100th birthday, was designed by the Frenchman Frédéric-Auguste Bartholdi, who devoted 21 years to the project. The unveiling on July 3, 1986 after the $100-million centennial restoration, was the occasion for one of the largest firework displays ever seen in the US.

1 Boat Ride
The views from the ferries **(above)** that carry a constant stream of visitors from Manhattan and Jersey City to the Statue of Liberty and on to Ellis Island are dramatic.

2 Castle Clinton National Monument
Built as a fort in 1808, it now serves as a boarding point for Statue of Liberty and Ellis Island ferry passengers, and exhibits panoramas of New York history. The fort was built 300 ft (91 m) offshore, but landfill gradually joined it to Battery Park.

3 Battery Park
With statues and monuments honoring everyone from New York's first Jewish immigrants to the U.S. Coast Guard, the park is also a great spot for sea-gazing.

GATEWAY TO THE NEW WORLD

The Statue of Liberty has symbolized the beginning of a new way of life for millions of immigrants fleeing poverty and hardship. She is an enduring symbol of the freedom and hope offered by the US and the subject of Emma Lazarus's poem *The New Colossus*: "… Give me your tired, your poor, Your huddled masses yearning to breathe free… Send these, the homeless, tempest-tost to me, I lift my lamp beside the golden door".

4 Close-up View of the Statue
A close-up view reveals the awesome size of the Statue of Liberty **(right)**. Dominating New York harbor, she stands 305 ft (93 m) tall and weighs 200 tons. Her right arm carrying the symbolic torch is 42 ft (13 m) long while her index finger measures 8 ft (2.4 m) and dwarfs most men.

5 Crown
Legend says that Bartholdi's mother was the model for Liberty, but the face was actually based on his early drawings for a never-commissioned statue in Egypt. The rays of her crown **(left)** represent the seven seas and continents.

⑥ Historical Exhibits

The museum inside the base documents the history of the Statue of Liberty using photos, prints, videos, oral histories, and replicas of the face and foot. A pedestal ticket is required to visit the museum and its observation deck.

⑦ Frame

Gustave Eiffel, best known for his Paris tower, created the inner framework. The copper sheeting shell, weighing 31 tons, is hung on bars from a massive central iron pylon that anchors the statue to the base.

⑧ Torch and Book

The new, gold-leaf-coated torch was added in 1986. The original is on display in the museum **(right)**. The book in Liberty's left hand is inscribed July 4, 1776, in Roman numerals.

⑨ Views

The observation decks in the pedestal and crown of the Liberty Statue offer spectacular views. The crown reopened in 2009 following closure after September 11, 2001. Advance reservation is required.

⑩ Pedestal

Prestigious American architect Richard Morris Hunt was chosen to design the 89-ft (27-m) pedestal. It sits within the 11-pointed, star-shaped walls **(above)** of Fort Wood, a fortress erected for the War of 1812.

TOP 10 ⭐ Ellis Island

Ellis Island is the symbol of America's immigrant heritage. From 1892 to 1954, it was the arrival point for over 12 million people searching for a better life. Their descendants, more than 100 million people, comprise almost 40 percent of today's population. First and second class passengers were processed for immigration on board ship, but the poor traveling in steerage class were ferried to the crowded island for medical and legal checks. As many as 5,000 passed through in a day. The museum not only retraces their experience here, but is a complete picture of the immigrant experience in America.

1 Arrival Area
Crowds of steerage passengers entered through the original gateway having been ferried from their arrival vessels. Instructions were given by interpreters in a babel of languages as they lined up for immigration.

2 Dormitory
Immigrants who were detained for further examinations slept here in separate quarters for men and women. Although the process was nerve-racking, only two percent of those seeking refuge were sent back.

Aerial view of Ellis Island and the Statue of Liberty

4 Railroad Ticket Office
Those traveling beyond New York were ferried to railroad terminals in New Jersey to continue their onward journeys. Agents could sell as many as 25 tickets per minute.

NEW JERSEY'S ELLIS ISLAND
Although a federal property, a long-fought battle over territorial jurisdiction of Ellis Island was settled in 1998. Originally a 3-acre (1-ha) site, Ellis Island's landmass was increased with landfill to more than 27 acres (11 ha) in the 1900s. A US Supreme Court ruling in 1998 adjudged the added landfill to be in the territory of New Jersey, and the original portion to be in New York State's jurisdiction.

3 Great Hall
In this hall (above), immigrants awaited examinations that would determine whether they would be granted entry. A doctor marked those needing special inspection with chalk.

6 The Peopling of America

Four hundred years of immigration history are displayed in more than 30 galleries. Exhibits such as *The Peopling of America* have heirlooms, posters, maps, and photos donated by immigrants' families.

5 Medical Examining Line

The most dreaded inspectors were the "eye men" **(above)**, looking for trachoma, a disease that lead to blindness and certain deportation.

7 Baggage Room

In this room, inspection officers checked the baskets, boxes, and trunks **(right)** that held the immigrants' meager belongings, which at that point constituted all their worldly possessions.

8 American Family Immigration History Center

Using computer and multimedia technology, visitors can access passenger arrival records of more than 25 million people entering New York between 1892 and 1924 **(below)**.

9 American Immigration Wall of Honor

To honor their forebears, Americans pay to have their names inscribed on this list. Including the families of John F. Kennedy and Barbra Streisand, the wall contains over 700,000 names.

10 Immigrants' Living Theater

Daily theatrical productions that are based on actual immigrant accounts are given by actors who recreate the experiences of Ellis Island. The museum has two movie theaters, a Library and an Oral History Studio with taped reminiscences.

NEED TO KNOW

For a map, see Lower Manhattan to Midtown inset on p10 ▪ 212 363 3200 ▪ www.nps.gov/elis

Open Jun–Aug: 9am–6pm daily; Sep–May: 9am–5:15pm daily

Ferry rides to Statue of Liberty and Ellis Island: adults $18, seniors $14, children (4–12) $9; statue crown access add $3; children under 4 free

▪ The island's cafeteria and picnic areas are great spots for lunch.

▪ Try to catch an early ferry from Battery Park to avoid the crowds.

▪ Stop at the museum information desk for tickets to the free 30-minute film *Island of Hope, Island of Tears*.

Milestones in Immigration History

Peter Stuyvesant forced to leave

1 **1624**
The first Dutch arrived in New Amsterdam, which thrived as a trading center, attracting settlers from many other nations. By 1643, the 500-strong population spoke 18 different languages.

2 **1664**
The dislike of Dutch governor Peter Stuyvesant and unpopular tax demands by the Dutch West India Company meant little resistance to their ousting by the British, who renamed the city New York.

3 **1790**
For the first US Census, New York's population of 33,131 was the second largest in the Colonies. This consisted of mostly British and Dutch expatriates.

4 **Mid-1800s**
Ireland's 1845–8 Great Famine and economic hardship in Germany led many to seek new lives in New York, where the city's rapid growth as a seaport and manufacturing center opened many jobs.

5 **1880–1910**
Thousands of Russian and Polish Jews, Italians and Scandinavians arrived, fleeing persecution or hard economic times.

Polish immigrant

6 **1892**
When Castle Island, an immigrant depot set up in 1855, could no longer handle the inflow, Ellis Island took over. "Settlement Houses" were set up in the city to help those living in squalid tenements, and "Americanization" programs encouraged assimilation.

7 **1924**
Nearly 40 percent of New York's population was foreign-born. US laws set national quotas on immigration; inhabitants of Great Britain's Caribbean colonies benefited from the British quota and arrived in large numbers.

8 **1965**
The Hart-Cellar Act ended discrimination based on national origin beginning a new wave of immigration to the city.

Chinatown, Manhattan

9 **1980s**
One million mainly Asian and Latin American newcomers arrived. The Chinese population topped 300,000 (mostly in Chinatown), Koreans became visible elements, and Dominican numbers grew.

10 **1990–present**
Over 1.2 million newcomers entered, swelling the city's foreign-born population to over 40 percent of the total population – the highest since 1910. The New York borough of Queens is classified as the most ethnically diverse in the US.

THE RESTORATION OF ELLIS ISLAND

Museum visitor

Laws enacted in 1924 defining immigration quotas drastically curtailed the numbers of foreigners coming into the US, and Ellis Island was no longer needed to serve as an immigration depot. It became a detention and deportation center for undesirable aliens, a training center for the US Coast Guard, and a hospital for wounded servicemen during World War II. In 1954, the US government closed the island. It remained abandoned until 1984, when a $156 million project replaced the copper roof domes, cleaned the mosaic tiles, and restored the interior, preserving any surviving original fixtures in the largest historic restoration in US history. The restoration included the establishment of the Ellis Island Immigration Museum (see pp22–3), telling the immigrant story through more than 2,000 artifacts. It also has an interactive children's exhibit, plus an oral history archive that can be visited by appointment. Reopened in 1990, Ellis Island receives almost 3 million visitors every year.

TOP 10 NATIONALITIES ENTERING ELLIS ISLAND

(Between 1892–7, 1901–31)

1 **Italy**: 2,502,310
2 **Austria and Hungary**: 2,275,852
3 **Russia**: 1,893,542
4 **Germany**: 633,148
5 **England**: 551,969
6 **Ireland**: 520,904
7 **Sweden**: 348,036
8 **Greece**: 245,058
9 **Norway**: 226,278
10 **Ottoman Empire**: 212,825

The restored entrance to the Ellis Island Immigration Museum

Following pages The Statue of Liberty and Manhattan skyline at sunset

🔟⭐ Times Square and Theater District

Known as the "Crossroads of the World," Times Square is New York's most famous intersection and center of the lively theater district. It was called Longacre Square until 1904, when the *New York Times* built One Times Square, a 25-story tower, on the site. Its occupancy on New Year's Eve was marked with fireworks, a celebration that continues today. A giant crystal ball descends the building at midnight to herald the new year, cheered by thousands packed into the square.

1 Broadway Lights

The city's longest street is known best for the section north of 42nd Street dubbed the "Great White Way" for its dazzle of neon **(main image)**.

3 Times Square News Ticker

In 1928, the *New York Times* erected the world's first moving electronic sign to post breaking news, a fixture that remains although the *Times* has now moved to 8th Avenue.

4 Nasdaq Headquarters

The headquarters of this over-the-counter stock market dominates the corner of Broadway and 43rd Street with a screen that regularly broadcasts financial news and live stock information **(left)**.

2 ABC Times Square Studios

The show *Good Morning America* **(below)** is taped at these Disney-owned studios (7–9am Mon–Fri). Large viewing windows allow passers-by to catch a glimpse of the celebrity guests or watch the occasional live pop concert.

NEED TO KNOW

MAP J3 ▪ Times Square is located where Broadway and 7th Ave intersect at 42nd St ▪ www.timessquarenyc.org

Madame Tussauds New York: 234 West 42nd St; 1 800 246 8872; Jun–Aug: 9am–10pm daily (Jul & Aug: to midnight), Sep–May: 10am–8pm daily (to 10pm Fri & Sat); www.nycwax.com; Adm: adults $37, children (4–12) $30

▪ Go to the TKTS booth in Times Square at Broadway and 47th (212 221 0013; www.tdf.org) for half-price tickets to all kinds of Broadway shows.

▪ Times Square Visitor Center, 7th Ave between 46th and 47th streets, has discount coupons for shows as well as a mini-museum on the square's history.

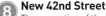

5 Brill Building
Everyone from Cole Porter to Jay-Z has produced hits in this legendary music industry building, a long-time home to famous music publishers and arrangers.

6 Condé Nast Building
The environmentally friendly, 48-story skyscraper, opened in 2000 to house its namesake magazine and remains a sign of the resurgence of Times Square.

8 New 42nd Street
The renovation of the New Amsterdam Theatre in the 1990s uplifted 42nd Street. Today, the New 42nd Street Studios and several theaters line the block.

9 Madame Tussauds, New York
Barack Obama, Brangelina, and Madonna are among the wax inhabitants of this 42nd Street tenant. The museum has exterior glass elevators and a huge hand holding the illuminated sign **(right)**.

THEATER DISTRICT

It was the move by the Metropolitan Opera House to Broadway in 1883 that drew lavish theaters and restaurants to this area. In the 1920s, movie palaces added the glamour of neon to Broadway. After World War II, the popularity of movies waned and sleaze replaced glitter. Since the 1990s, a redevelopment program has brought the public and bright lights back to this area.

10 Duffy Square
The block was revitalized with the unveiling of the TKTS area in 2008, a dramatic wedge of red overlaid with a set of stairs to nowhere **(left)**. A statue of World War I hero Father Duffy stands beneath the steps.

7 Off-Broadway
Before the rest of 42nd Street was rejuvenated, this block between 9th and 10th Avenues was resurrected by Off-Broadway theater companies needing inexpensive homes. New plays are premiered at Playwrights Horizons, one of the area's better-known tenants **(right)**.

Theaters

1 Lyceum
MAP J3 ▪ 149–57 West 45th St

The oldest playhouse boasts a vaulted ceiling, murals, and elaborate plasterwork. It is often used as an auxiliary for Lincoln Center *(see p142)*.

2 Lyric Theatre
MAP K3 ▪ 214 West 42nd St

The run-down Lyric and Apollo Theatres were combined to form this showcase for musicals in 1998, marking the arrival of corporate sponsorship for theaters.

3 Shubert Theatre
MAP J3 ▪ 221–33 West 44th St

Built in 1912–13 as a lavish site for musicals and headquarters for the Shubert Organization. The Booth, opposite, was built at this time.

4 New Amsterdam Theatre
MAP K3 ▪ 214 West 42nd St

This Art Nouveau beauty housed the famous *Ziegfeld Follies*. Restored by Disney, in the 1990s, it is now home to several hit Disney shows.

5 New Victory Theater
MAP K3 ▪ 209 West 42nd St

Built for Oscar Hammerstein in 1900, this theater had resorted to X-rated films until it was restored in 1995 to present family entertainment.

Detail of the Lyceum facade

6 Hudson Theatre
MAP J2 ▪ 139–41 West 44th St

A restrained facade belies the lavish interior, including an inner lobby with a Classical arcade and domes of Tiffany glass. It is currently used as a conference center.

7 Belasco Theatre
MAP J3 ▪ 111–21 West 44th St

This 1907 monument to impresario David Belasco, who supervised the unusual Georgian Revival design, was restored in 2010. The rooftop duplex, with the decor of a Gothic church, was his personal residence.

8 Lunt-Fontanne Theatre
MAP J3 ▪ 203–17 West 46th St

Originally the Globe (finished in 1910), part of the roof of this venue could be removed to create an open-air auditorium. It was rebuilt in 1958.

9 Palace Theatre
MAP J3 ▪ 1564 Broadway

Sarah Bernhardt inaugurated the stage, and playing here became the ultimate assignment. It is now restored as a venue for musicals.

10 Winter Garden Theatre
MAP J3 ▪ 1634 Broadway

Originally the American Horse Exchange in 1885, this was acquired by the Shuberts in 1911 and remodeled in 1922. Popular musicals have included *Cats* (1982–2000), *Mamma Mia!* (2001–2013), and *School of Rock* (from 2015).

Interior of New Victory Theater

A BRIEF HISTORY OF NEW YORK THEATER

Oscar Hammerstein

New York's first theater is thought to have been the New Theater, erected in 1732. The city's theatrical center steadily moved uptown to the Bowery, Astor Place, Union Square, and Herald Square, before finally settling around Longacre Square (now Times Square), after Oscar Hammerstein's Olympia Theater opened on Broadway in 1895. Some 85 theaters were built over the next three decades, many with grand Beaux Arts interiors by architects such as Herts & Tallant, who were responsible for designing cantilevered balconies that eliminated the need for columns. Impresarios like the Shuberts and the Chanins made theater-going more democratic by blurring the class distinction between orchestra and balcony, using a single entrance for all. As modern theaters replaced them, more than 40 of these beauties were demolished. Fortunately, the rest have now been designated landmarks.

**TOP 10
BROADWAY CLASSICS**

1 **The Phantom of the Opera**
2 **Jersey Boys**
3 **Chicago**
4 **The Lion King**
5 **Mamma Mia!**
6 **Billy Elliot**
7 **Annie**
8 **Wicked**
9 **Mary Poppins**
10 **Rain**

The Broadhurst Theatre, designed by Herbert J. Krapp in 1917, remains one of the Shubert Organization's most frequented theatres.

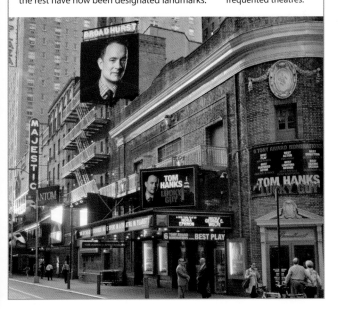

TOP10 ⭐ Central Park

New York's "backyard," an 843-acre (341-ha) swathe of green, provides recreation and beauty for around 38 million visitors a year. Designed by Frederick Law Olmsted and Calvert Vaux in 1858, the park took 16 years to create and involved the hauling in of vast amounts of stone and earth to form hills, lakes, and meadows, the planting of over 500,000 trees and shrubs, and the building of more than 30 bridges and arches.

1 Great Lawn

This is a 13-acre (5-ha) oval of green lawn **(above)**. In the summer, free concerts by the Metropolitan Opera and New York Philharmonic draw up to 100,000 people.

2 Bethesda Terrace

Overlooking the Ramble and the Lake, the ornate terrace and its fountain **(below)** form the focal point of the park. On the adjacent tree-lined Mall in-line skaters often show off acrobatic stunts.

3 Belvedere Castle

This 19th-century stone castle **(above)** offers peerless views in all directions. Inside is the Henry Luce Nature Observatory with exhibits covering the park's diverse wildlife.

4 The Ramble

This wooded 37 acres (15 ha) is a bird-watcher's paradise. Central Park is on the Atlantic migration flyway. Over 270 species have been spotted here, including the purple grackle **(right)**.

5 Reservoir
This 106-acre (43-ha) lake **(above)** is the largest of the park's five, which include Conservatory Water, where model boat races are often held.

CREATING CENTRAL PARK
Central Park was the first landscaping project of Frederick Law Olmsted, who was already 43. Rejecting the usual formal plantings, he created passages of contrasting scenery, the pastoral against the rugged. Areas for active and passive recreation were separated, and dense raised plantings shut out the city. The park brought him high praise and set a pattern for future landscapes. He went on to be America's most prolific designer of parks.

6 Strawberry Fields
This peaceful garden area was created by Yoko Ono in memory of John Lennon (shot in 1981), who lived in the nearby Dakota apartments. Gifts for the memorial came from all over the world.

7 Conservatory Garden
This formal garden with fountains and beautiful displays of flowering trees and bulbs is at its best in spring, when everything is in bloom.

NEED TO KNOW
MAP D3–H3 ■ From Central Park South to 110th St, and between 5th Ave and Central Park West ■ www.centralpark nyc.org

Open dawn–dusk

■ Refreshments and light lunches are available at the Boathouse snack bar. The Boathouse restaurant serves gourmet meals.

■ Make your first stop the Dairy, a Victorian Gothic building housing the Visitor Center. Ask about the free nature workshops and guided walks.

■ Rent bicycles, rowboats, and gondolas from the Boathouse, and skates from the Wollman Rink.

8 Hans Christian Andersen Statue
Children's storytelling sessions are held here **(right)** in the summer. Other activities for youngsters include nature workshops, a carousel, and a marionette theater.

9 Central Park Zoo
This conservation center and children's zoo has three climatic zones: temperate, Polar Circle, and rain forest. They are home to over 100 species including monkeys, seals, and penguins.

10 Delacorte Theater
Home of the two "Shakespeare in the Park" summer productions. Get in line early for free tickets. The SummerStage music and dance series offers free entertainment too.

TOP 10 ⭐ Metropolitan Museum of Art

One of the world's great art museums, the Metropolitan (Met) spans 5,000 years of culture from across the globe. Each specialized gallery holds an abundance of treasures. Founded in 1870 with three European collections and 174 paintings, the Gothic Revival building has been expanded many times and the present holdings number over 2 million.

1 European Paintings
The 2,500 European paintings form one of the world's greatest collections. Strengths include the Rembrandts, Vermeers, and the many Impressionist and Post-Impressionist canvases.

2 Egyptian Art
One of the largest collections of Egyptian art outside Cairo includes masks, mummies, statues, jewelry, the Tomb of Perneb, and the spectacular Temple of Dendur **(right)**, built around 15 BC and reassembled as it appeared on the banks of the Nile.

3 Michael C. Rockefeller Wing
Inca masks **(above)**, Pre-Columbian gold, ceramics from Mexico and Peru, and art from the court of Benin in Nigeria are highlights among 1,600 objects covering 3,000 years.

4 American Wing
This collection includes Tiffany glass, paintings, sculptures, and period rooms from the 17th to early 20th centuries **(right)**.

5 Robert Lehman Collection
This extraordinary private collection includes Renaissance masters, Dutch, Spanish, and French artists, Post-Impressionists and Fauvists, plus ceramics and furniture.

6 Costume Institute

Women's fashions from ball gowns to miniskirts, and menswear from the French courts **(left)** to the present day are on display here. The glamorous Gala draws massive crowds annually.

7 Asian Art

The West's most comprehensive collection features paintings, textiles, sculpture and ceramics.

8 Lila A. Wallace Wing

The Metropolitan has a growing collection of art, sculpture, and design from the 20th century, with works ranging from Picasso and Matisse to Émile-Jacques Ruhlmann and Jackson Pollock.

9 European Sculpture and Decorative Arts

This collection reflects the development of Western European design. It includes French and English period rooms, tapestries, and sculptures by Rodin and Degas **(right)**.

10 Roof Garden

From May to October the Iris and B. Gerald Cantor Roof Garden boasts outstanding annual displays of contemporary sculpture. It also offers an opportunity to enjoy a drink with a peerless view of Central Park and the surrounding skyline.

European Paintings 1
Roof Garden 10
Lila A. Wallace Wing 8
Asian Art 7
Michael C. Rockefeller Wing 3
American Wing 4
Egyptian Art 2
European Sculpture and Decorative Arts 9
Robert Lehman Collection 5
Costume Institute 6

Key to Floor Plan
- Ground Floor
- First Floor
- Second Floor

NEED TO KNOW

MAP F3 ■ 1000 5th Ave ■ 212 535 7710 ■ www.metmuseum.org

Open 10am–5:30pm Mon–Thu & Sun, 10am–9pm Fri & Sat (galleries cleared 15 mins before closing)

Adm: recommended fee: adults $25, seniors $17, students $12, children under 12 and members free

■ If time is short, the European Paintings, Egyptian Art, and American Wing will give you a sense of this institution's greatness.

■ Less-crowded weekend evenings have bar service and live music.

Paintings in the Met

1 Self-Portrait
Rembrandt (1606–69) painted a self-portrait each decade of his whole career. In this moving study from 1660, when he was 54, he portrayed age very honestly.

2 View of Toledo
Darkening clouds set an eerie mood for one of El Greco's (1541–1614) most memorable paintings, depicting the capital city of the Spanish Empire until 1561.

3 Young Woman with a Water Pitcher
Painted between 1660 and 1667, this is a classic example of the subtle and sensitive use of light that has made Vermeer (1632–75) one of the most revered Dutch masters.

The Harvesters **(1565), Bruegel**

4 The Harvesters
This is Bruegel (1551–69) at his best, an example of the use of light and detail that set him apart. It is one of five remaining panels depicting different times of the year.

5 Madame X
Part of the excellent American art collection, this canvas by John Singer Sargent (1856–1925) is of an American woman who married a French banker, becoming a notorious Paris beauty in the 1880s.

6 Garden at Sainte-Adresse
This resort town on the English Channel where Monet spent the

Garden at Sainte-Adresse **(1867), Monet**

summer of 1867 is portrayed with sparkling color and intricate brushwork. The work combines illusion and reality, demonstrating why Monet (1840–1926) was considered to be one of the greatest of the Impressionists.

7 Gertrude Stein
This portrait, created when Picasso (1881–1973) was just 24 years old, shows the influence of African, Roman, and Iberian sculpture and a shift from the slender figures of his early years, foreshadowing his adoption of Cubism.

8 The Card Players
Better known for landscapes and still lifes, Cézanne (1839–1906) was intrigued by a scene of peasants intent on their card game. This ambitious project emphasizes the concentration of the participants.

9 Cypresses
Painted in 1889, soon after Van Gogh's (1853–90) voluntary confinement at an asylum in Saint-Rémy, this painting shows the swirling and heavy brushwork typical of his work from this period.

10 Autumn Rhythm
This work by Jackson Pollock (1912–56), the Abstract Expressionist famous for his radical "drip" paintings, is part of the modern collection. Pollock dripped paint onto a canvas that lay flat on the floor.

THE CLOISTERS

Reliquary Shrine ("The Elizabeth Shrine")

As well as the medieval treasures in the main building, the Met oversees this spectacular branch, built in medieval architectural style, overlooking the Hudson River in Fort Tryon Park in northern Manhattan. Opened in 1938, it consists of elements from five medieval cloisters and other monastic sites in France. The collections are noted for Romanesque and Gothic sculptures and include manuscripts, tapestries, stained glass, enamels, ivories, and paintings. The gardens are serene. John D. Rockefeller Jr. *(see p17 & p46)*, who donated items to the collection, is largely responsible for funding the Cloisters. To reach the complex, take the A train to 190th Street.

TOP 10
CLOISTERS SIGHTS

1 Gothic Chapel

2 Boppard Room

3 Mérode Altarpiece (Annunciation Triptych)

4 Nine Heroes Tapestries

5 Hunt of the Unicorn Tapestries

6 The Treasury

7 Reliquary Shrine ("The Elizabeth Shrine")

8 Virgin Statue

9 Altar Angels

10 Medieval Gardens

The medieval gardens of the Cloisters make for a peaceful escape from the city.

TOP 10 ⭐ Solomon R. Guggenheim Museum

One of the great architectural achievements of the 20th century, Frank Lloyd Wright's 1959 spiral design alone would make this museum a must. Solomon Guggenheim's core collection of Abstract art has been widened by donations of several important collections. The museum owns a host of work by Gauguin, Chagall, Kandinsky, Van Gogh, Mondrian, Picasso and Miró. Only a small portion is on show, as the main gallery is used for temporary exhibits.

1 Woman Ironing
Picasso's early paintings showed sympathy for the working class. This striking 1904 canvas uses angular contours and a bleak palette of whites and grays to make the subject a symbol of the misfortunes of the poor.

2 Black Lines
Kandinsky wanted the undulating, richly-colored ovals and animated black brushstrokes to elicit specific reactions from viewers. *Black Lines* (1913) is one of his best-known nonobjective works.

3 Mountains at Saint-Remy
Van Gogh was recovering from an attack of mental distress when he painted this scene **(below)** in July 1889, a year before his suicide. The subject was the low range of the Alpilles mountains in southern France, visible from his hospital grounds.

4 Before the Mirror
Edouard Manet scandalized Paris with his paintings of prostitutes and courtesans. This private scene is of a partially undressed woman, an actress perhaps, contemplating her image.

5 Paris Through the Window
Painted after Marc Chagall moved to Paris from Russia in 1910, the surreal scene reflects the latest avant-garde styles. The Eiffel Tower seen in the distance is a metaphor for Paris and for modernity.

6 Still Life: Flask, Glass, and Jug

Paul Cézanne's later style, based on the interplay of surface and depth, is shown in this 1877 painting **(left)**. His mastery of space and depth make him the foremost precursor to the Cubist movement of the 1900s.

7 Bibémus

In Bibémus, the abandoned quarries outside Aix-en-Provence, France, Cézanne found a man-made landscape that suited his increasingly geometric style.

8 The Hermitage at Pontoise

This unsentimental rendering **(left)** of the village where Pisarro lived on and off from 1866 to 1883 emphasizes the use of light and shade. The depiction of villagers was thought vulgar by some painters of the day.

9 Woman with Yellow Hair

In this memorable portrait from 1931, Picasso portrays the supple body of his mistress, Marie-Thérèse. He employed the continuous arched line from forehead to nose that he would often repeat in the many paintings of her.

FRANK LLOYD WRIGHT

Though Frank Lloyd Wright (1867–1959) designed many public buildings, he was best known for residential designs, "organic architecture" that followed the natural contours of the land, and tradition-breaking open interior spaces that have had lasting worldwide influence. The New York Guggenheim, one of his last projects, was a complete departure. So intent was Wright on his spiral design that when told some walls were too short for large works, he reportedly responded, "cut the paintings in half."

10 Haere Mai

Gauguin made his first trip to Tahiti in 1891. This idyllic village landscape **(below)** was painted during that trip; the rich hues and flattened forms show the simplicity he sought.

TOP 10 ⭐ American Museum of Natural History

Few city children grow up without visiting the dinosaurs, the life-size dioramas of animal life, and natural wonders in this popular museum. Since its founding in 1869, the museum has grown to 46 permanent exhibition halls spanning 4 city blocks. Holdings include 32 million specimens and cultural artifacts, many unique in the world. Newer areas, such as the Hall of Biodiversity, the Fossil Halls, and the Rose Center *(see pp42–3)*, bring recent research to visitors through multimedia displays.

① Dinosaurs and Fossils

The best-known hallmark of the museum, the collection of dinosaur fossils is the world's largest. The giant Barosaurus in the rotunda is the highest free-standing exhibit **(right)**.

② Mammals

Dramatic dioramas of life-size animals are divided by continent and shown in accurate natural habitats. The wildlife ranges from African elephants to Asian lions and leopards.

③ Ocean Life

The Milstein Hall of Ocean Life explores the waters of the earth and their inhabitants. A 94-ft (29-m) life-size blue whale presides over the hall **(below)**.

④ Hall of Asian Peoples

Exquisite artifacts, artwork, costumes, and dioramas of daily life show the different religions and lifestyles of Chinese, Korean, Indian, Japanese, and other Asian cultures.

⑤ Hall of African Peoples

These depictions of tribes living in various environments reflect many years of research. The displays include dwellings, clothing, masks, musical instruments, weapons, and tools.

⑥ Northwest Coast Indians

This area features Native American totem poles showing the wood-working skills of tribes living in Northwest America. Also on show is a 63-ft (19-m) canoe built in 1878.

⑦ Human Biology and Evolution

This display of human origins and physical characteristics includes reconstructed heads of early hominids.

8 Hall of Biodiversity

Opened in 1998 to encourage conservation, the hall contains a rainforest with accurate sounds, plants, and inhabitants **(left)**. The 100-ft- (30-m-) long Spectrum of Life wall displays 1,500 different specimens.

American Museum of Natural History floorplan

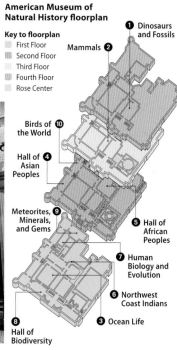

Key to floorplan
- First Floor
- Second Floor
- Third Floor
- Fourth Floor
- Rose Center

1 Dinosaurs and Fossils
2 Mammals
10 Birds of the World
4 Hall of Asian Peoples
9 Meteorites, Minerals, and Gems
5 Hall of African Peoples
7 Human Biology and Evolution
6 Northwest Coast Indians
3 Ocean Life
8 Hall of Biodiversity

NEED TO KNOW

MAP F2 ■ Central Park West, between 77th & 81st Sts ■ 212 769 5100 ■ www.amnh.org

Open 10am–5:45pm daily; Rose Center open until 8:45pm on first Fri of month

Adm: adults $22, students and seniors $17, children (2–12) $12.50, members free; Plus One (museum & planetarium or IMAX films) $27/$22/$16; Super Saver (museum, planetarium, IMAX films & special exhibitions) $35/$28/$22

■ Eat at the lower-level food court, or one of the three cafés.

■ Join a free tour at 15 minutes past the hour, 10:15am–3:15pm, daily.

9 Meteorites, Minerals, and Gems

Wonders include the 563-carat sapphire Star of India **(right)**, a 596-lb (270-kg) Brazilian topaz crystal, and the Cape York meteorite, 4.5 billion years old and weighing 34 tons.

10 Birds of the World

The world's most complete collection of birds. More than a million specimens are organized geographically, with dioramas of oceanic, North American, and other birds of the world.

Rose Center for Earth and Space

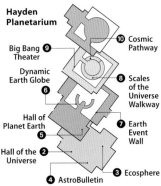

Hayden Planetarium

Big Bang Theater **9**

Dynamic Earth Globe **6**

Hall of Planet Earth **5**

Hall of the Universe **2**

AstroBulletin **4**

10 Cosmic Pathway

8 Scales of the Universe Walkway

7 Earth Event Wall

3 Ecosphere

5 Hall of Planet Earth
Geological samples from around the world and videos explain the various processes that formed the earth and continue to shape it.

Hall of Planet Earth

1 The Building
Opened in 2000 to explore inner earth and the outer universe, the dramatic exhibit building is a huge glass cube enclosing a three-story, 87-ft- (27-m-) wide sphere containing the Hayden Planetarium.

2 Hall of the Universe
Exhibits, divided into the universe, galaxies, stars, and planets, show the discoveries of modern astrophysics. Digital scales measure your weight on Saturn, Jupiter, and the Sun.

Hall of the Universe

3 Ecosphere
A sealed spherical aquarium in the Hall of the Universe holds a complete, self-sustaining ecosystem of plants, algae and animals that recycle nutrients and obtain energy solely from sunlight. The exhibit explores the basis of life on Earth.

4 AstroBulletin
This high-definition screen displays the latest imagery from telescope observations worldwide and current NASA missions.

6 Dynamic Earth Globe
This globe, suspended above an amphitheater in the Hall of Planet Earth, uses a projection system to recreate views of a rotating earth as seen from space.

7 Earth Event Wall
Events such as earthquakes or volcanoes are broadcast on a screen as they unfold. Other video stations show scientists at work.

8 Scales of the Universe Walkway
Models show the relative sizes of cosmic, human, and microscopic objects, from galaxies, stars, and planets down to the human brain and the smallest atom.

9 Big Bang Theater
Glass flooring around a circular opening lets visitors look down into a multisensory interpretation of the first movements of the universe. Explanatory narration is by Liam Neeson.

10 Cosmic Pathway
The Big Bang exits to this sloping 360-ft (110-m) pathway with astronomical images tracing landmarks through 13 billion years of cosmic evolution.

THE HAYDEN PLANETARIUM

Entrance to the Rose Center for Earth and Space

The Hayden Planetarium, a remarkable advance in the study of astronomy and astrophysics, boasts a highly sophisticated Digital Dome System that is the most advanced high-resolution virtual reality simulator ever built. The space shows take place in a 429-seat Space Theater and are virtual flights through a scientifically accurate universe. It is advisable to order tickets for the space shows in advance, or to pick them up early in the day to secure a spot. Don't miss *Dark Universe*, a spectacular space show that launches visitors into the night sky on an epic voyage through time and space.

TOP 10 FEATURES

1 **3D Milky Way** model

2 **High speed** simulators

3 **In-depth study** of galaxy

4 **Advanced** star projector

5 **Up-to-date** planetary data supported by NASA

6 **Onyx 2 Infinite Reality** supercomputer

7 **3D map** of the galaxy

8 **Continuous calculation** of star locations

9 **"Flyby"** of Orion Nebula

10 **Simulations** of current events

Dark Universe **space show at the Hayden Planetarium**

The Top 10
of Everything

Interior of the historic St. Patrick's
Cathedral, Lower Manhattan

🔟 Figures in New York History

1 Peter Stuyvesant

Sent from the Netherlands in 1647 to govern New Amsterdam, Peter Stuyvesant (1612–1672) was so disliked by his subjects that they welcomed British occupation.

2 Alexander Hamilton

Revolutionary leader and first Secretary of the Treasury, Hamilton (1755–1804) introduced business-friendly policies, instrumental in New York's emergence as the financial center of the US. He lost his life in a duel with political opponent Aaron Burr and is buried in Trinity Church graveyard.

Alexander Hamilton

3 William "Boss" Tweed

The political leader of Tammany Hall, Tweed (1823–78) became the living embodiment of political corruption, kickbacks, and payoffs. It is estimated that he and his associates took up to $200 million from the city. To hide his crime, he did good works, building orphanages, public baths, and hospitals, but he died in prison.

4 DeWitt Clinton

Mayor of the city, governor of the state, and US senator, Clinton (1769–1828) is best remembered for negotiating

Clinton opens Erie Canal

the construction of the Erie Canal in 1817–25. By connecting the Great Lakes to the Hudson River, he helped to secure New York's future as a predominant seaport.

5 Jacob Riis

Appalled by immigrant living conditions, Riis (1849–1914), a social reformer, writer, and photographer, used photos taken in tenements to illustrate his stories, shocking the middle class and motivating them to act. His 1888 article, "Flashes from the Slums," as well as his book, *How the Other Half Lives*, brought national attention.

6 John D. Rockefeller, Jr.

The largest of John D. Rockefeller, Jr. (1874–1960) helped support housing in Harlem, the Bronx, and Queens, created Fort Tryon Park and the Cloisters, and provided land for the United Nations. Construction of Rockefeller Center (see pp16–19) employed thousands at the height of the Depression, giving the city an enduring landmark.

John D. Rockefeller, Jr.

7 Fiorello H. LaGuardia

Considered to have been the best mayor of the city, after his election in 1933 Fiorello H. LaGuardia (1882–1947) modernized and centralized a chaotic city government, eliminated waste, unified the transit system, and obtained federal funds to help the city. A man of the people, he is popularly remembered for his reading of comics on the radio during a city newspaper strike.

8 ## Robert Moses
As construction supervisor and parks commissioner from the 1930s to the 1950s, Robert Moses (1888–1981) vastly enlarged and upgraded the city's recreational areas, but he also covered the city with highways rather than develop a public transport system and was responsible for urban renewal projects that razed many neighborhoods in favor of high-rises.

9 ## Donald Trump
"The Donald" (b. 1946), the flamboyant real estate wheeler–dealer, has left an indelible mark on New York. The huge Trump Place development overlooks the Hudson River, while the cheapest condo in Trump World Tower (the world's highest residential building 2001–3) costs over $1 million.

10 ## Rudolph Giuliani
Mayor "Rudy" Giuliani (b. 1944) is widely credited with reducing crime, making the city cleaner, and upgrading quality of life for most New York citizens during his tenure, 1993–2001. Once controversial for his strong personality, he rallied a stunned city following the attack on the World Trade Center and won praise at home and abroad.

Rudolph "Rudy" Giuliani

TOP 10 DATES IN NEW YORK HISTORY

Peter Minuit buys Manhattan

1 1626
Peter Minuit buys Manhattan from the Lenape Indians. Beads and trinkets worth about 60 Dutch guilders at the time accomplished the deal.

2 1664
The British take Manhattan from the Dutch. New Amsterdam becomes New York.

3 1789
George Washington is inaugurated as first President and takes his oath of office in Federal Hall. New York serves as the first US capital.

4 1792
New York Stock Exchange is established; 24 traders sign an agreement beneath a tree on Wall Street, and the city becomes a financial center.

5 1857
Central Park opens and the city gains a green expanse enjoyed by millions every year.

6 1886
The Statue of Liberty is unveiled, becoming the symbol of freedom for millions of immigrants, who form a "melting pot" of nationalities.

7 1898
The five boroughs unite to form New York, the world's second largest city.

8 1931
The Empire State Building establishes New York as the skyscraper capital of the world.

9 1952
The city becomes home to the headquarters of the United Nations.

10 2001
Terrorists use hijacked planes to destroy the World Trade Center.

🔟 Museums

1 Metropolitan Museum of Art

It would take weeks to take in all the treasures of this mammoth, ever-changing museum that includes a collection of more than 3,000 European paintings. The Greek, Roman, Cypriot, and Asian halls attract a good number of visitors, and the Joyce and Robert Menschel Hall for Modern Photography is also well attended *(see pp34–7)*.

2 Museum of Modern Art

The renovation of MoMA for the museum's 75th anniversary in 2004 cost $425 million and doubled the capacity of the building. MoMA has one of the most comprehensive collections of modern art in the world, including works by Picasso, Van Gogh, and Warhol *(see p132)*.

3 American Museum of Natural History

Exhibiting everything from dinosaurs to Chinese costumes and rare gems,

Museum of Modern Art

this is the largest museum of its kind in the world. In addition to the planetarium show in the Rose Center, there are films screened in a giant IMAX theater *(see pp40–43)*.

4 Solomon R. Guggenheim Museum

The Guggenheim has expanded its collection with several major donations, including Justin Thannhauser's Impressionist masters, Peggy Guggenheim's Cubist, Surrealist, and Abstract Expressionist works, a collection of American Minimalist and Conceptual art, and the most extensive collection of Kandinsky's works in the US *(see pp38–9)*.

5 Whitney Museum of American Art

MAP M2 ■ 99 Gansevoort St
■ Open 10:30am–6pm Sun, Mon, Wed & Thu; 10:30am–10pm Fri & Sat ■ 212 570 3600 ■ Adm (7–10pm Fri is pay-what-you-wish)
■ www.whitney.org

The entire range of 20th- and 21st-century American art can be seen in the permanent collection in this striking Renzo Piano building, along with changing contemporary exhibitions. The museum showcases works by renowned artists such as Warhol, Calder, O'Keeffe, and Hopper

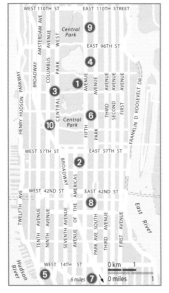

6 Frick Collection

MAP G4 ■ 1 East 70th St at 5th Ave ■ Open 10am–6pm Tue–Sat, 11am–5pm Sun ■ Adm ■ www.frick.org

The mansion of industrialist Henry Clay Frick, with an indoor garden court and fountain, is the setting for his exceptional collection of Old Masters, French furniture, and Limoges enamels. You can view works by Rembrandt, Vermeer, and Hals in the West Gallery, with ones by Holbein, Titian, and Bellini on display in the Living Hall.

7 Brooklyn Museum

200 Eastern Pkwy, Brooklyn ■ Subway 2, 3 to Eastern Pkwy ■ Open 11am–6pm Wed–Sun (to 10pm Thu), 11am–11pm first Sat of month (except Sep) ■ Adm ■ www.brooklynmuseum.org

Housed in a fine Beaux Arts building, this museum presents a wide range of special exhibitions alongside its permanent collections of Asian, Egyptian, African, and American art. The Elizabeth A. Sackler Center for Feminist Art is the first public space of its kind in the country.

8 Morgan Library and Museum

MAP K4 ■ 225 Madison Ave at 36th St ■ Open 10:30am–5pm Tue–Thu, 10:30am–9pm Fri, 10am–6pm Sat, 11am–6pm Sun ■ Adm ■ www.themorgan.org

This Italian Renaissance-style palazzo was designed in 1902 to hold the collection of billionaire J. Pierpont Morgan – an extraordinary assemblage of rare manuscripts, books, prints, drawings, and ancient artifacts. Morgan's original opulent study and library are highlights. There are also galleries with changing exhibitions.

Museum of the City of New York

9 Museum of the City of New York

MAP D3 ■ 1220 5th Ave at 103rd St ■ Open 10am–6pm daily ■ Adm ■ www.mcny.org

The toy collection is a highlight and rotating exhibitions explore fashion, architecture, entertainment, cultural identity, ethnic traditions, and social history. A film documenting the evolution of the city is featured.

10 American Folk Art Museum

MAP G2 ■ 2 Lincoln Square (Columbus Ave at 66th St) ■ Open 11:30am–7pm Tue–Thu & Sat, noon–7:30pm Fri, noon–6pm Sun ■ www.folkartmuseum.org

The first New York museum built from the ground up has critiqued the country's cultural history since opening in 1961. The eight-level, innovative structure shows off a collection of whimsical, all-American paintings, sculptures, quilts, and furniture.

Egyptian exhibit, Brooklyn Museum

American Folk Art Museum

🔟 Art Galleries

Balloon Swan by Jeff Koons at the Gagosian gallery

① Gagosian
MAP E4 ■ 980 Madison Ave; Chelsea: 555 West 24th St & 522 West 21st St ■ Open 10am–6pm Tue–Sat ■ www.gagosian.com

Expect big names and equivalent price tags at this blue-ribbon gallery with three locations (one uptown and two Chelsea addresses, each with the lofty spaces necessary for exhibiting large-scale art. Damien Hirst, Anselm Kiefer, Richard Serra, and Jeff Koons are among the contemporary artists represented.

② Marlborough
MAP H3 ■ 40 West 57th St, Floor 2; Chelsea: 545 West 25th St ■ Open 10am–5:30pm Mon–Sat ■ www.marlboroughgallery.com

This top-of-the-art-world gallery, representing the estates of artists including Larry Rivers, Red Grooms, and R. B. Kitaj, has opted for two locations. The midtown gallery has shown work by sculptors such as Anthony Caro and Jacques Lipchitz. New sculptures and paintings are found at the Chelsea location.

③ Mary Boone
MAP L2 ■ 541 West 24th St between 10th & 11th Aves; Uptown: 745 5th Ave ■ Open 10am–6pm Tue–Sat (by appointment only on Sat in summer) ■ www.maryboonegallery.com

One of the art world's big names has a sleek Chelsea gallery. The work on display has a downtown edge and talented newcomers share space with established artists. Occasional intriguing group shows, assembled by independent curators, include sculpture, photography, and painting.

④ Pace
MAP H4 ■ 32 East 57th St, Floor 4; Chelsea: 508, 510, & 534 West 25th St ■ Open 10am–6pm Tue–Sat ■ www.pacegallery.com/newyork

Expect the likes of Picasso, Rothko, Chuck Close, or Agnes Martin at this ultra-prestigious gallery exhibiting modern masters of the 20th and 21st centuries.

At 57th Street the galleries are for photographs, prints, and fine art, while the gallery located in Chelsea shows large-scale pieces.

5 Sperone Westwater
MAP N4 ■ 257 Bowery
■ Open 10am–6pm Tue–Sat
■ www.speronewestwater.com
This is an excellent place to see some of the most creative contemporary art being produced today. The gallery was set up in 1975 to showcase European artists who had little recognition in the US. In 2010 it moved to a building designed by Foster + Partners. Exhibitions have included works by Bruce Nauman and Donald Judd.

The Drawing Center

6 The Drawing Center
MAP P4 ■ 35 Wooster St
■ Open noon–6pm Wed & Fri–Sun, noon–8pm Thu; closed Nov 25–6, Dec 24–Jan 1 ■ Adm
■ www.drawingcenter.org
Formed in 1977 to promote the art of drawing, this non-profit center has displayed the drawings of more than 2,500 emerging artists, including the early work of Shahzia Sikander and Kara Walker, as well as the work of the Old Masters. The center also hosts monthly events, including book signings and panel discussions.

7 apexart
MAP P3–4 ■ 291 Church St
■ Open 11am–6pm Tue–Sat
■ www.apexart.org
Contemporary visual arts exhibitions, as well as public lectures, readings, children's workshops, and innovative performances are on offer at this not-for-profit organization, which aims to promote cultural and intellectual diversity. Over 17,000 visitors pass through its doors each year to see the latest works by artists such as Dave Hickey, Martha Rosler, and David Byrne.

8 Matthew Marks
This was one of the first commercial galleries to open in Chelsea, in a converted garage in 1994. Matthew Marks specializes in displaying the work of big-name artists such as Ellsworth Kelly, Jasper Johns, Nan Goldin, and Brice Marden. Three other Chelsea locations show new works by painters, photographers, and sculptors (see p124).

9 Paula Cooper
Paula Cooper, the first gallery to open in SoHo in 1968, deserted the area in 1996 to move to Chelsea (see p124). There, the vast, creatively designed space filtering natural light through a cathedral ceiling is a superb setting for conceptual and minimalist art by Donald Judd, Sol LeWitt, Sophie Calle, and others.

10 Paul Kasmin
Kasmin is the son of a bohemian London art dealer and continues the family tradition of taking chances on new artists. He usually features these artists in group shows. More established names, including those of sculptors and photographers, regularly appear here in solo exhibitions (see p124).

Gallery shop, Paul Kasmin

🔟 New York Skyscrapers

1 Empire State Building

The Empire State Building (1930–1) was eclipsed as the tallest structure in New York for 28 years by the World Trade Center, which was destroyed in the 9/11 terrorist attack. It was overtaken again upon completion of One World Trade Center in 2014. With an 86th-floor observatory, the Empire State Building receives some 4 million visitors a year (see pp12–13).

2 Chrysler Building

The gleaming, stainless-steel, tiered spire of the Chrysler Building (1928–30) adds grace to the city skyline. William Van Alen fashioned this Art Deco classic as a tribute to the automobile. The building has a decorative frieze of stylized hubcaps and silver gargoyles, much like the winged radiator caps of a Chrysler automobile (see p127).

Woolworth Building

3 Woolworth Building
MAP Q4 ■ 233 Broadway, between Park Pl & Barclay St

Prominent architect Cass Gilbert was responsible for this flamboyant 1913 Neo-Gothic building, the tallest in the world for two decades after it was completed. The rich terra-cotta ornamentation accentuates the structure's steel frame, which soars to a graceful crown 60 stories above Broadway. The small lobby boasts a luxurious marble interior using stone from Greece and Vermont (see p85).

4 Comcast Building
MAP J3 ■ 30 Rockefeller Plaza, between 50th & 51st Sts
■ Closed to public

This dramatic 70-story skyscraper (1931–3), designed by Raymond Hood, has shallow setbacks that recede into the distance. Part of the greatness of Hood's design is the contrast between the building's height and the surrounding Rockefeller Center (see pp16–17).

5 Flatiron Building

This 21-story, triangular-shaped building has intrigued New Yorkers since it was built by Daniel Burnham in 1902; the shape was so unusual that people took bets on whether it would topple. The secret

Spire of the Chrysler Building

helps blur the division between indoor and outdoor space. Inside is the Four Seasons restaurant, offering American cuisine.

8 601 Lexington Avenue
MAP J4 ■ 601 Lexington Ave ■ Closed to public

This was considered New York's first Postmodern skyscraper upon its completion in 1978. The triangular top never served its original purpose as a solar panel, but it did make the building instantly recognizable. An open base on four tall columns and a reflective aluminum-and-glass exterior give it an airy quality.

9 World Wide Plaza
MAP J2 ■ Between 8th & 9th Aves and 49th & 50th Sts

The copper roof and frosted-glass crown atop this 48-story tower bring some traditional romance to a 1989 Postmodern building. The World Wide Plaza complex transformed a decaying neighborhood.

10 One World Trade Center
MAP Q3 ■ 285 Fulton St ■ Open 9am–8pm daily (to 12am Jun–Sep)

Marking the rebirth of Lower Manhattan after 9/11, the One World Trade Center opened in 2014. The tallest building in the city, it rises to a height of 1,776 ft (541 m), reflecting the year of the Declaration of Independence.

One World Trade Center

of this successful design was in the steel frame support, which was used instead of traditional heavy stone walls: a precursor of skyscrapers to come *(see p116)*.

6 Lever House
MAP J4 ■ 390 Park Ave, between 53rd and 54th Sts ■ Open during office hours (plaza and lobby only)

Gordon Bunshaft's 24-story Lever House, completed in 1952, was revolutionary; it was New York's first skyscraper built in the form of a vertical slab of glass and steel. It began the eventual transformation of Park Avenue into an avenue of glass towers.

7 Seagram Building
MAP J4 ■ 375 Park Ave, between 52nd & 53rd Sts ■ Open during office hours (plaza and lobby only)

The first New York building by Mies van der Rohe is this landmark "glass box" with slender bands of bronze amid walls of smoked glass rising from the open plaza. The glass-walled lobby by Philip Johnson

🔟 Historic Buildings

Interior of St. Patrick's Cathedral

1 St. Paul's Chapel
Completed in 1766, this church has a glorious Georgian interior lit by Waterford Crystal chandeliers. The pew where George Washington prayed after his inauguration as President has been preserved (see p86).

2 City Hall
This Georgian building (1803–12) with French Renaissance influences is one of New York's finest. The interior features a rotunda circled by ten Corinthian columns, opening to twin spiral marble staircases (see p86).

City Hall

3 Trinity Church
This lovely, square-towered church, built 1839–46 (see p79), has bronze doors designed by Richard Morris Hunt. The spire, once the tall-est structure in Manhattan, is now dwarfed by Wall Street towers. Alexander Hamilton (see p46) and Robert Fulton are buried here.

4 St. Patrick's Cathedral
James Renwick, Jr. designed America's largest Catholic cathedral (opened in 1879) in French Gothic style with twin 330-ft (100-m) towers. The interior has side altars dedicated to saints and holy figures, chapels, and stained-glass windows (see p128).

5 Carnegie Hall
Industrialist Andrew Carnegie financed the city's first great concert hall, built in 1891. Major renovation in 1996 restored the wonderful interior bronze balconies and ornamental plaster, and a museum was added. The corridors of the hall are lined with memorabilia of the great artists who have performed here (see p129).

6 Cathedral of St. John the Divine
The world's largest cathedral was begun in 1892 and is still a work in progress. The part-Romanesque, part-Gothic building is impressive for its stonework, enormous nave, bay altar windows, and rose window. The seat of New York's episcopal arch-diocese, the church is the scene of many avant-garde musical and theatrical events (see p148).

7 New York Stock Exchange

Opened in 1903, the facade of this 17-story edifice is appropriately monumental for the building at the center of the US economy. The figures on the pediment represent the "sources of American prosperity." "Black Thursday," the start of the Great Depression, began here in 1929 *(see p79)*.

8 US Custom House

One of the city's best Neo-Classical buildings, this eight-story structure, built in 1907, features an elaborate mansard roof and fine sculptures, including four by Daniel Chester French. A 1927 nautical mural by Reginald Marsh adorns the huge, oval rotunda *(see p79)*.

9 New York Public Library

This white marble, 1911 Beaux Arts edifice is magnificent both inside and out. Imposing stairways, terraces, and fountains inspire awe, while reading rooms invite repose. Events and lectures are frequently held here *(see p128)*.

10 Grand Central Terminal

This 1913 public facility is remarkable for its beauty; the main concourse is suffused with natural light and the vaulted ceiling is decorated with myriad twinkling constellations *(see p127)*.

The main concourse of Grand Central Terminal

TOP 10 CHURCHES AND TEMPLES

Temple Emanu-El

1 Zion St. Mark's Evangelical Lutheran Church
MAP F5 ▪ 339 East 84th St
Built in 1892, this church is a reminder of the Upper East's German past.

2 St. George Ukrainian Catholic Church
MAP M4 ▪ 30 East 7th St
A contemporary church built in Byzantine style.

3 St. Nicholas Russian Orthodox Cathedral
MAP E4 ▪ 15 East 97th St
Five onion domes mark this Russian Baroque church.

4 St. Sava Serbian Orthodox Cathedral
MAP L3 ▪ 16–20 West 26th St
Byzantine windows were added to this 1856 church.

5 St. Vartan Armenian Cathedral
MAP K4 ▪ 630 2nd Ave
The gold-leaf dome was inspired by the churches of Armenia.

6 St. Elizabeth of Hungary Church
MAP F4 ▪ 211 East 83rd St
This Neo-Gothic church has a painted vaulted ceiling.

7 Holy Trinity Cathedral
MAP G5 ▪ 319 East 74th St
Built in 1931 in Byzantine style as the seat of the Greek Orthodox diocese.

8 Temple Emanu-El
MAP G4 ▪ 1 East 65th St
World's largest synagogue, built in 1929.

9 First Chinese Presbyterian Church
MAP P5 ▪ 61 Henry St
The stone sanctuary dates from 1819.

10 Islamic Cultural Center
MAP E4 ▪ 1711 3rd Ave at 96th St
Ninety bulbs hang from the dome.

🔟 Off The Beaten Path

Aerial view of Governors Island

1 Governors Island
New York Harbor ■ Open late May–late Sep: 10am–6pm daily (to 7pm Sat & Sun) ■ www.govisland.com

The ferry ride only takes 10 minutes to this former Coast Guard base in the middle of New York harbor. It features open-air sculpture exhibits, summer concerts, and festivals.

2 Socrates Sculpture Park
MAP F6 ■ 32-01 Vernon Blvd, Queens ■ Open 10am–sunset daily ■ www.socratessculpturepark.org

Tap into New York City's vibrant out-door art scene at this free sculpture park. It hosts lots of free events, from summer solstice to Halloween.

3 Green-Wood Cemetery
500 25th St, Brooklyn ■ Open Mar–Apr & Oct–Mar: 7:45am–6pm; May–Sep: 7:45am–7pm ■ www.green-wood.com

Roam the final resting place of many New York personalities, from Jean-Michel Basquiat to Leonard Bernstein, at this landscaped beauty.

4 Roosevelt Island and Tramway
MAP H5

Climb aboard the Roosevelt Island Tramway, one of the oldest aerial commuter tramways in the US, to this island in the East River, with everything from a 19th-century lighthouse to the quiet, riverfront Franklin D. Roosevelt Four Freedoms Park.

5 New York Earth Room
MAP N4 ■ 141 Wooster St ■ Open Sep–Jun: noon–3pm & 3:30–6pm Wed–Sun ■ www.diart.org/sites/main/earthroom

The draw of this modern installation by Walter De Maria is the juxtaposition – in SoHo, amid the most expensive real estate in the world, is a massive room filled with nothing but dirt.

6 Wave Hill
West 249th St, Riverdale, Bronx ■ Open 9am–5:30pm daily (Nov–mid-Mar: to 4:30pm) ■ Adm ■ www.wavehill.org

Walk in the footsteps of Mark Twain and Theodore Roosevelt, who once resided in the stately Wave Hill House, which presides over this historic garden and cultural center overlooking the Hudson River.

7 Alice Austen House
2 Hylan Blvd, Staten Island ■ Open Mar–Dec: 11am–5pm Tue–Sun ■ www.aliceausten.org ■ Donation

See historic New York City through the photos of Alice Austen, one of the

Alice Austen House, Staten Island

nation's pioneering photographers, in this museum on the shores of the Narrows on Staten Island.

8 Museum of the Moving Image

It's a long way from Hollywood, but Queens has one of the finest movie museums in the nation – and it's free on Friday nights (4–8pm). The permanent exhibition includes historic cameras and vintage TVs, but the real draw is the museum's interactive exhibits; for example, you can dub in your own voice over famous movie scenes (see p158).

Museum of the Moving Image

9 Greenacre Park

MAP J4 ▪ East 51st St, between 2nd and 3rd Aves ▪ www.sasaki.com/project/111/greenacre-park

A waterfall in Midtown Manhattan? Your eyes do not deceive you. This often overlooked but lovely "vest-pocket" park features leafy corners, fragrant flowers and a tumbling 25-ft- (8-m-) high waterfall that sends off a refreshing spray of cooling water over passersby.

10 Red Hook
South Brooklyn

▪ www.redhookwaterfront.com

Take in gorgeous vistas of the New York City skyline and a straight-on view of the iconic Statue of Liberty (Manhattan and New Jersey only get views of the back and side) from this waterfront Brooklyn neighborhood, dotted with homey spots like the Red Hook Lobster Pound and Steve's Authentic Key Lime Pies.

TOP 10 PARKS AND GARDENS

Madison Square Park in spring

1 Central Park
The grand dame of New York City's parks (see pp32–3).

2 The High Line
This elevated train-track-turned-stylish-park has transformed the surrounding Meatpacking District (see p121).

3 Bryant Park
MAP K3 ▪ 6th Ave, between 41st and 42nd Sts
A swath of green with formal planting in Midtown, behind the New York Public Library.

4 Madison Square Park
MAP L3 ▪ 5th Ave and Broadway, at 23rd St
This landscaped park has striking displays of public art.

5 91st Street Community Garden
MAP E2 ▪ Riverside Park, at 91st St
A lovely grove filled with flowers.

6 Hudson River Park
MAP N2 ▪ From 59th St to Battery Park
The longest waterfront park in the US.

7 New York Botanical Garden
The city's premiere botanical garden with plants and flowers from all around the world (see p155).

8 The Cloisters' Gardens
An oasis of serene beauty, where over 250 kinds of plants grown in the Middle Ages can be found (see p37).

9 Battery Park
MAP R3 ▪ Southern tip of Manhattan
Waterfront park with views of New York Harbor and the Statue of Liberty.

10 John Jay Park
MAP F5 ▪ East 77th St and FDR Drive
Past the playgrounds is a placid seating area with East River views.

TOP 10 Places for Children

Chelsea Piers sports complex

1 Central Park

Myriad activities include storytelling, carousel rides, boating, and guided walks. The Central Park Zoo is excellent and the Tisch Children's Zoo allows petting and feeding of farm animals *(see pp32–3)*.

2 Chelsea Piers

Opportunities to work off energy are many at this family-friendly sports complex with an indoor bowling alley and ice-skating rink. Seasonal outdoor activities include a golf driving range and batting cages for baseball *(see p122)*.

3 Children's Museum of Manhattan

Educational fun with exhibits like Body Odyssey, exploring a giant crawl-through body, and a TV studio where kids produce their own shows. Under-fours have their own play area *(see p144)*.

4 American Museum of Natural History

Introduce children to the world-famous dioramas of wild animals in realistic natural habitats and the fascinating dinosaur exhibits. The enormous meteorites and mineral rock specimens are also favorites. The Rose Center will intrigue older children and teens *(see pp40–41)*.

5 Sony Wonder Technology Lab

MAP H4 ■ Sony Plaza at 56th St & Madison Ave ■ 212 833 8100
■ www.sonywondertechlab.com
Go on a digital adventure in this four-story technology and entertainment centre that appeals to all ages. Children can create video games, movies, and music for free, or perform dance moves with animated characters. It is recommended to make reservations.

6 New Victory Theater

MAP J3 ■ 209 West 42nd St, between 7th & 8th Aves ■ Box office open noon–7pm Tue–Sat, 11am–5pm Sun & Mon ■ Adm ■ www.new victory.org
New York's first major theater devoted to family entertainment. Pre-performance workshops with staff and cast offer interesting insights into how a theater works.

New Victory performer

7 Coney Island

Coney Island has undergone major redevelopments after years of neglect. Features of the island include Luna Park, which has thrilling rides, the landmark Ferris wheel, a long sandy beach, and a beachside boardwalk with a carnival atmosphere that is peppered with marine mosaics, gaming arcades, concession stands hawking prizes, and sideshows. It is a fabulous children's playground. Summer is the best time to visit, as most of the attractions are outdoors, but the crowds can get heavy on weekends.

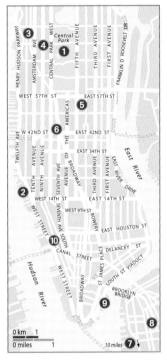

Rides at Coney Island

8 New York Transit Museum

130 Livingston St, Brooklyn ■ 718 694 1600 ■ 10am–4pm Tue–Fri, 11am–5pm Sat–Sun ■ Adm ■ www.mta.info/mta/museum/

Discover the intricate world of New York City's subways, trains, buses, and bridge and tunnel systems at this lively museum, filled with interactive exhibits. A gallery annex is also at Grand Central Terminal (*see p132*).

9 Tall Ship Cruises

MAP Q4 ■ South Street Seaport Museum: Pier 16 at South Street Seaport ■ May–Sep: Tue–Sun ■ Adm

A boat ride in Manhattan harbor is always a thrill, and what better way to go to sea than aboard the 1885 schooner *Pioneer* at South Street Seaport? Lunchtime 90-minute sails are good for those with short attention spans; 2-hour cruises depart afternoon and evening.

10 Children's Museum of the Arts

MAP N3 ■ 103 Charlton St, between Hudson & Greenwich Sts ■ Open noon–5pm Mon, noon–6pm Thu & Fri, 10am–5pm Sat & Sun ■ Adm ■ www.cmany.org

When little ones get fed up with sightseeing, bring them to this SoHo stop to enjoy interactive exhibits. Kids are invited to create works of art using a range of materials, and work off energy in play areas. Under-fives have their own WEE (wondrous experimenting and exploring) Arts drop-in sessions. Children's art from other nations is on show.

Gay and Lesbian New York

Exterior of Stonewall Inn

1 Stonewall Inn
MAP N3 ■ 53 Christopher St

A police raid on this bar on June 27, 1969 turned into a riot as gays rose up against constant police harassment. The present bar is a far more peaceful spot.

2 Christopher Street
MAP N3

The profusion of bars, shops, and cruisers between 6th and 7th Avenues used to be the epicenter of gay Greenwich Village before the boys moved on to Chelsea and Hell's Kitchen. It still retains a sense of history, however. Now the crowd in the area tends to be a bit older.

3 Bluestockings Bookstore
MAP N5 ■ 172 Allen St at Stanton St

This Lower East Side haunt, named after an 18th-century feminist group, changes its clothes (so to speak) throughout the day. It's a solid source for women's literature, a Fair Trade organic café, and a platform for a full calendar of readings, performances, and other community events.

4 Chelsea
MAP M2/L2 ■ 8th Ave between West 14th & West 23rd Sts

This neighborhood is where it all happens these days. Gay revelers pack the bars and spill onto the sidewalks at the weekend, and a scene of some sort can be found in every café and club.

5 Lesbian, Gay, Bisexual, and Transgender Community Center
MAP M2 ■ 208 West 13th St ■ Open 9am–10pm daily

Since 1983 this center has been a nucleus of the gay community, serving as a meeting space for local organizations, a leader in public education, health, and emotional counseling, and a destination for social events. It also documents gay and lesbian history in the extensive library it maintains.

6 Publications

Next is a weekly magazine reviewing the club and entertainment scene. Other publications include *Gay City News*, a newspaper covering politics, health, and arts; and *Metrosource*, a glossy lifestyle magazine. *Time Out New York*, a general entertainment weekly

Bluestockings Bookstore

handed out free every Wednesday, has a big section on gay and lesbian events, from lectures to clubs.

7 Club Nights
Check listings publications for details
Many bars and clubs have party nights, like Thursdays at The Eagle, Saturdays at HK, and Sundays at The Monster. The Cock is lively most nights. New York nightlife is under pressure from rising rents and complaining neighbors, and venues frequently change.

8 Lesbian Herstory Archives
484 14th St, Brooklyn ▪ Subway (F) 15th St, Prospect Park ▪ 718 768 3953 ▪ Open by appointment
The world's largest and oldest lesbian archive, founded in 1973, is located in Park Slope, a popular lesbian neighborhood. The volunteer-run archive houses art, books, photos, periodicals, video, and films recording lesbian lives. It also holds events supporting lesbian writers and artists in all media.

9 David Barton Gym
MAP L3 ▪ 656 6th Avenue at 20th St ▪ Open 5:30am–midnight Mon–Fri, 8am–9pm Sat & Sun ▪ Adm
The muscle boys in Chelsea flock to this upscale gym, which relocated in 2015 to the one-time Limelight nightclub space in what used to be an Episcopal church. Besides yoga, spin classes, steam rooms, and Russian baths, you will find a DJ and a Bumble and Bumble hair salon.

10 The Leslie Lohman Museum of Gay and Lesbian Art
MAP P3 ▪ 26 Wooster St ▪ Open noon–6pm Tue–Sun, noon–8pm Thu ▪ 212 431 2609 ▪ www.leslielohman.org
One of the nation's oldest gay and lesbian art museums, the Leslie Lohman Museum features exhibits across all mediums, ranging from photography and video to paintings and drawings.

TOP 10 EATING AND MEETING PLACES

Henrietta Hudson logo

1 Eastern Bloc
MAP N5 ▪ 505 East 6th St
This Soviet-themed East Village hole-in-the-wall is frequently packed.

2 Gym
MAP L2 ▪ 167 8th Ave
This friendly, casual site is home to New York City's first gay sports bar.

3 Therapy
MAP H2 ▪ 348 West 52nd St
Chic two-level lounge with cabaret shows, nightly DJs, and great drinks.

4 G
MAP L3 ▪ 225 West 19th St
This trendy lounge has a live DJ, a round stainless steel bar, and a conversation pit.

5 Flaming Saddles
MAP H2 ▪ 793 9th Ave
A casual saloon-style boys bar complete with chaps-clad dancers.

6 Phoenix
MAP M5 ▪ 447 East 13th St
An East Village hangout with an old-school vibe. Unpretentious, with cheap drinks.

7 The Eagle
MAP L2 ▪ 554 West 28th St
In this place, it's all about Levi's, leather and fetish.

8 Posh Bar
MAP J2 ▪ 405 West 51st St
An elegant, laid-back bar with half-price drinks during Happy Hour.

9 Henrietta Hudson
MAP N3 ▪ 438 Hudson St
Warm, down-to-earth, lesbian lair in Greenwich Village.

10 The Cubby Hole
MAP M2 ▪ 281 West 12th St
A cozy, unpretentious lesbian bar where the regulars sing along to the songs on the jukebox.

🔟 Performing Arts Venues

A ballet dancer performs at David H. Koch Theater

1 Carnegie Hall

This historic concert hall opened in 1891 with Tchaikovsky making his US debut on the podium. A campaign led by violinist Isaac Stern saved the hall from demolition after Lincoln Center (see p142) was completed in 1969, and it entered its second century with old-world style intact after being lavishly renovated (see p129).

2 Metropolitan Opera House

Lincoln Center's most elegant performance venue shows off glorious oversize murals by Marc Chagall inside great arched windows. The interior boasts exquisite star-burst chandeliers that are raised to the ceiling before each performance. The theater presents the American Ballet Theater and many traveling groups, as well as its famous opera company (see p142).

3 David Geffen Hall

Thanks to the generosity of entertainment mogul David Geffen, the hall is expected to begin renovation in 2019. It is home to the New York Philharmonic, the oldest symphony orchestra in the US. A bust by Rodin of composer and once Philharmonic Music Director Gustav Mahler, on the west side of the building, is one of the finest pieces of public sculpture in Lincoln Center (see p142).

4 David H. Koch Theater

Formerly known as the New York State Theater, this famous stage was built in 1964 to the specification of legendary choreographer George Balanchine, the founder of the New York City Ballet company, which dances here in winter and spring. The venue also hosts performances from several international dance troupes (see p142).

⑤ Alice Tully Hall

This hall, with its stunning modern facade, was built in 1969 for the Chamber Music Society of Lincoln Center. Besides chamber and vocal concerts, it is used for shows by the Juilliard School students and faculty, many of which are free to the public *(see p142)*.

⑥ New York City Center

MAP H3 ■ 131 West 55th St, between 6th & 7th Aves ■ 212 581 1212 ■ Adm ■ www.nycity center.org

The ornate, Moorish-style building with a dome of Spanish tiles was opened in 1923 as a Shriners Temple. Having been saved from developers by city mayor Fiorello H. LaGuardia *(see p46)*, it survived after losing its companies to Lincoln Center, and is now a major venue for touring dance companies. The center was extensively renovated in 2011.

The ornate New York City Center

⑦ Joyce Theater

MAP L2 ■ 175 8th Ave at 19th St; Joyce Soho: 155 Mercer St ■ 212 242 0800 ■ Adm ■ www.joyce.org

This 1941 Art Deco movie theater was converted in 1982 to become an intimate home for dance. Small and medium-sized modern dance companies from around the world present an exciting range of work that can't be seen elsewhere in Manhattan. Question-and-answer sessions with artists and performers follow some of the shows.

The neon lights of Radio City

⑧ Radio City Music Hall

MAP J3 ■ 1260 6th Ave at 50th St ■ 212 247 4777 ■ Tours: 11am–3pm Mon–Sat ■ Adm ■ www.radiocity.com

Opened in 1932, the largest theater in the US has an opulent, Art Deco interior. Once a movie palace, it now hosts musical performances and special events. The Christmas show starring the Rockettes, a troupe of long-legged dancers, is a festive New York tradition.

⑨ Brooklyn Academy of Music (BAM)

30 Lafayette Ave, Brooklyn ■ Subway 2, 3, 4, 5, B, Q to Atlantic Ave ■ 718 636 4100 ■ Adm ■ www.bam.org

This Neo-Italianate 1908 building draws city-wide audiences for New York's most avant-garde program of international music, theater, and dance, most notably the Next Wave Festival, a fixture since 1981.

⑩ Madison Square Garden

MAP K3 ■ 7th Ave at 32nd St ■ 212 465 6741 ■ Adm ■ www.thegarden.com

Home court for the New York Knicks basketball team and the New York Rangers hockey team, this 20,000-seat venue is also used for rock concerts, ice shows, tennis, boxing, dog shows, and the circus.

🔟 Music Venues

Auditorium of the Beacon Theatre

1 Beacon Theatre
MAP G2 ■ Broadway at West 74th St ■ Open 1 hour before show ■ Adm

Name the star and they've probably been on stage at Beacon Theatre, where the likes of Bob Dylan and B. B. King have performed. Shows range from pop and light rock to gospel.

2 Village Vanguard
MAP M3 ■ 178 7th Ave South ■ Open 8pm–midnight ■ Adm

Since 1935, this club has featured a "who's who" of jazz. The early years were eclectic, also launching calypso singer Harry Belafonte.

3 Birdland
MAP J2 ■ 315 West 44th St, between 8th & 9th Aves ■ Open 5pm–3am Mon–Sun ■ Adm

Another legendary venue, although no longer in the location Charlie Parker in 1949; it is now near Times Square. The Birdland Big Band plays on Mondays.

4 SOBs
MAP N3 ■ 204 Varick St at West Houston St ■ Opening times vary ■ Adm

The letters stand for Sounds of Brazil, but the music ranges from African to reggae and hip-hop via soul or jazz. The beat is contagious, and the dance floor gets crowded.

5 Highline Ballroom
MAP M2 ■ 431 West 16th St between 9th & 10th Aves ■ Adm

This industrial-looking space on the edge of the Meatpacking District offers an intimate experience. Mos Def, Lou Reed, Jonatha Brooke, and Lady Sovereign are among the artists who have graced the stage here.

6 The Iridium
MAP J3 ■ 1650 Broadway at West 51st St ■ Open 7pm–2am Fri–Sat, 5pm–midnight Sun–Thu ■ Adm

Opened in 1994, Iridium has funky decor, good food, and excellent established and new jazz groups. The great guitarist Les Paul used to play here from 1996 to 2009. The Les Paul Trio continues the tradition every Monday night.

7 Dizzy's Club Coca Cola
MAP H2 ■ Broadway at 60th St ■ Sets at 7:30, 9:30, & 11:30pm daily ■ Adm

Part of Jazz at Lincoln Center, this dazzling club features changing line-ups of top jazz groups. The cover charge is steep, but "after-hours sets" are usually $10 maximum, and the food is reasonably priced.

⑧ Jazz Standard
MAP L4 ■ 116 East 27th St, between Park Ave Sth & Lexington Ave ■ Open 7pm–3am Tue–Sat (from 6pm Sun) ■ Adm

First-rate acoustics and a mix of music from traditional to avant-garde, plus a great restaurant, Blue Smoke (see p119). The Mingus Big Band plays most Monday nights.

⑨ Bowery Ballroom
MAP N4 ■ 6 Delancey St, between Bowery & Chrystie Sts ■ Opening times vary ■ Adm

The opening of the Bowery Ballroom in 1998 helped spearhead a Lower East Side renaissance. It boasts great acoustics and sight-lines. Well-known touring acts, mid-scale indie rockers, and local bands feature.

⑩ Blue Note
MAP N3 ■ 131 West 3rd St, between MacDougal St & 6th Ave ■ Open 7pm–2am Sun–Thu, 7pm–4am Fri & Sat ■ Adm & cover charge

Tony Bennett, Natalie Cole, and Ray Charles have all played this Greenwich Village venue. The emphasis is on jazz, but blues, Latin, R&B, soul, and big band also feature.

Blue Note jazz club

TOP 10 DANCE CLUBS

DJ playing at Webster Hall

1 Bar 13
MAP M4 ■ 35 East 13th St
Three floors, roof deck and rocking DJs.

2 Output
78 Wythe Ave, Williamsburg
Lots of techno and ambient music at this trendy place in Brooklyn.

3 Webster Hall
MAP M4 ■ 125 East 11th St
Headlining bands and DJs, as well as weekly dance parties.

4 Santos Party House
MAP P4 ■ 96 Lafayette St
Partygoers swing to the beat in this multi-level club in Lower Manhattan.

5 Marquee
MAP L2 ■ 289 10th Ave
Tough to get in, but worth it. House and hip-hop.

6 Verboten
54 North 11th St, Williamsburg
Hip Brooklyn club showcasing all forms of underground dance music.

7 Beauty Bar
MAP M4 ■ 231 East 14th St
Part dive bar, part salon with nightly dance parties with throwback DJs playing 80s and 90s music.

8 The 40/40 Club
MAP L3 ■ 6 West 25th St
Rapper Jay-Z's swanky sports bar and R&B dance spot also boasts exclusive VIP sections.

9 Cielo
MAP M2 ■ 18 Little West 12th St
The beautiful set come for soulful and deep house.

10 Pacha New York
MAP J2 ■ 618 West 46th St
Dance music and urban style over four floors from the Ibiza superclub.

🔟 Restaurants

The luxurious interior of Le Bernardin

① Le Bernardin

Seafood doesn't come any better than at this quietly luxurious French restaurant lauded for revolutionizing the way fish is served in New York city. Chef Eric Ripert seems to have no critics. Of course, perfection has its price and you'll pay dearly, but the meal will be memorable *(see p133)*.

Customers dining at Nobu

② Nobu

Reservations are hard to come by for Nobu Matsuhisa's Japanese/Peruvian fusion that produces inspired dishes. Say *"Omakase"* ("I'll leave it to you") and let the chef choose from the surprising and always sublime offerings. David Rockwell's whimsical setting adds to the experience *(see p107)*. Nobu Next Door, at the same address, needs no reservations and is more reasonable.

③ Eleven Madison Park
MAP L4 ■ 11 Madison Ave ■ 212 889 0905 ■ $$$

Indulge in a French-inspired feast – from suckling pig to tender duck to a dizzyingly delicious chocolate tart drizzled with caramel – at this grand Madison Avenue restaurant helmed by famed restaurateur Danny Meyer and chef Daniel Humm.

④ Gotham Bar and Grill
MAP M3 ■ 12 East 12th St, between 5th Ave & University Pl ■ 212 620 4020 ■ $$$

A perennial favorite. Alfred Portale was one of the first with "vertical food," delicious layers so artfully stacked you can hardly bear to disturb them. The new American fare is elegant, and the lofty space is sophisticated and casual. The three-course lunch is a great buy.

⑤ Jean-Georges

Already a culinary star from his Jo Jo and Vong restaurants, in his namesake restaurant Jean-Georges Vongerichten turns out food that is among the very best in New York, transformed by the French master's delicate sauces and creative combinations. Designer Adam Tihany has created a polished, almost austere, setting that does not upstage the four-star chef *(see p147)*.

6 Daniel
Another luminary, Daniel Boulud has a Venetian Renaissance-inspired dining room worthy of his talents. Seasonal menus with choices like black truffle-crusted cod are divine. Lunch is a less expensive way to sample the master *(see p141)*.

7 Momofuku Ssäm Bar
Wunderkind David Chang brings humor (and lots of pork products) to this inventive restaurant. The steamed pork buns are legendary, and one can always count on some unusual seafood and market vegetables to appear *(see p101)*.

8 Per Se
You need to call two months in advance to get a seat in Thomas Keller's expensive restaurant. One of a handful of eateries to receive 4 stars from *The New York Times*, diners come for the food, service, and views of Central Park. Patrons can also visit the kitchen *(see p147)*.

9 Four Seasons
This New York institution with landmark decor by Philip Johnson is always among the top-rated for Continental food. The Grill Room is still the prime place for power lunches, and the Pool Room is a perfect setting for special occasion dinners *(see p133)*.

Exterior of Gramercy Tavern

10 Gramercy Tavern
Another Danny Meyer success offers perhaps New York's most unpretentious fine dining. Chef Michael Anthony has maintained the high standard here *(see p119)*.

TOP 10 CHEAP EATS

Pork sandwich from Porchetta

1 Lombardi's Pizza
On everybody's list of best-in-town for its thin-crust, coal-oven pizza *(see p95)*.

2 Salaam Bombay
MAP Q3 ▪ 319 Greenwich St ▪ 212 226 9400
A top-ranked Indian restaurant with bargain lunch and brunch.

3 Porchetta
MAP M5 ▪ 110 East 7th St ▪ 212 777 2151
Phenomenal pork sandwiches.

4 Nyonya
MAP P4 ▪ 199 Grand St ▪ 212 334 3669
Good, traditional Malaysian food.

5 Streetbird
MAP E2 ▪ 2149 Frederick Douglass Blvd ▪ 212 206 2557
Top-quality rotisserie chicken and sides.

6 Flor de Mayo
MAP D2 ▪ 2651 Broadway ▪ 212 595 2525
A mix of Peruvian, Cuban, and Chinese cuisine; rotisserie chicken is a specialty.

7 Shake Shack
MAP L4 ▪ Southeast corner of Madison Square Park ▪ 212 889 6600
Sink your teeth into juicy burgers and crisp fries at this friendly burger joint.

8 Il Bagatto
MAP N5 ▪ 192 East 2nd St ▪ 212 228 0977
Even uptowners head for this East Village Italian. Good food and prices.

9 La Bonne Soupe
Midtown's best bet for onion soup and other bistro specialties *(see p133)*.

10 Corner Bistro
MAP M2 ▪ 331 West 4th St ▪ 212 242 9502
Giant burgers in the West Village.

For a key to restaurant price ranges see p83 ←

TOP10 **Bars and Lounges**

1 King Cole Bar and Lounge

MAP H4 ■ St. Regis Hotel, 2 East 55th St, between 5th & Madison Aves ■ 212 753 4500

Maxfield Parrish's famous mural of Old King Cole, rich mahogany paneling, and sumptuous seating set the stage for New York's most famous hotel bar, where the Bloody Mary is believed to have first been created. Lush, luxurious, and very expensive.

2 The Dead Rabbit Grocery and Grog

MAP R4 ■ 30 Water St ■ 646 422 7906

Step back into the 1800s at this convivial bar in a 200-year-old building on the Lower Manhattan waterfront. Dimly lit and cozy, this is the perfect hybrid of cocktail lounge and old Irish tavern, with gleaming wooden bars, sawdust-strewn floors and complimentary spiked punch as you wait for your drink order.

3 Plunge

MAP M2 ■ Gansevoort Hotel, 18 9th Ave at 13th St ■ 212 206 6700

Enjoy superb views of the New York skyline and the Hudson River from this rooftop bar at the trendy Gansevoort Hotel, located in the Meatpacking District. Although a little on the expensive side, this is a great spot to hang out in during the summer months.

4 Angel's Share

MAP M4 ■ 8 Stuyvesant St ■ 212 777 5415

All visitors must pass through a bustling Japanese restaurant to reach this Asian-influenced East Village hideaway. The stylishly dressed clientele drink pricey cocktails and order sharing plates of dim sum and fried oysters from the neighboring restaurant.

5 Flute

MAP H3 ■ 205 West 54th St, between 7th Ave & Broadway ■ 212 265 5169

Proudly stocking over 150 different types of champagne, several of which are available by the glass, this former speakeasy blends high-end opulence with a romantic atmosphere and friendly service. It was operated during Prohibition by notorious showgirl manager, Texas Guinan.

Plunge rooftop bar at the Gansevoort Hotel

⑥ Campbell Apartment
MAP J4 ■ West balcony, Grand Central Terminal, 15 Vanderbilt Ave at 42nd St ■ 212 953 0409

Set in the luxurious former offices of 1920s railroad tycoon John W. Campbell, this bar features a beautifully painted ceiling and a carved-wood balcony, inspired by a Florentine palazzo. This elegant setting is complemented by single-malt scotches, old-world cocktails, and vintage wines. The dress code is business-casual.

Wine at Campbell Apartment

⑦ Salon de Ning
MAP H3 ■ Peninsula Hotel, 700 5th Ave at 55th St ■ 212 956 2888

This swanky Asian-themed bar features breathtaking views of the Manhattan skyline from its 23rd-floor perch. The outdoor terrace is an unbeatable spot.

⑧ Boathouse Bar
MAP G2 ■ Central Park near East 72nd St ■ 212 517 2233

Watch the sun set and the lights come on across the skyline at this outdoor bar beside the lake in Central Park. Particularly romantic on warm nights as gondolas glide by.

⑨ Hudson Common
MAP H2 ■ Hudson Hotel, 356 West 58th St ■ 212 554 6217

With a backlit glass floor and Louis XV meets *Star Wars* decor, this bar draws a stylish crowd despite high prices. Those looking for a quieter spot can head for the Library Bar's fireplace and comfortable sofas.

⑩ Employees Only
MAP N3 ■ 510 Hudson St ■ 212 242 3021

Sip impeccably mixed cocktails at this stylish bar and restaurant. From the fortune teller at the entrance to the mahogany paneling and warm lighting, it is soaked in a retro allure.

TOP 10 ROOFTOP BARS

1 230 Fifth
MAP L3 ■ 230 5th Ave
■ www.230-fifth.com
Terrace with skyline views, cozy lounge.

2 Metropolitan Museum Roof Terrace & Bar
MAP F3 ■ 5th Ave and 82nd St
■ www.metmuseum.org
Cocktails with views of Central Park.

3 Hotel Chantelle
MAP N5 ■ 92 Ludlow St
■ www.hotelchantelle.com
Parisian-style rooftop lounge with old-fashioned lampposts and greenery.

4 Gansevoort Meatpacking NYC
MAP M2 ■ 18 9th Ave
■ www.gansevoorthotelgroup.com
One of the top places to party in NYC.

5 Rare View Murray Hill
MAP K4 ■ 303 Lexington Ave
■ www.rarebarandgrill.com
Gaze at the Chrysler and Empire State.

6 Jimmy at the James
MAP P3 ■ 15 Thompson St
■ www.jimmysoho.com
A 360-degree vista of Manhattan.

7 Berry Park
5 Berry St, Brooklyn ■ www.berryparkbk.com
Brooklyn rooftop with Manhattan views.

8 Empire Hotel
MAP H2 ■ 4 West 63rd St
■ www.empirehotelnyc.com
Jazz, with views of the Upper West Side.

9 Loopy Doopy at Conrad
MAP Q3 ■ 102 North End Ave
■ www.conradnewyork.com
Refined bar with Statue of Liberty views.

10 La Birreria
MAP L3 ■ 200 5th Ave
■ www.eataly.com
Beer garden atop an Italian emporium.

Rooftop terrace at 230 Fifth

🔟 New York Stores

Macy's department store

① Macy's
What can you say about the city's largest store? From food to futons, the selection is vast. And Macy's is a major part of the New York scene, from the spring flower show to Tap-O-Mania, when thousands of tap dancers converge on Herald Square *(see p123)*.

② Bloomingdale's
MAP H4 ▪ 1000 Lexington Ave at 59th St
After Macy's, this is New York's best-known department store, renowned for high fashion for men and women. The main floor, with cosmetics, jewelry, and accessories, is a mob scene, but don't be discouraged; the upper floors are more manageable.

Shoes at Bloomingdale's

③ 5th Avenue Department Stores
MAP H3–K3 ▪ Bergdorf Goodman: 754 5th Ave at 57th St ▪ Saks Fifth Avenue: 611 5th Ave at 50th St ▪ Lord & Taylor: 424 5th Ave at 38th St
Bergdorf Goodman, Saks Fifth Avenue, and Lord & Taylor have a full range of well-known brand clothing for men, women, and children, as well as an upscale selection of home accessories. All of these stores have ultra-stylish seasonal window displays that are worth checking out.

④ Barneys New York
MAP H4 ▪ 660 Madison Ave at 61st St
If you have the wherewithal, this is the place to find the latest designer labels to please a well-heeled, young and trendy clientele. The semi-annual clearance sales are legendary and draw hordes of shoppers on the hunt for chic on the cheap.

⑤ Henri Bendel
MAP H3 ▪ 712 5th Ave at 55th St
Set up like a series of boutiques, Bendel's displays innovative women's fashion for glamorous shoppers. The signature brown and white shopping bag is such a status symbol that the pattern is used for accessories.

⑥ Century 21
MAP Q4 ▪ 22 Cortlandt St
Savvy uptown shoppers know it is worth the trek downtown to Century 21 to sift through racks full

of designer labels at ridiculously cheap prices. You will even see celebrities toting its distinctive red bags. As well as fashion and sportswear, the store is also especially good for cosmetics and ladies' accessories.

Century 21

⑦ H&M
MAP K3, & N4 respectively ▪ 34th St and Herald Square; 558 Broadway

Hennes & Mauritz, a Swedish retailer, was a smash success when the 5th Avenue store opened in New York in 2000. What's the secret? Kicky, young designs for men, women, and children sold at rock bottom prices, but creating a look that belies the price tag.

⑧ Madison Avenue Designers
MAP F4–H4 ▪ Giorgio Armani: 760 Madison Ave ▪ Ralph Lauren: 867 Madison Ave

The epicenter of designer boutiques in New York used to be 57th Street between 5th and Madison Avenues, where shops like Burberry are still found. But as stores like Nike and Levi's have invaded this territory, the designers, from Giorgio Armani to Ralph Lauren, have moved to Madison Avenue.

⑨ SoHo Boutiques
MAP N3–N4 ▪ Anna Sui: 484 Broome St ▪ A.P.C.: 131 Mercer St ▪ Miu Miu: 100 Prince St ▪ Prada: 575 Broadway ▪ Portico: 139 Spring St ▪ Kirna Zabête: 477 Broome St

SoHo is home to trendy boutiques such as Anna Sui, A.P.C., Miu Miu, and Prada. The stores are between Thompson Street and Broadway and between Prince and Greene Streets, though any block in this area may yield a special find. This is also prime hunting ground for home furnishings at stores such as Portico.

Miu Miu's SoHo boutique

⑩ Union Square and 6th Avenue
MAP L3 ▪ Whole Foods Market: 4 Union Square South

Union Square is ringed by various stores and places to refuel, including a massive Whole Foods Market. Nearby, around 18th Street, is the shopping mecca of 6th Avenue, lined with historic buildings now housing homeware and clothing stores.

 New York for Free

Glorious views across the water from the Staten Island Ferry

1 Staten Island Ferry
MAP R4

This ferry journey is one of the greatest deals the city of New York has to offer. You will see sweeping views of New York Harbor, the Statue of Liberty, and the glittering Manhattan skyline on its journey between Lower Manhattan and Staten Island – all to be enjoyed without paying a cent *(see p159)*.

2 New York Philharmonic Concerts in the Parks
Jul–Aug ■ www.nyphil.org

Ease yourself into the night with some soaring classical music, played in the open air during the New York Philharmonic's annual summer concerts, which are staged in parks throughout all five of the boroughs of New York.

Philharmonic summer concert

3 Recording of TV Shows
The Late Show with Stephen Colbert: www.cbs.com/shows/the-late-show-with-stephen-colbert ■ *Rachael Ray:* www.rachaelrayshow.com

New York City is the land of TV talk shows, from *The Late Show with Stephen Colbert* to *Rachael Ray*. You can watch these shows being recorded for free as a member of the studio audience. Apply for tickets via the shows' websites.

4 Downtown Boathouse Kayaks
MAP P2 ■ Pier 26, Hudson River Greenway at North Moore ■ mid-May–mid-Oct: 9am–4:30pm Sat, Sun, & public hols; Jul–Aug: 5–6:30pm Mon–Fri, 9am–4:30pm Sat, Sun, & public hols ■ www.downtownboathouse.org

The Hudson River is ideal for kayaking and the Downtown Boathouse offers complimentary use of kayaks at locations on the river and Governors Island.

5 Chelsea Art Galleries
MAP L2 ■ Between 10th and 11th Aves, from West 18th to West 28th Sts

Saunter through Chelsea on a Thursday night, when many of the area's formidable galleries have free art openings, along with complimentary nibbles and wine.

6 Open House New York
Runs over a weekend, October
■ www.ohny.com

Open House New York opens up the city's most fascinating architectural structures, from churches to government buildings, to the public every October. Tours, talks, performances, and other special events also take place.

7 Brooklyn Brewery
79 North 11th St, Williamsburg, Brooklyn ■ Free tours 1–5pm Sat, 1–4pm Sun

There are free tours of the handsome Brooklyn Brewery in Williamsburg on the half hour every Saturday and Sunday, when visitors can also sample some of the great brews made in Brooklyn.

Brooklyn Brewery beer

8 New York Public Library
MAP K3

This stately library hosts all manner of free events, from lectures and readings to career-enhancing classes (see p128).

9 El Museo del Barrio
MAP D4 ■ 1230 5th Ave ■ Free 3rd Sat of month ■ www.elmuseo.org

Super Sábado is celebrated on the third Saturday of the month with free admission and entertainment at this colorful museum showcasing over 800 years of Latino art and culture.

10 Stand-up Comedy
MAP L2 ■ 307 West 26th St ■ Select nights free ■ newyork.ucbtheatre.com

From Jack Benny to Woody Allen to Jerry Seinfeld, New York has a long comedy legacy, and the city continues to host regular comedy shows, many of which are free, including select nights at Upright Citizens Brigade, an improvisational and sketch comedy theater.

TOP 10 BUDGET TIPS

Union Square Greenmarket

1 TKTS Theater Tickets
MAP J3 ■ 47th St & Broadway ■ www.tdf.org
Same-day theater tickets are discounted.

2 Free Museum Days
Includes Fridays at MoMA (see p48) and first Saturday of the month at Brooklyn Museum (see p49). Check websites.

3 Farmers' Markets
Try the Union Square Greenmarket (see p115) for cheaper prices than at some supermarkets.

4 Changing Money
Transaction fees are generally lower at ATMs than at currency exchanges.

5 Saving on Transit
Metropolitan Transportation Authority: www.mta.info
There is a 11 per cent bonus on the $10 Pay-Per-Ride MetroCard; the 7-day one allows unlimited subway and bus rides.

6 Restaurant Week
Jan & Jun ■ www.nycgo.com/restaurant-week
Three-course lunches $25; dinners $38.

7 Discount Passes to Sights
CityPass: www.citypass.com ■ New York Pass: www.newyorkpass.com
CityPass ($114, nine days) covers 6 top sights; New York Pass covers 80 ($90, one day). Longer periods available.

8 Sale Periods
Coats are on sale in November and February, bathing suits after July 4, and everything before and after Christmas.

9 Free Happy Hour Nibbles
Many bars include snacks with a drink.

10 Discount Stores and Malls
From Century 21 (see p70) to 200 outlets at Woodbury Common, an hour away (www.coachusa.com; tickets from $42).

 Festivals and Events

Fireworks display, 4th of July

1 St. Patrick's Day Parade
MAP H3 ■ 5th Ave ■ 11am Mar 17 ■ Check press for exact route

People dress up in green for this big spectacle when marching bands, politicos, and civic groups march down 5th Avenue to proclaim their love of the Emerald Isle. Millions come to watch and the citywide celebrations last way into the night.

2 Easter Parade
MAP H3–J3 ■ 5th Ave ■ 11am Easter Sunday

Following a long-time tradition, 5th Avenue closes to traffic in Midtown, and New York families in their Sunday best stroll up the avenue, with ladies sporting amazing hats, both traditional and outrageous.

3 9th Avenue Food Festival
MAP H2–K2 ■ 9th Ave, 37th to 57th Sts ■ Mid-May

New York's biggest food extravaganza has been running since 1974. Vendors come from all over and thousands of people jam the streets to sample a United Nations of food, from burritos to samosas.

4 4th of July Fireworks
MAP R3 ■ East River ■ 9:30pm Jul 4

Huge crowds come out to enjoy this pyrotechnic spectacular over the Hudson River. Macy's spends over $1 million each year for this salute to the red, white, and blue.

5 West Indian Day Carnival
MAP R6 ■ Eastern Parkway, Brooklyn ■ Subway C to Franklin Ave ■ Labor Day (1st Mon in Sep)

Brooklyn's West Indian population celebrates its heritage with a parade of enormous floats, lavish, feathered costumes in rainbow hues, and contagious Caribbean music. Street stands offer Caribbean specialties.

6 Feast of San Gennaro
MAP P4 ■ Mulberry St ■ 3rd week in Sep for 10 days

The patron saint of Naples is carried through the streets of Little Italy, and Mulberry Street is packed with music, game booths, and tons of tasty, traditional food. Sausage and pepper sandwiches are the trademark of this 10-day event, but there is an Italian treat for every taste.

7 **New York City Marathon**
MAP H5 ■ 1st Ave above 59th St is a good viewpoint ■ 10:45am 1st Sun in Nov

An amazing 30,000 entrants run the 26-mile (42-km) marathon that starts on Staten Island, takes in all five boroughs, and finishes in Central Park. New Yorkers line the route, cheering and offering water to the runners along the way.

8 **Macy's Thanksgiving Day Parade**
MAP G2 ■ Central Park West at 77th St along Broadway to 34th St ■ 9am Thanksgiving Day (4th Thu in Nov)

New Yorkers take to the streets and America watches on television as cartoon character balloons, marching bands, lavish TV and movie star-laden floats, and the dancing Rockettes announce the start of the Christmas season.

Macy's Parade

9 **Christmas Tree Lighting Ceremony**
MAP J3 ■ Rockefeller Center ■ 1st week in Dec

America's tallest Christmas tree, festooned with miles of twinkling lights, stands next to the skating rink in Rockefeller Center. Trumpeting angel decorations in the Channel Gardens and window displays on 5th Avenue add to the atmosphere.

10 **New Year's Eve Ball Drop**
MAP K3 ■ Times Square ■ Midnight Dec 31

Huge crowds gather to cheer when a giant Waterford Crystal ball lowered at midnight marks the official start of the New Year. There's also a midnight run, with a costume parade and fireworks, in Central Park.

TOP 10 SPORTS EVENTS

New York Knicks in action

1 US Open Tennis Championships
USTA National Tennis Center, Queens ■ Aug–Sep
The last Grand Slam of the year.

2 New York Yankees & Mets Baseball
Yankee Stadium: Bronx ■ Citi Field: Queens ■ Apr–Sep
Perennial rivals compete in America's favorite pastime.

3 New York Knicks Basketball
Madison Square Garden, 7th Ave ■ Oct–Apr
Fast-paced games that always sell out.

4 New York Liberty
Madison Square Garden, 7th Ave ■ May–Sep
Women's professional basketball.

5 New York Jets and Giants Football
MetLife Stadium, New Jersey ■ Sep–Dec
Both teams play in New Jersey, but tickets for games are scarce.

6 New York Rangers Hockey
Madison Square Garden, 7th Ave ■ Sep–Apr
Played on ice, requiring speed and skill.

7 Millrose Games
216 Fort Washington Avenue ■ Feb
America's fastest runners compete in this indoor track meet.

8 Wood Memorial
Aqueduct Raceway, Queens ■ Mid–Apr
This horse race features Kentucky Derby contenders.

9 Belmont Stakes
Belmont Park, Long Island ■ 2nd Sat in Jun
The last of racing's "triple crown."

10 New York Red Bulls
Red Bull Arena, New Jersey ■ Mar–Oct
Soccer's growing popularity draws fans.

New York
Area by Area

Aerial view of Central Park

🔟 Lower Manhattan

This is where old and new New York meet. The city was born here under Dutch rule and became the nation's first capital after the Revolutionary War (1775–83). At the intersection of Broad and Wall Streets are the Federal Hall National Memorial, marking where George Washington was sworn in as President, and the New York Stock Exchange, founded in 1817, whose influence is felt worldwide. In the 20th century, skyscrapers added drama to the skyline. The area's recovery after the destruction of the Twin Towers has been striking, and the National September 11 Memorial and Museum offers an opportunity to remember the events of September 2001. The 104-story One World Trade Center opened in 2014.

September 11 Museum

AREA MAP OF LOWER MANHATTAN

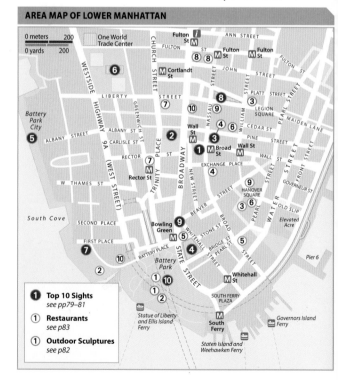

1 **Top 10 Sights**
see pp79–81

1 **Restaurants**
see p83

1 **Outdoor Sculptures**
see p82

1 New York Stock Exchange

MAP R4 ■ 20 Broad St at Wall St ■ Closed to public ■ www.nyse.com

The present building opened in 1903, and behind its Neo-Classical facade is the financial heart of the US (see p55). The New York Stock Exchange has grown from dealing with local businesses to a global enterprise. On the busiest

Antique stock ticker tape

days, billions of shares are traded for more than 8,500 listed issues, although the action is much calmer now that everything is computerized. On its most active days, between five and seven billion shares trade hands on the exchange.

2 Trinity Church

MAP Q4 ■ 75 Broadway at Wall St ■ Open 7am–6pm Mon–Fri, 8am–4pm Sat, 7am–4pm Sun (church), 7am–4pm Mon–Fri, 8am–3pm Sat, 7am–3pm Sun (churchyard); tours 2pm daily and after 11:15am Sun service

This much-admired Gothic building is the third church on this site serving one of the oldest Anglican parishes in the US, founded in 1697. The church has had notable additions since its completion in 1846, including the sacristy, the chapel, and the Manhattan wing. The bronze doors were donated as a memorial to John Jacob Astor III. Trinity Church is known for its musical programs, with concerts each Monday and Thursday at 1pm and occasional Sunday concerts by the full choir. Trinity Church also oversees the programs at St. Paul's Chapel (see p86).

3 Federal Hall National Memorial

MAP R4 ■ 26 Wall St at Nassau St ■ Open 9am–5pm Mon–Fri ■ Free ■ www.nps.gov/feha

Although the bronze statue of George Washington on the steps marks the site where the nation's first president took his oath of office in 1789, the original building was replaced by this handsome, columned Greek Revival structure in 1842. It served as the US Custom House and as a branch of the Federal Reserve Bank before being turned into a museum in 1955, with exhibits of the Constitution and the Bill of Rights. Guided tours are available several times daily.

4 US Custom House

MAP R4 ■ 1 Bowling Green, between State & Whitehall Sts ■ Museum open 10am–5pm Fri–Wed, 10am–8pm Thu

The galleries that encircle the grand rotunda were installed during a renovation of this classic building in 1994. It now houses the George Gustav Heye Center of the Smithsonian's National Museum of the American Indian, which displays changing exhibits of Native American life, including costumes and fine crafts. The ceremonial objects, toys, and musical instruments on display in the research room can be examined and researched further using the computer that is available there (see p55).

Stained-glass window, Trinity Church

Public art, Battery Park City

5 Battery Park City

MAP Q3–R3 ■ Off West St, Battery Place to Chambers St, bounded by the Hudson River

Several prestigious architects were involved in this extension of Manhattan, a commercial and residential enclave built on a 92-acre (37-ha) landfill created with earth displaced by excavation for the World Trade Center. A 2-mile (3-km) esplanade offers grand Statue of Liberty views. Enjoy the public works of art or visit the Skyscraper Museum.

6 National September 11 Memorial and Museum

MAP Q3 ■ 180 Greenwich St ■ Museum open 9am–8pm daily (to 9pm Fri & Sat) ■ Adm (museum only); reserve tickets online ■ www.911 memorial.org

Opened on September 11, 2011, on the 10th anniversary of the attacks, this memorial features the name of every person who died, inscribed in bronze panels around the two memorial pools that sit where the towers once stood. Artifacts, memorabilia, and photographs in the museum pay tribute to the victims. Nearby, One World Trade Center, the tallest building in the western hemisphere, is the centerpiece of the plaza's development.

7 Museum of Jewish Heritage

MAP R3 ■ 36 Battery Place, Battery Park City ■ Open 10am–5:45pm Sun–Thu (to 8pm Wed), 10am–3pm Fri & Jewish holiday evenings (mid-Mar–Oct: to 5pm) ■ Adm, free Wed evenings ■ www.mjhnyc.org

A memorable experience for all faiths is this chronicle of the 20th-century Jewish experience before, during, and after the Holocaust, told with a collection of over 2,000 photographs and hundreds of artifacts, as well as original documentary films.

8 Federal Reserve Bank

MAP Q4 ■ 33 Liberty St, between William & Nassau Sts ■ Tours at 1pm and 2pm Mon–Fri (except bank hols) ■ Free; reserve ahead at www.newyorkfed.org

Though gold is no longer transferred between nations, much of the gold reserves of the world remains stored in the vault below this building. All bank notes from here have the letter B in the Federal Reserve seal.

Memorial pool at National September 11 Memorial and Museum

GEORGE WASHINGTON IN NEW YORK

A statue (right) at the Federal Hall National Memorial (see p79) where George Washington was sworn into office is testament to the time he spent in New York. So too is the pew where he worshipped at St. Paul's Chapel (see p86), and the museum at Frauces Tavern where he said farewell to his officers in 1789.

9 Charging Bull
MAP R4 ■ Broadway at Bowling Green Park

Sculptor Arturo di Modica secretly unloaded this bronze statue in front of the New York Stock Exchange late at night in December 1989. It was later removed, but has since been given a permanent spot on Broadway. The bull signifies the strength of the American people after the 1987 stock market crash.

Castle Clinton, Battery Park

10 Battery Park
MAP R3–4 ■ Broadway and Battery Place ■ Open daily

This park at New York harbor – built largely on 18th- and 19th-century landfill – is usually visited for Castle Clinton, the 1811 fort and embarkation point for Ellis Island and Statue of Liberty ferries. This welcome swath of green is of interest for its many monuments and statues.

A DAY EXPLORING LOWER MANHATTAN

▶ MORNING

Begin at **Battery Park** for a view of the waterfront, and look into **Castle Clinton** (see p20), an 1807 fort, to see dioramas of a changing New York. Then visit the **Museum of the American Indian** at the **US Custom House**. Cross over to **Bowling Green**, the city's first park, then turn right onto Whitehall, and left on Pearl Street for the **Frauces Tavern Museum**, a restoration of the 1719 building where George Washington bade farewell to his troops.

Head up Broad Street to Wall Street and the **New York Stock Exchange**, where there is chaos on the trading floor. Close by is the **Federal Hall National Memorial** (see p79), where the country's first president took his oath of office. Steak is a specialty of the Financial District, so take a break for lunch at **Bobby Van's Steakhouse** (see p83), on Broad Street and Exchange Place.

AFTERNOON

Continue uptown on Nassau Street (which is a continuation of Broad Street) to see **Chase Plaza** and its famous sculptures. At the end of the plaza on Liberty Street is the ornate **Federal Reserve Bank** and then Louise Nevelson Square, which features the artist's Shadows and Flags.

Go back onto Liberty Street and take in the **9/11 Tribute Center**, which is located at No. 120. End the day by treating yourself to dinner at the lively Parisian bistro, **Les Halles** (see p83).

See map on p78 ←

Outdoor Sculptures

1 The Immigrants
MAP R3 ■ Battery Park

Reflecting the diversity of new-comers to the US from 1855–90, Luis Sanguino's 1973 work includes an African, a Jew, a family, a priest, and a worker.

2 Giovanni da Verrazzano
MAP R3 ■ Battery Park

The first European to sail into New York Harbor in 1524 was honored by fellow Italians with this 1909 statue by Ettore Ximenes.

3 Shadows and Flags
MAP Q4 ■ Between Maiden Lane, William, & Liberty Sts

Louise Nevelson's 1977 figures enliven the traffic island they inhabit. The largest is rooted to the ground, others are on stilts.

4 George Washington
MAP R4 ■ Federal Hall National Memorial, 26 Wall St

Designed and cast in 1883, a bronze Washington on a massive granite pedestal lifts his hand from the Bible after being sworn in.

5 The Four Continents
MAP R4 ■ US Custom House, 1 Bowling Green

Here, sculptor Daniel Chester French reflects 19th-century US

views – meditative Asia and exotic Africa to the sides, regal Europe and a dynamic US in the center.

6 Sunken Garden
MAP R4 ■ Chase Manhattan Plaza, between Pine & Liberty Sts

The spray from a central fountain covers the floor of the circular garden. Isamu Noguchi's 1960s work suggests rocks rising from the sea.

Double Check, bronze sculpture

7 Double Check
MAP Q4 ■ Zuccotti Park, between Broadway & Church St

The briefcase of J. Seward Johnson, Jr.'s 1982 bronze figure contains a stapler, calculator, and the occasional sandwich provided by a passerby.

8 Sky Reflector-Net
MAP Q4 ■ Fulton St Subway Station

A brilliant cable net of aluminum panels hanging from the ceiling of this gleaming new subway station.

9 Group of Four Trees
MAP R4 ■ 1 Chase Manhattan Plaza, between Nassau & Liberty Sts

Jean Dubuffet's 1972 amusing mushroom-like sculptures hover over pedestrians nearby.

10 Red Cube
MAP Q4 ■ Marine Midland Plaza, 140 Broadway

Isamu Noguchi's 1967 red, 28-ft (9-m) high, metal cube balances on one corner defying gravity.

The Four Continents

Restaurants

PRICE CATEGORIES

For a three-course meal for one with a glass of house wine, and all unavoidable charges including tax.

$ under $25 $$ $25–$75 $$$ over $75

1 Battery Gardens
MAP R4 ■ Battery Park, opposite 17 State St ■ 212 809 5508 ■ $$

This restaurant offers decent New American fare with Asian accents, but come for the stunning panoramic views of the harbor.

2 Gigino at Wagner Park
MAP R3 ■ 20 Battery Place, next to the Jewish Heritage Museum ■ 212 528 2228 ■ $$

Gigino's delivers excellent Italian food from the Amalfi coast and dazzling views from the sophisticated dining room and the waterfront terrace.

3 Smorgas Chef
MAP R4 ■ 53 Stone St at William St ■ 212 422 3500 ■ $$

The Swedish meatballs are famous, and there's a range of lighter fare. The setting is charming.

4 Bobby Van's Steakhouse
MAP R4 ■ 25 Broad St at Exchange Place ■ 212 344 8463 ■ $$$

The excellent steaks, views of the Stock Exchange, and a setting within an 1898 Beaux Arts landmark are all highlights. Part of a high-end chain.

Bobby Van's Steakhouse

5 Fraunces Tavern
MAP R4 ■ 54 Pearl St at Broad St ■ 212 968 1776 ■ $$

This unique 18th-century tavern is where George Washington bade farewell to his officers in 1783. The historic site features a restaurant as well as a museum.

Fraunces Tavern

6 Harry's Café & Steak
MAP R4 ■ 1 Hanover Square between Pearl & Stone Sts ■ 212 785 9200 ■ $$–$$$

The historic India House is home to a downstairs café-steakhouse that draws Wall Street types in droves.

7 George's
MAP R3 ■ 89 Greenwich St at Rector St ■ 212 269 8026 ■ $$

For hearty American diner fare downtown. Burgers, soups, omelets, sandwiches, and salads are on offer.

8 Les Halles
MAP Q4 ■ 15 John St between Broadway and Nassau St ■ 212 285 8585 ■ $$

Financial district meets Parisian bistro at this sister restaurant of the Park Avenue spot with celebrity chef Anthony Bourdain.

9 Joseph's
MAP R4 ■ 3 Hanover Square ■ 212 747 1300 ■ $$

When Wall Streeters require Italian food, they often head for Joseph's. The menu includes *fettucine Alfredo* and fried calamari.

10 2West
MAP R3 ■ 2 West St at Battery Park ■ 917 790 2525 ■ $$

A contemporary steakhouse with French influences. Located in the Ritz Carlton Hotel, with views across the Hudson and Battery Park.

See map on p78

TOP 10 Civic Center and South Street Seaport

Some of the finest architecture in New York City is to be found at its Civic Center, which serves as the headquarters for city government. The impressive buildings in this area span several centuries, from the 18th-century St. Paul's Chapel to the pioneering 20th-century Woolworth Building. The famous Brooklyn Bridge is located nearby, as well as the old maritime center of the city, South Street Seaport. The piers and buildings of South Street Seaport have now been restored and are home to a lively hub of cafés, restaurants, and museums.

Woolworth Building

AREA MAP OF CIVIC CENTER AND SOUTH STREET SEAPORT

❶ **Top 10 Sights**
see pp85–7

① **Restaurants**
see p89

① **Maritime Sights**
see p88

Brooklyn Bridge makes for an enjoyable stroll

① South Street Seaport
MAP Q4 ▪ Museum open
Jan–Mar: 11am–5pm Fri–Sun;
Apr–Dec: 11am–5pm Wed–Sun
▪ www.southstseaport.org

The cobbled streets, piers, and buildings that were the center of New York's 19th-century seafaring activity have been restored as a tourist center, although redevelopment is still in progress. There are shops, restaurants, bars, a museum with seafaring exhibits, a fleet of ships for boarding, and plenty of outdoor entertainment.

South Street Seaport

② Brooklyn Bridge
MAP Q4 ▪ (Manhattan side)
Park Row near Municipal Building

Linking Manhattan and Brooklyn, when it was completed in 1883 this was the largest suspension bridge in the world and the first to be built of steel. It took 600 workmen and 16 years to build, claiming 20 lives during construction, including that of the designing engineer, John A. Roebling. Now an iconic symbol of New York, its 1-mile (1.8-km) span rewards those who walk it with fabulous views of city towers seen through the artistic cablework.

③ Woolworth Building
MAP Q4 ▪ Broadway, between
**Park Pl & Barclay St ▪ Open for tours
only ▪ www.woolworthtours.com**

Built in 1913, this has one of New York's great interiors; marble walls, bronze filigree, a mosaic ceiling, and stained glass combine to magical effect. Architect Cass Gilbert also had a sense of humor – sculptures include Five and Dime mogul Woolworth counting nickels and Gilbert himself cradling a model of the building. It set the standard for the skyscrapers that followed in the 1920s and 1930s (see p52).

THE "BOSS TWEED" COURTHOUSE

The first New York County Courthouse at 52 Chambers Street, completed in 1881, was built by "Boss" Tweed (right), a corrupt politician (see p46) who spent fortunes on this grand marble monument to himself. The elaborate interior has been restored, and it is now the headquarters of the Department of Education.

4 Former AT&T Building
MAP Q4 ■ 195 Broadway
■ Open office hours

Built in 1922, this is a monument to excess, but fun to see nevertheless. In its day, the facade was said to have more columns than any other building in the world; the vast lobby is a forest of marble pillars. Not far away at 120 Broadway, the former Equitable Building, built in 1915, is of note for another excess: its immense bulk was responsible for the nation's first skyscraper zoning regulations.

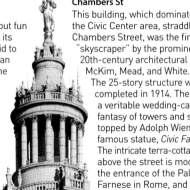

Municipal Building

5 St. Paul's Chapel
MAP Q4 ■ 209 Broadway, between Fulton & Vesey Sts ■ Open 10am–6pm Mon–Sat, 7am–6pm Sun ■ Episcopal service 8 & 9:15am Sun ■ www.trinitywallstreet.org

Manhattan's oldest church was built in 1766 as an "uptown" chapel for Trinity Church and took on added importance while Trinity was being rebuilt after the great fire of 1776. St. Paul's Chapel was modeled after London's St. Martin-in-the-Fields. Situated one block away from Ground Zero, the church has an interactive 9/11 exhibit (see p54).

6 City Hall
MAP Q4 ■ Broadway and Park Row ■ Open for pre-arranged tours only, call 212 788 2656 ■ www.nyc.gov

The seat of city government since 1812, City Hall is considered one of the most beautiful early 19th-century public buildings in the US. The design, by architects Mangin and McComb, Jr., won a competition held in 1802. A statue of Justice crowns the structure. The rear of the building, facing north, was not clad in marble until 1954, since the architects never expected the city to develop further north (see p54).

7 Municipal Building
MAP Q4 ■ 1 Center St at Chambers St

This building, which dominates the Civic Center area, straddling Chambers Street, was the first "skyscraper" by the prominent 20th-century architectural firm McKim, Mead, and White. The 25-story structure was completed in 1914. The top is a veritable wedding-cake fantasy of towers and spires topped by Adolph Wienman's famous statue, *Civic Fame*. The intricate terra-cotta vaulting above the street is modeled on the entrance of the Palazzo Farnese in Rome, and the subway entrance at the south end, an arcaded plaza, is a dramatic vault of Guastavino tiles.

8 New York County Courthouse
MAP P4 ■ 60 Center St ■ Open 9am–5pm Mon–Fri

Ascend the wide staircase of the 1926 New York County Courthouse (adjacent to the 31-story, pyramid-topped US Courthouse which dates from 1933), and enter to admire the marble-columned rotunda with its Tiffany lighting fixtures. Note, too, the ceiling murals depicting Law and Justice. The hexagonal building has a courtroom in each of its six wings.

Surrogate's Court/Hall of Records

⑨ Surrogate's Court/ Hall of Records

MAP Q4 ■ 31 Chambers St ■ Lobby open 9am–5pm Mon–Fri

With an interior inspired by the Paris Opéra, this 1907 Beaux Arts beauty boasts a magnificent central hall with marble stairways and ceiling mosaics. The facade features statues representing Justice, the seasons, and notable New Yorkers, as well as figures depicting the stages of life.

⑩ Police Plaza

MAP Q4 ■ Park Row at Pearl St

Constructed in 1973, the city's police headquarters can be found on a spacious pedestrian plaza, a welcome area in a district with very few public spaces. The Tony Rosenthal abstract sculpture, *Five in One*, made of five sloping interlocked discs, symbolizes the city's five boroughs.

Police Headquarters, Police Plaza

A WALK THROUGH CIVIC CENTER AND SOUTH STREET SEAPORT

▶ MORNING

Most subway routes lead to City Hall. When you come up to street level, walk down Broadway to see the lobbies of the **Woolworth Building** (see p85) and the former **AT&T Building**, as well as the beautiful Georgian interior of **St. Paul's Chapel**.

Return via Park Row, once known as Newspaper Row because it was lined with their offices. **Printing House Square** has a statue of Benjamin Franklin holding a copy of his *Pennsylvania Gazette*. West of the Row lies small but beautiful **City Hall Park**, where the Declaration of Independence was read to George Washington's troops in July 1776. The park has a granite time wheel telling the city's history.

A walk along Center and Chambers Streets takes you past the ornate **Municipal Building**.

AFTERNOON

At midday, head east for a seafood lunch at the **Bridge Café** (see p89), which is housed in a 1794 wood-framed building. From here the East River is a short stroll away, offering excellent views of lower Manhattan.

Spend the afternoon at **South Street Seaport** (see p85), visiting the museum and the maritime crafts center, and perhaps even taking a cruise on one of the ships. Head to **Keg 229** (see p89) for dinner, where you can enjoy revisted kiddie comfort foods, or perhaps try some delicious Italian fare at **Acqua** restaurant and wine bar (see p89).

See map on p84 ←

Maritime Sights

Ambrose, Seaport Museum New York

① Seaport Museum New York

MAP Q4 ■ 12 Fulton St ■ Open Jan–Mar: 11am–5pm Fri–Sun; Apr–Dec: 11am–5pm Wed–Sun ■ www.south streetseaportmuseum.org

A small portion of the city's maritime artifacts are open due to the damage caused by Hurricane Sandy and the resulting ongoing redevelopment.

② Schermerhorn Row

MAP Q4 ■ Fulton St, between Front & South Sts

Federal-style houses built by Peter Schermerhorn in 1811–12 now house a permanent exhibition space, as well as shops and restaurants.

③ Peking

MAP Q4 ■ Piers 16, South Street Seaport ■ Open Apr–Dec: 11am–5pm Tue–Sun ■ Adm

This four-masted vessel was built in 1911 as a German merchant ship before serving as a British training boat in the 1930s.

④ Bowne & Co.

MAP Q4 ■ 211 Water St ■ Open 11am–7pm daily

An atmospheric re-creation of a 19th-century print shop, complete with working printing presses.

Titanic Memorial

⑤ Ambrose

MAP Q4 ■ Pier 16, South Street Seaport ■ Open Apr–Dec: 11am–5pm Tue–Sun ■ Admission charge

Part of the South Street Seaport Museum, this 1907 lightship remained in service until 1964.

⑥ Pilot House

MAP Q4 ■ South Street Seaport ■ Open 11am–5pm Tue–Sun

The South Street Seaport ticket and information center is housed in this pilot house, taken from a steam tugboat built in 1923 by the New York Central Railroad.

⑦ Pier 17

MAP Q5 ■ South Street Seaport ■ Closed for redevelopment

A pier with three floors of food stands, restaurants, and views of the East River and Brooklyn Bridge.

⑧ Harbor Excursions

MAP Q4 ■ Pier 16, South Street Seaport ■ May–Sep: Tue–Sun ■ Adm

The 1885 schooner *Pioneer* offers 90-minute family sails and 2-hour cruises in the afternoon and evening.

⑨ Titanic Memorial

MAP Q4 ■ Fulton St at Water St

This lighthouse was built to commemorate the tragic sinking of the *Titanic*, the largest steamship ever made, in April 1912.

⑩ Audubon Summer & Winter EcoCruise

MAP Q4 ■ Pier 16, South Street Seaport ■ Adm

A thrilling 90-minute ride offers views of egrets, herons, seals and more in their habitats.

Restaurants

1 Bridge Café
MAP Q4 ▪ 279 Water St at
Dover St ▪ 212 227 3344 ▪ $$

Dating back to 1794, this is one of
the oldest establishments in the city.
Inside the quaint building beside the
Brooklyn Bridge, there are checked
tablecloths, and the American menu
is surprisingly sophisticated.

Bridge Café

2 Il Brigante
MAP Q4 ▪ 214 Front St
▪ 212 285 0222 ▪ $$

Dig into hearty pastas, crisp pizzas
from a wood-burning oven, and
sausage ragù accompanied by silky
red wines at this cozy trattoria.

3 Nelson Blue
MAP Q4 ▪ 233–5 Front St
▪ 212 346 9090 ▪ $$

One of the city's few restaurants
specializing in food from New
Zealand. Dishes are made using
imported ingredients.

4 Acqua
MAP Q4 ▪ 21–3 Peck Slip
▪ 212 349 4433 ▪ $$

New American-influenced Italian
food is served here, prepared with
organic ingredients. A cozy ambience
is provided by the vaulted ceilings
and warm lighting.

5 Bin 220
MAP Q4 ▪ 220 Front St
▪ 212 374 9463 ▪ $$

Italian-inspired wine bar and café set
in a 1798 building that once held the

offices of a shipping agent. The café
serves good charcuterie and panini,
salads, and antipasti.

6 El Luchador
MAP Q4 ▪ 87 South St
▪ 646 398 7499 ▪ $

No-frills, fresh Mexican cuisine is
served up at this popular eatery,
named after the colorfully-masked
Mexican wrestlers called *luchadores*.

7 Fish Market
MAP Q4 ▪ 111 South St
▪ 212 227 4468 ▪ $$

Located on the site of a 19th-century
fish market, this restaurant serves
briny staples in a dark, authentic
wood-and-brick room.

8 Suteishi
MAP Q5 ▪ 24 Peck Slip St
▪ 212 766 2344 ▪ $$

Nestled in the shadow of the
Brooklyn Bridge, just to the north of
South Street Seaport, this spot is a
favorite among area workers and
nearby residents for its fresh,
reasonably priced sushi.

9 Fresh Salt
MAP Q4 ▪ 146 Beekman St
▪ 212 962 0053 ▪ $$

Come to this convivial bar and café
for soups, gourmet sandwiches, and
salads. Also on offer is a good
weekend brunch.

10 Keg 229
MAP Q4 ▪ 229 Front St
▪ 212 566 2337 ▪ $$

Childhood favorites for all ages are
available at this fun beer bar and
café. Wax nostalgic over pigs in a
blanket, mac and cheese and
chicken tenders.

See map on p84 ←

TOP 10 Chinatown and Little Italy

Settled by immigrants in the 19th century, these two ethnic enclaves are among the most colorful parts of the city. Little Italy has dwindled to a few blocks, but it is still an atmospheric center of authentic Italian food and shops. Chinatown, however, continues to grow. Up to 150,000 Chinese live here in crowded quarters. The shops and sidewalk markets overflow with exotic foods, fine antiques and novelty gifts.

Chinatown

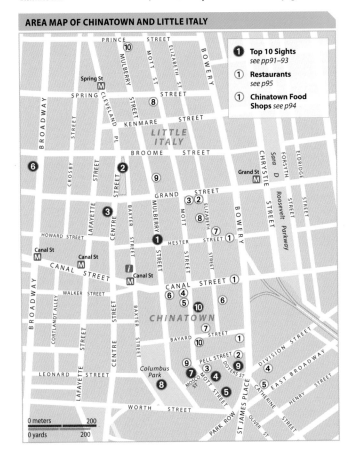

AREA MAP OF CHINATOWN AND LITTLE ITALY

1 Top 10 Sights
see pp91–93

1 Restaurants
see p95

1 Chinatown Food
Shops *see p94*

0 meters 200
0 yards 200

Mulberry Street, Little Italy

① Mulberry Street
MAP P4 ▪ Mulberry St, between Broome & Canal Sts

There are many trendy shops on Mulberry Street from Houston down to Spring Street and though Chinatown is overrunning much of Little Italy, the section between Broome and Canal remains strictly Italian. It is filled with restaurants, coffee shops with tempting Italian pastries, and stores selling pasta implements, statues of saints, and T-shirts saying "Kiss Me, I'm Italian." The Feast of San Gennaro packs the street each September *(see p74)*.

② Old Police Headquarters Building
MAP P4 ▪ 240 Centre St
▪ Closed to public

After the boroughs merged into Greater New York in 1898, the city's police department expanded rapidly. This 1905 headquarters near Little Italy was the result – a monumental, columned Baroque structure fit for "New York's Finest," with an ornate dome tall enough to be seen from City Hall. The strange shape of the building fits a wedge-shaped lot. Empty for more than a decade after the department relocated in 1973, the building has since been converted into luxury condos, the Police Building Apartments.

③ Museum of Chinese in America
MAP P4 ▪ 211–215 Centre St ▪ Open 11am–6pm Tue, Wed & Fri–Sun, 11am–9pm Thu ▪ Adm, free Thu ▪ www.mocanyc.org

This fascinating museum, devoted to the Chinese experience in the West, features an exhibit called "Where is Home?," with personal stories, photographs, and poetry culled from the community. Among the topics explored are women's roles, religion, and the "bachelor society." Changing exhibits range from art to the experience of gay Chinese people. Books, area guides, and free flyers on cultural events are also available.

Old Police Headquarters

④ Good Fortune Gifts
MAP P4 ▪ 32 Mott St

Originally known as Quong Yeun Shing & Company, this is Chinatown's oldest store, established in 1891. The store was a social hub for Chinese men, who were not allowed to bring their wives to the US under old immigration laws.

CHINATOWN'S EARLY DAYS

The 1882 Chinese Exclusion Act prevented Chinese workers from bringing their families with them to New York, so the original Chinatown (left), bounded by Pell, Doyers, and Mott streets, was mostly male and dominated by tongs. These were sometimes social clubs and sometimes rival criminal fraternities, giving the old locale its dangerous reputation.

Mott Street Shopping
MAP P4 ▪ Mott St

Clustered on this street are a variety of shops with a wonderful selection of Oriental goods. Iki Iki Gift Shop (No. 2) is a paradise for fans of Yu-Gi-Oh! and Hello Kitty. Vintage jewelry, bags, and candles are the specialty of Uniqulee (No. 36), while New Age Designer (No. 38) makes clothing to order in your choice of jewel-hued silks. For beautifully designed chopsticks, head to the Yunhong Chopsticks (No. 50).

6 Pearl River Chinese Products Emporium
MAP P4 ▪ 477 Broadway

The largest department store in Chinatown has a fascinating pot-pourri of goods for sale. There are Chinese musical instruments, paper lanterns, kites, dried herbs, embroidered silk tops, dresses and pajamas with mandarin collars, purses, dolls, pillows, and sandal-wood and jasmine soaps.

7 Church of the Transfiguration
MAP P4 ▪ 29 Mott St ▪ Open 7:30–9am & 11:30am–1pm daily, 5:30–7pm Sat, 8am–2pm Sun

Built by the English Lutheran Church in 1801 and sold to the Roman Catholic Church of the Transfiguration in 1853, this Georgian-style stone church with Gothic windows is typical of the influence of successive influxes of immigrants in New York. The church has changed with the nationalities of the community it

serves, first Irish, then Italian, and now Chinese. As the focal point of today's Chinese Roman Catholic community, it offers classes and services to help newcomers and holds services in Cantonese and Mandarin.

Church of the Transfiguration

8 Columbus Park
MAP P4 ▪ Bayard & Mulberry Sts

Chinatown's only park was created in the late 1890s as a result of the cam-paigning of the newspaper reporter Jacob Riis and other social reformers. It filled a stretch of the city that at the time was New York's worst slum, where Riis reported a stabbing or shooting at least once a week. Though it features more concrete than greenery, the park is popular today, filled with Chinese kids at play,

Xiangqi players in Columbus Park

xiangqi (Chinese chess) players, and people practicing *tai chi*. On the weekends, Chinese fortune-tellers sometimes set up shop in the park.

9 Bloody Angle

MAP P4 ■ Doyers St near Pell St

The name for this sharp curve on Doyers Street was coined by a newspaper because this was the site of so many gangland ambushes during the 1920s. It was a period when the Hip Sing and On Leong *tongs*, groups similar to criminal gangs, were fighting for control of the opium trade and gambling rackets in Chinatown. The *tong* wars continued off and on until at least the 1940s, and their rivalries continue in the present-day youth gangs.

10 Eastern States Buddhist Temple

MAP P4 ■ 64B Mott St
■ Open 8am–6pm daily

Step into the incense-scented interior of this temple, where offerings of fresh fruit are piled high, and more than 100 gold Buddhas gleam in the candlelight. The temple takes advantage of Chinatown's tourist traffic by offering $1 fortunes for sale near the front.

Inside Eastern States Buddhist Temple

A STROLL AROUND CHINATOWN AND LITTLE ITALY

Spring St Subway
Caffè Roma
Museum of Chinese in America
Alleva Dairy, Piemonte Ravioli Co.
Di Palo Fine Foods
Ferrara's
Ten Ren's Tea
Jing Fong
Eastern States Buddhist Temple
Golden Unicorn

MORNING

Take the No. 6 train to Spring Street, walk past Lafayette, and turn down **Mulberry Street** *(see p91)* for a stroll through Little Italy. Don't miss the old-fashioned food shops on Grand Street, such as cheese specialist **Alleva Dairy** (188 Mulberry Street at Grand) and Piemonte Ravioli Co. (190 Grand Street), where two dozen shapes and varieties of pasta can be bought. At 206 Grand Street is **Di Palo Fine Foods**, where you can watch fresh mozzarella being made. Take a break at a classic Italian café, like **Caffè Roma**, 385 Broome Street, or **Ferrara**'s, 195–201 Grand Street.

Take Grand Street west to Centre Street, then turn left and you'll find an introduction to what's ahead, the **Museum of Chinese in America** *(see p91)*. Walk east back to Mott Street, the center of Chinatown. Enjoy a dim sum lunch at **Jing Fong** or the **Golden Unicorn** *(see p95)*.

AFTERNOON

Remaining on Mott Street, spend some time browsing the many shops, exotic food stores, markets, and galleries that line the street. Step into Ten Ren's Tea (79 Mott Street) to sample a fad imported from Taiwan called "bubble tea": tall glasses of flavored teas served with "pearls" of tapioca in the bottom.

End the afternoon with a visit to the golden Buddhas of the **Eastern States Buddhist Temple** and have your fortune read.

See map on p90

Chinatown Food Shops

Market stall, Chinatown

1 Street Markets
MAP P4 ■ Chinatown, including Canal & Hester Sts

Canal Street and Hester Street are among the many blocks crowded with stands selling exotic Chinese vegetables, fruits, and dried foods.

2 Paris Sandwich Bakery Café
MAP P4 ■ 213 Grand St

This takeaway spot is renowned for its Vietnamese treats, such as *báhn mì* (baguettes typically filled with meat) and green-tea waffles.

3 Kamwo Herbal Pharmacy
MAP P4 ■ 209–11 Grand St

One of the better-known shops offering Chinese herbs said to cure anything from arthritis to impotence. Ginseng is available in teas or supplement form.

4 Fay Da Bakery
MAP P4 ■ 83 Mott St at Canal St

Sample a delicious soft bun filled with roasted pork or beef for less than $1, then try almond cookies, red bean cakes, custard tarts, or cream buns for dessert.

5 Ten Ren Tea & Ginseng Company
MAP P4 ■ 75 Mott St

An array of golden canisters holds many varieties of Chinese teas; knowledgeable clerks will explain the properties of each and how to brew them properly.

6 New Kam Man
MAP P4 ■ 200 Canal St

One of the largest food emporiums in Chinatown stocks tonics, teas, ginseng, vegetables of every shape, and row upon row of sauces.

7 Hong Kong Supermarket
MAP P4 ■ 157 Hester St at Elizabeth St

This huge store offers all manner of dried seafood, noodles, imported goods, watermelon seeds, and food products from China. Try one of the inexpensive, wrapped hard candies.

8 Deluxe Food Market
MAP P4 ■ 79 Elizabeth St

The Chinese come here for prepared foods, marinated meats, and the fully stocked meat and fish counters.

9 Aji Ichiban USA
MAP P4 ■ 37 Mott St

The name of this snack emporium means "the best and superior" in Japanese, and this tiny store in the heart of Chinatown lives up to its moniker. Look out for exotic treats such as spicy dried fish.

10 Chinatown Ice Cream Factory
MAP P4 ■ 65 Bayard St at Mott St

Ginger, lychee, pumpkin, mango, and red bean are among the flavors of ice cream that can be sampled at this popular dessert stop, a favorite with young visitors.

Chinatown Ice Cream Factory

Restaurants

PRICE CATEGORIES
For a three-course meal for one with a glass of house wine, and all unavoidable charges including tax.

$ under $25 $$ $25–$75 $$$ over $75

1 Great N.Y. Noodletown
MAP P4 ▪ 28½ Bowery St at Bayard St ▪ 212 349 0923 ▪ **No credit cards** ▪ $

The decor is simple and so is the menu, with wonderful soups, meat dishes, noodles, and creatively prepared seafood.

Great N.Y. Noodletown

2 Joe's Shanghai
MAP P4 ▪ 9 Pell St at Bowery ▪ 212 233 8888 ▪ **No credit cards** ▪ $$

The Chinatown branch of the Flushing (Queens) restaurant famous for its soup dumplings (look for steamed buns on the menu).

3 Peking Duck House
MAP P4 ▪ 28 Mott St ▪ 212 227 1810 ▪ $$

A pretty escape from Chinatown's surrounding bustle, the Peking Duck House serves diners its time-tested signature duck as well as elegant takes on Chinese classics.

4 Fuleen Seafood
MAP P4 ▪ 11 Division St, off Bowery ▪ 212 941 6888 ▪ $$

Fresh, well-prepared seafood dishes at bargain prices can be had at this Chinatown favorite. The Dungeness crab and lobster appetizers (four ways) are a steal.

5 Golden Unicorn
MAP P4 ▪ 18 East Broadway at Catherine St ▪ 212 941 0911 ▪ $

Dim sum is the star but all the dishes are well prepared in this crowded, third-floor restaurant.

6 Jing Fong
MAP P4 ▪ 20 Elizabeth St, between Bayard & Canal Sts ▪ 212 964 5256 ▪ $$

This glittery room is packed daily for the vast selection of freshly made dim sum. Just point at your choices as the carts roll by.

7 Nice Green Bo
MAP P4 ▪ 66 Bayard St, between Mott & Elizabeth Sts ▪ 212 625 2359 ▪ **No credit cards** ▪ $

This busy Shanghai spot is famous for its dumplings and scallion pancakes. Service is perfunctory, but the lines move quickly.

8 Lombardi's Pizza
MAP P4 ▪ 32 Spring St, between Mott & Mulberry Sts ▪ 212 941 7994 ▪ **No credit cards** ▪ $$

Pizza doesn't come much better than at "America's First Pizzeria." This unpretentious old-timer turns out delectable thin-crust pies.

9 Da Nico
MAP P4 ▪ 164 Mulberry St, between Broome & Grand Sts ▪ 212 343 1212 ▪ $$

A rustic setting and a wonderful courtyard garden make this family-run restaurant with a dozen varieties of pizza a favorite.

Chef at Da Nico

10 Parm
MAP P4 ▪ 248 Mulberry St ▪ 212 965 0955 ▪ $

Known for its Italian-American cuisine, sensational sandwiches are served at this popular Nolita spot. Try their Turkey Hero or Saratoga Club. Dine in or take-away.

See map on p90 ←

TOP 10 Lower East Side and East Village

The Lower East Side still seems to echo the calls of immigrants living in the area's tenements. Early churches became synagogues for the Jews who came here in record numbers. Recently, Latinos and Chinese have added to the rich history of the area, now being rediscovered by a hip, young generation. Nearby is the East Village, an early Dutch enclave that changed from German to Jewish before becoming a hippie haven and the birthplace of punk rock. A Ukrainian community here has tenaciously survived these changes.

Steam iron, Tenement Museum

AREA MAP OF LOWER EAST SIDE AND EAST VILLAGE

1 Top 10 Sights
see pp97–9

1 Restaurants
see p101

1 Bargain Stores and Boutiques
see p100

1 Lower East Side Tenement Museum

MAP N5 ■ 108 Orchard St ■ 212 431 0233 ■ Tours: run regularly 10am–6pm daily from 103 Orchard St (call ahead) ■ Adm ■ www.tenement.org

Guided tours inside this tenement building give an insight into the carefully researched lives of three of the families who lived here; a German-Jewish clan in 1874, an Orthodox Jewish family from Lithuania in 1918, and a Sicilian Catholic family during the Depression in the 1930s.

2 Orchard Street

MAP P5 ■ Lower East Side Visitor Center, 54 Orchard St ■ 212 226 9010 ■ Open 10am–6pm Mon–Fri, noon–5pm Sat & Sun ■ www.lowereastside.org

Orchard Street turned into a street of shops in 1940, when Mayor Fiorello La Guardia outlawed pushcarts throughout New York City. Many of the street's merchants continue to put some of their wares out on the sidewalk on Sundays and lure customers in with offers of 20 to 30 percent off brand names. The Lower East Side Visitor Center gives a free tour of the street every Sunday between April and December.

3 New Museum of Contemporary Art

MAP N4 ■ 235 Bowery St ■ Open 11am–6pm Wed–Sun (to 9pm Thu) ■ Adm ■ www.newmuseum.org

This provocative museum mounts shows of experimental work that other museums often overlook, particularly new multimedia forms, which sometimes include intriguing window displays. It moved into a cutting-edge building by Tokyo-based architects Sejima and Nishizawa in 2007, with a bookstore, theater, learning center, and café.

4 Museum at Eldridge Street

MAP P5 ■ 12 Eldridge St ■ Open 10am–5pm Sun–Fri (to 3pm Fri) ■ Tours: hourly until 4pm ■ Adm, free Mon ■ www.eldridgestreet.org

This 1887 synagogue was the first built in the US by Jewish immigrants from Eastern Europe. As many as 1,000 people attended services here at the turn of the 20th century. As congregants left the neighborhood, attendance waned, and the temple closed in the 1950s. After a 20-year restoration initiative, the synagogue has been transformed into a museum and a vibrant cultural center.

Restored interior of the Museum at Eldridge Street

Beth Hamedrash Hagadol Synagogue

5 Beth Hamedrash Hagadol Synagogue

MAP P5 ▪ 60–4 Norfolk St
▪ Closed to public

Artists can often be seen sketching this small, picturesque building. It was constructed in 1850 as the Norfolk Street Baptist Church, but as the neighborhood changed, the membership moved uptown, and in 1885 the structure was converted to a synagogue by America's oldest Russian-born Orthodox Jewish congregation. Gothic woodwork and the iron fence from the original church remain.

6 Russ & Daughters

MAP N5 ▪ 179 East Houston St
▪ Open 8am–8pm Mon–Fri, 8am–7pm Sat, 8am–5:30pm Sun (times may vary due to Jewish holidays)
▪ www.russanddaughters.com

In 1907, Joel Russ began trading strings of Polish mushrooms that he carried on his shoulders while he saved up to buy a handcart. In 1920, he opened this landmark store, which also sold salt-cured herring and salmon. Nowadays, a fourth generation of the family, including Russ's great-granddaughter, is in charge. The smoked salmon and other goods are of top quality and delicious, and caviar is a specialty.

7 St. Mark's Place

MAP M4 ▪ East 8th St, between 3rd Ave & Ave A

Once the heart of hippiedom, this block still has a counter-culture feel and is the headquarters of the East Village youth scene. Sidewalks are crowded until late into the night with patrons of funky, punky bars and shops selling music, books, T-shirts, vintage clothing, beads, posters, and black-leather everything. This is the place to get pierced or tattooed.

Comics store, St Mark's Place

(8) St. Mark's in-the-Bowery Church

MAP M4 ▪ 131 East 10th St ▪ Open 8:30am–4pm Mon–Fri, service 10:30am Sun

The second-oldest church in New York stands on land where Peter Stuyvesant, Dutch governor of the settlement in the 1600s, had his private chapel. He is also buried here. In the 1960s it served as one of the city's most politically committed congregations and continues to live on the avant-garde edge.

(9) Renwick Triangle

MAP M4 ▪ 114–128 East 10th St, 23–5 Stuyvesant St, between 2nd & 3rd Aves

These handsome townhouses were created in 1861 by James Renwick, Jr., a prominent architect of the day, on land that was once Peter Stuyvesant's farm.

(10) Ukrainian Museum

MAP N4 ▪ 222 East 6th St, between 2nd & 3rd Aves ▪ Open 11:30am–5pm Wed–Sun ▪ Adm ▪ www.ukrainian museum.org

The museum showcases a beguiling collection of Ukrainian costumes (embroidered blouses, colorful sashes, sheepskin and fur vests) and wedding wreaths of yarn and ribbons. There are also ceramics, jewelry, and intricate Ukrainian Easter eggs known as *pysanky*.

Ukrainian costume

THE CHANGING SCENE

Proving that change is the rule in New York City, the Lower East Side has emerged as the newest trendy area for clubs, restaurants, bars, cafés, and hip boutiques. Some residents are even moving into the tenement buildings that their great-grandparents fought so hard to escape. Ludlow Street is one of the best streets to get a feel for the current scene in the area.

EAST SIDE EXPLORATION

▶ MORNING

From the Delancey Street subway walk south to Grand Street and **Kossar's Bialys Bakery**, 367 Grand, famous for chewy, onion-flavored rolls, or the **Doughnut Plant**, 379 Grand, where the treats achieve gourmet status. Walk east for two historic houses of worship, the **Beth Hamedrash Hagadol Synagogue** and the **Bialystoker Synagogue**. Return along East Broadway, passing the **Henry Street Settlement** at No. 281. The community center at No. 197, the **Manny Cantor Center**, has good art exhibits. Walk to Orchard and pick up a bargain at the shops here or visit the **Lower East Side Tenement Museum** (see p97). Try one of the 50 delicious flavors of ice cream at **Il Laboratorio del Gelato** at 188 Ludlow, or continue to East Houston Street and have lunch at **Katz's Delicatessen** (see p101), or pick up some bagels at **Russ & Daughters**.

AFTERNOON

After lunch, walk uptown on 2nd Avenue. Turn left on East 6th to visit the **Ukrainian Museum**, a small and hidden gem of costumes and culture. Walk to **St. Mark's Place**, browsing the funky shops and bars on your way, then walk east on Stuyvesant Street, admiring the landmark townhouses of the **Renwick Triangle**. Lastly, stop at **St. Mark's in-the-Bowery Church**, one of the oldest in the city, where you can pay your respects at the grave of Peter Stuyvesant.

See map on p96 ←

Bargain Stores and Boutiques

1 Zarin Fabric Home Furnishings
MAP P5 ▪ 69 Orchard St
Since 1936 this mammoth showroom and workshop has provided upholstery and fabrics to the public at wholesale prices.

2 Katinka
MAP M4 ▪ 303 East 9th St
Miniature treasure featuring exotic Indian textiles, clothing, and jewelry for shockingly low prices.

The Dressing Room

3 The Dressing Room
MAP P5 ▪ 75A Orchard St
More than just a boutique, it showcases the work of young designers, offers a clothing exchange, and also has a cocktail bar with live DJ sets.

4 Exit 9 Gift Emporium
MAP N5 ▪ 51 Ave A
An independent store with a large collection of kitsch, gifts, and all sorts of novelties. This is a great places to pick up inexpensive, fun gifts, from inflatable moose heads to colorful tote bags.

5 Giselle
MAP N5 ▪ 143 Orchard St
Four floors of designer clothing by European names such as Valentino, Escada, and Ungaro, promising 20 to 30 percent off retail.

6 A. W. Kaufman
MAP P5 ▪ 73 Orchard St
Fine-quality European lingerie is sold at an excellent price with personalized service. This third-generation store, set up in 1924, offers a range of underwear for men and women, as well as some stunning bridal sets.

7 Jodamo
MAP N5 ▪ 321 Grand St
An extensive range of European designer menswear can be found in this large store, including Versace, Valentino, and Missoni, as well as leather goods and shoes.

8 Altman Luggage
MAP N5 ▪ 135 Orchard St
From computer cases to carry-ons, brand names like Lark, Travelpro, and American Tourister are sold for less at this well-stocked emporium.

9 Moo Shoes
MAP P5 ▪ 78 Orchard St
You can shop for funky, colorful footwear at this vegan-owned store that sells cruelty-free shoes, bags, T-shirts, wallets, books, and various other accessories.

10 Economy Candy
MAP N5 ▪ 108 Rivington St
Since 1937, this old-fashioned, family-run candy store has been doling out gumballs, hand-dipped chocolates, and fun New York-themed goodies.

Economy Candy

Restaurants

PRICE CATEGORIES
For a three-course meal for one with a glass of house wine, and all unavoidable charges including tax.

$ under $25 $$ $25–$75 $$$ over $75

1 Schiller's Liquor Bar
MAP N5 ▪ 131 Rivington St at Norfolk St ▪ 212 260 4555 ▪ $$

An eclectic menu is served at this French-inspired restaurant by Keith McNally. Arrive early for dinner if you do not want to wait. The brunch menu is also very good.

2 Katz's Delicatessen
MAP N5 ▪ 205 East Houston St at Ludlow St ▪ 212 254 2246 ▪ $

Savor a pastrami sandwich on rye here, and you'll understand why New York delis are famous.

3 Sammy's Roumanian
MAP N4 ▪ 157 Chrystie St ▪ 212 673 0330 ▪ No vegetarian options ▪ $$

This steakhouse is like a Jewish wedding every night. You'll enjoy the chopped liver and every minute of the schmaltzy entertainment.

4 Mission Chinese Food
MAP P5 ▪ 171 East Broadway ▪ 212 529 8800 ▪ $$

Dine on reinvented Chinese food – from mapo tofu with simmered pork to salt-cod fried rice – at Danny Bowien's wildly popular restaurant.

5 Macondo
MAP N5 ▪ 157 East Houston St, between Allen & Eldridge Sts ▪ 212 473 9900 ▪ $$

This fun bar-restaurant gives Latino street food a gourmet rework, serving seven signature dishes.

6 Veselka
MAP M4 ▪ 144 2nd Ave at 9th St ▪ 212 228 9682 ▪ $$

This funky and cozy Ukrainian diner is open 24 hours a day, and for over 60 years has been serving borscht, blintzes, and pierogi for a pittance. The tables at the back are quieter.

7 The Dumpling Man
MAP M4 ▪ 100 St Mark's Place ▪ 212 505 2121 ▪ $

The pork, chicken, and vegetarian dumplings are a big draw, but save room for the shaved ice dessert.

8 Freemans
MAP N4 ▪ 191 Chrystie St ▪ 212 420 0012 ▪ $$

Hiding at the end of a graffitied alley, this hunting lodge-style restaurant serves a 1950s-inspired menu, from rum-soaked ribs to prunes wrapped in bacon, oozing Stilton cheese.

Freemans restaurant

9 Prune
MAP N4 ▪ 54 East 1st St, between 1st & 2nd Aves ▪ 212 677 6221 ▪ $$

Updated homestyle American is the game here, with dishes like lamb chop with leeks and braised potatoes. Brunch is also a hit.

10 Momofuku Ssäm Bar
MAP M4 ▪ 207 2nd Ave at 13th St ▪ 212 254 3500 ▪ $$

This popular spot serves American food that usually veers through Asia on its way to the plate. Offal often figures in, but don't be intimidated – it's all delicious *(see p67)*.

See map on p96 ←

SoHo and TriBeCa

The area named for its shape (Triangle Below Canal) long consisted mostly of abandoned warehouses. When Robert De Niro set up his Tribeca Film Center in 1988, stylish restaurants opened, and the area started to draw celebrity residents. Now TriBeCa is one of New York's hottest neighborhoods and home to the TriBeCa Film Festival. SoHo's (South of Houston) once empty loft spaces first drew artists, then galleries, then crowds of browsers and restaurants to serve them. Only some galleries remain, and the streets are now lined with designer clothing and home furnishing boutiques. Both areas boast the famous New York cast-iron architecture.

Statue, Fire Museum

1 Greene Street
MAP N4

Cast-iron architecture flourished in New York in the late 1800s, as a way to produce decorative elements such as columns and arches and create impressive buildings inexpensively. Greene Street, between Canal and Grand streets, and between Broome and Spring streets, has 50 examples. The rows of columned facades creating a striking streetscape.

Cast-iron building on Greene Street

2 Children's Museum of the Arts
MAP N3 ■ 103 Charlton St, between Hudson & Greenwich Sts ■ 212 274 0986 ■ Open noon–5pm Mon, noon–6pm Thu & Fri, 10am–5pm Sat & Sun ■ Adm ■ www.cmany.org

Founded in 1988, the CMA's mission is to enable children aged one to 12 to reach their full potential in the visual and performing arts. Children can work with paint, glue, paper, and recycled materials to paint, build, sculpt, and imagine. They can also play in the ball pond and art house, design projects, explore exhibitions, and meet other children visting the museum.

3 Prada
MAP N4 ■ 575 Broadway at Prince St ■ Open 11am–7pm Mon– Sat (to 8pm Thu), 11am–6pm Sun

This extraordinary flagship store for trend-setting Italian designer Prada is a sign of SoHo's shift from art to fashion. Dutch architect Rem Koolhaas is responsible for the ultra-hip floating stairs, undulating walls, futuristic elevators, and hi-tech dressing rooms. A visit here is a must for fans of both high-end fashion and architecture.

AREA MAP OF SOHO AND TRIBECA

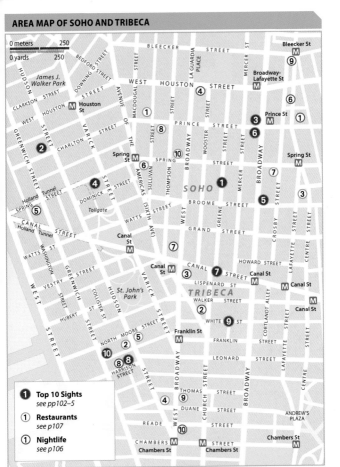

0 meters 250
0 yards 250

Top 10 Sights
see pp102–5

Restaurants
see p107

Nightlife
see p106

4 New York City Fire Museum

MAP N3 ■ 278 Spring St
■ Open 10am–5pm daily ■ Adm
■ www.nycfiremuseum.org

A nostalgic treasure housed in a 1904 firehouse, this splendid collection includes the city's fire-fighting engines, equipment, garb, and memorabilia from the 18th century to the present. A moving photo display depicts the World Trade Center attack on September 11, 2001 and honors the hundreds of firefighters lost there.

New York City Fire Museum

Impressive cast-iron facade of the Haughwout Building

(5) Haughwout Building
MAP P4 ■ 488–492 Broadway at Broome St

A cast-iron masterpiece, this structure was built in 1857 to house a fashionable china and glassware emporium. The design of colonnaded arches flanked by taller Corinthian columns was adapted from the facade of the Sansovino Library in Venice. This motif is repeated 92 times across the front of the building. A 1995 renovation removed grime and restored the elegant original pale color. This building boasted the first Otis safety elevator, an innovation that made the skyscraper possible.

(6) "Little" Singer Building
MAP N4 ■ 561–563 Broadway, between Prince & Spring Sts

By the early 1900s, cast iron was giving way to steel-framed brick and

"Little" Singer Building

terra-cotta. One notable example is Ernest Flagg's 1904 "Little" Singer Building (to distinguish it from a taller tower also built for Singer). Influenced by Parisian architecture of the period, it has a charming 12-story facade adorned with wrought-iron balconies and graceful arches painted in dark green.

(7) Canal Street
MAP P3–4

The end of SoHo, the beginning of TriBeCa, and a world of its own, no street better shows the contrasts of New York. Canal Street is crowded with peddlers selling fake Rolex watches and Gucci bags, electronics that may or may not be new, and bargain stores offering sneakers, jeans, and flea-market finds. Keep walking east into Chinatown, and the goods shift to vegetables and displays of live and dried fish.

8 Harrison Street
MAP P3

This rare group of Federal town-houses, built between 1796 and 1828, did not exist as a row until 1975, when the houses were moved to this site to be saved from the urban renewal that razed much of the area. At the end of the block (No. 6) is the former New York Mercantile Exchange, a Queen Anne building dating from 1884 and in use until 1977 when the Exchange moved to 4 World Trade Center.

9 White Street
MAP P3–4

The best example of cast-iron architecture in TriBeCa is a sampling of several styles. No. 2 has Federal features and a gambrel roof; Nos. 8–10, designed by Henry Fernbach in 1869, sport Tuscan columns and arches and use the Neo-Renaissance device of building shorter upper stories to give an illusion of height. There is a complete change of pace at No. 38, which houses neon artist Rudi Stern's gallery, Let There Be Neon.

10 TriBeCa Film Center
MAP P3 ■ 375 Greenwich St

A turn-of-the-century coffee warehouse has been converted into office space for the film and entertainment industry. The guiding spirit was Robert De Niro, whose TriBeCa Productions was founded in 1988. Miramax has set up offices here and the building is also home to the TriBeCa Grill, owned by De Niro and restaurateur Drew Nieporent.

TRIBECA'S MOVIE BUSINESS

Robert De Niro organized the first TriBeCa Film Festival in 2002 to help the neighborhood's recovery from the effects of the 9/11 attacks. The 10-day spring event is now one of the highest profile film festivals in the country. Outside the festival period, big name stars have been sighted heading for the Grand Screening Room at the TriBeCa Grand Hotel (see p174).

A STROLL AROUND SOHO AND TRIBECA

▶ MORNING

Bleecker Street subway is a good starting point to explore Soho. Galleries worth a visit include **Spencer Brownstone** at 3 Wooster St, and **Franklin Bowles Galleries** at 431 West Broadway. **Greene Street** (see p102) has a number of interesting boutiques, such as Moss, Helmut Lang, Paul Smith, and Kirna Zabête.

The Drawing Center (see p51) exhibits work from emerging artists and has poetry readings. This is also a prime area for photography galleries. The most interesting are **Janet Borden** and **Staley-Wise**, both located at 560 Broadway. Afterwards, stop for Asian noodles at **Kelley & Ping**, 127 Greene St, between Houston and Prince streets.

AFTERNOON

Drop in on designer boutiques **Miu Miu**, 100 Prince Street, and **Anna Sui**, 484 Broome Street, before proceeding to TriBeCa. Take a stroll along **White** and **Harrison** streets to admire their historic architecture before stopping for a drink at the **Roxy Lounge** (see p106).

Spend the rest of the afternoon taking in the varied exhibits at **apexart** (see p51), which also hosts free public events. Afterward, sample the best of TriBeCa cuisine with a meal at one of the area's many leading restaurants, such as **Nobu** (see p107) or **Bouley** (see p107).

See map on p103 ←

Nightlife

1 Pravda
MAP N4 ▪ 281 Lafayette St, between Prince & Houston Sts ▪ 212 226 4696

Vodkas from across the world are served in this bar featuring Russian mementos, leather chairs, and a low gold ceiling.

2 Roxy Lounge
MAP N3 ▪ Roxy Hotel Tribeca, 2 6th Ave ▪ 212 519 6600

Almost the entire ground floor of the hotel is devoted to this popular bar with plush seats and a dramatic eight-story atrium.

3 Nancy Whiskey Pub
MAP P3 ▪ 1 Lispenard St ▪ 212 226 9943

Popular with local workers, this no-frills hangout is one of TriBeCa's most beloved neighborhood bars.

Cocktail mixologist at work, Pegu Club

4 Pegu Club
MAP N3 ▪ 77 West Houston St ▪ 212 473 7348

Cocktails are taken to a high art at this sultry drinking den – try the Earl Grey "Marteani," with tea-infused gin, lemon juice, and egg white to froth it all up.

5 Ear Inn
MAP P3 ▪ 326 Spring St at Greenwich St ▪ 212 226 9060

This classy but cozy and casual spot is likely the oldest bar in the city (it dates to 1830). Fairly buzzy at night and at lunch, it's also good for a respectable cheap meal.

The bar at Puck Fair

6 Puck Fair
MAP N4 ▪ 298 Lafayette St, between Houston & Prince Sts ▪ 212 431 1200

At this cozy multi-level pub you can settle in to enjoy a pint along with tasty Irish snacks.

7 Grand Bar
MAP P3 ▪ SoHo Grand Hotel, 310 West Broadway, between Canal & Grand Sts ▪ 212 965 3588

The SoHo Grand is a neighborhood nightlife mecca; comfortable and softly lit, with food if you want it.

8 Terroir Tribeca
MAP P3 ▪ 24 Harrison St ▪ 212 625 9463

Toast the New York night at this lively wine bar with wines from around the world and creative nibbles, from duck salad to mozzarella balls.

9 Temple Bar
MAP N4 ▪ 332 Lafayette St, between Bleecker & East Houston Sts ▪ 212 925 4242

Dark, swanky, sexy, and pricey, but the martinis are mammoth.

10 Ward III
MAP Q3 ▪ 111 Reade St ▪ 212 240 9194

A neighborhood mainstay for great cocktails – both off the menu and bespoke concoctions – and an unpretentious yet chic atmosphere.

Restaurants

PRICE CATEGORIES

For a three-course meal for one with a glass of house wine, and all unavoidable charges including tax.

$ under $25 $$ $25–$75 $$$ over $75

① The Dutch
MAP N3 ▪ 131 Sullivan St
▪ 212 677 6200 ▪ $$

Oysters and bold dishes, from strip steak to lamb neck, are the highlights at this wood-paneled tavern helmed by Andrew Carmellini.

Seafood platter at The Dutch

② Nobu
MAP P3 ▪ 105 Hudson St
▪ 212 219 0500 ▪ $$$

Nobu Matsuhisa's sublime Japanese/Peruvian fusion fare served in a whimsical setting *(see p66)*. An outpost, Nobu 57, is at 40 West 57th Street (212 757 3000).

③ La Esquina
MAP P4 ▪ 114 Kenmare St
▪ 646 613 7100 ▪ $$

At this colorful Mexican spot, customers choose between the inexpensive *taquería* counter and the stylish cocktail lounge.

④ Bouley
MAP P3 ▪ 163 Duane St
▪ 212 964 2525 ▪ $$$

David Bouley demonstrates his legendary culinary skills in a vaulted dining room. The prix fixe dinner menu features seasonal dishes like porcini flan and New England black sea bass.

⑤ Bubby's
MAP P3 ▪ 120 Hudson St
▪ 212 219 0666 ▪ $$

In TriBeCa, this sunny, family-friendly restaurant churns out comfort fare at all hours from a varied menu that includes full meals as well as light bites.

⑥ Aquagrill
MAP N3 ▪ 210 Spring St at 6th Ave ▪ 212 274 0505 ▪ $$

The draw at this popular SoHo restaurant is the ultra-fresh seafood it serves. Save some room for choices from the raw bar.

⑦ Balthazar
MAP N3 ▪ 80 Spring St at Broadway ▪ 212 965 1414 ▪ $$$

As close to a Parisian bistro as you're likely to find in SoHo, the only problem with Balthazar is its popularity. A buzzing scene.

⑧ Raoul's
MAP N4 ▪ 180 Prince St, between Sullivan & Thompson Sts ▪ 212 966 3518 ▪ $$$

Another taste of the Left Bank in SoHo, with an updated French menu as well as a great garden.

⑨ The Odeon
MAP P3 ▪ 145 West Broadway at Thomas St ▪ 212 233 0507 ▪ $$

Art Deco decor, consistently good French-American food, and a star-studded crowd have been keeping the vibe right since 1980.

⑩ Boqueria
MAP N3 ▪ 171 Spring St
▪ 212 343 4255 ▪ $$

Head to lively Boqueria for superb tapas, such as blistered *padrón* peppers sprinkled with sea salt or juicy marinated lamb, all washed down with a potent jug of sangria.

See map on p103

🔟 Greenwich Village

New York University

It was different from the start, a crazy pattern of streets that broke from the city's grid plan, reflecting the boundaries of a rural village. As a bohemian haven, the leafy lanes of the Village have been home to artists and writers. Jazz musicians, beat poets, and performers like the young Bob Dylan found their places here. Later it became popular with gays, and today cafés and funky shops attract young people from all over the city. The Village really comes to life at night, when cafés, theaters, and clubs beckon at every turn.

AREA MAP OF GREENWICH VILLAGE

- ❶ **Top 10 Sights**
  see pp108–11
- ① **Restaurants**
  see p113
- ① **Literary Landmarks**
  see p112

❶ Washington Square Park

MAP N3 ■ 5th Ave, between Waverly Pl & 4th St

In 1826, a marshy area was filled to form this popular park. The marble arch by Stanford White went up in 1892, replacing a wooden version that marked the centenary of George Washington's inauguration. Mothers with strollers, chess players, and

Marble arch, Washington Square Park

The mid-19th-century town houses in Grove Court, Greenwich Village

young lovers now occupy benches where drug dealers once reigned. The fountain in the center is where Bob Dylan sang his first folk songs.

② MacDougal Alley
MAP M3 ■ East of MacDougal St, between 8th St & Waverly Pl

These 19th-century stables for the fine homes on Washington Square North were converted into studios by artists early in the 20th century, causing the street to be known as "Art Alley de Luxe." Among the residents were painter Guy Pene du Bois and sculptor Gertrude Vanderbilt Whitney, who established the first Whitney Museum in 1914 at 8 West 8th Street, adjoining her studio.

③ Washington Mews
MAP M3 ■ University Place to 5th Ave

Another group of stables turned into houses around 1900, the mews attracted both writers and artists. No. 14A housed, at various times, author John

Washington Mews

Dos Passos and artists Edward Hopper, William Glackens, and Rockwell Kent. Writer Sherwood Anderson often stayed at No. 54 with his friend and patron, Mary Emmett. In contrast to the modern buildings in much of Manhattan, this type of quaint enclave is the reason many find the Village so appealing.

④ Grove Court
MAP N3 ■ Grove St near Bedford St

This group of six town houses in a bend in the street was developed by grocer Samuel Cocks, who thought that having residents nearby would help his business at No. 18. But while such private courts are prized today, they were not considered respectable in the 1850s, and the disreputable types who moved in earned it the nickname "Mixed Ale Alley." American writer O. Henry later used the block as the setting for his 1902 novel *The Last Leaf*.

5 Jefferson Market Courthouse

MAP M3 ■ 425 6th Ave, between 9th & 10th Sts ■ Open 10am–8pm Mon, Wed, 11am–6pm Tue, Thu, 10am–5pm Fri, Sat

The site was a market in 1833, named after the former president, Thomas Jefferson. The fire lookout tower had a giant bell that alerted volunteer firefighters. When the courthouse was built in 1877, the bell was installed in its clock tower. The treasured Village landmark was saved from demolition after a spirited local campaign and converted into a branch of the New York Public Library (see p128) in the 1950s.

Jefferson Market Courthouse

6 Cherry Lane Theatre

MAP N3 ■ 38 Commerce St, between Bedford & Barrow Sts ■ 212 989 2020 ■ www. cherrylanetheatre.org

In 1924, a warehouse was converted into one of the first Off-Broadway theaters and showcased plays by the likes of Edward Albee, Eugene Ionesco, David Mamet, Samuel Beckett, and Harold Pinter. Today, the "Cherry Lane Alternative" uses established playwrights to mentor talented newcomers.

Bleecker Street

7 Bleecker Street

MAP N3 ■ Between 6th Ave & West Broadway

The present line-up of ordinary shops and restaurants belies the history of this street. James Fenimore Cooper lived at No. 145 in 1833, Theodore Dreiser stayed at No. 160 when he came to New York in 1895, and James Agee lived at No. 172 from 1941 to 1951. The café at No. 189, on the corner of Bleecker and MacDougal, was the San Remo bar, the favorite gathering place for William Burroughs, Allen Ginsberg, Gregory Corso, and Jack Kerouac, leading lights of the Beat Generation.

8 New York University

MAP N4 ■ Washington Square ■ www.nyu.edu

Founded in 1831, NYU enlarged the scope of early 19th-century study from its previous concentration on Greek and Latin to contemporary subjects: a "rational and practical education" for those aspiring to careers in business, industry, science, and the arts, as well as in law, medicine, and the ministry. It has grown into the largest private university in America and now occupies buildings in many blocks around Washington Square.

⑨ Judson Memorial Church

MAP N3 ■ 55 Washington Square South ■ Open for services 11am Sun

An elegant work in Romanesque style by Stanford White, with stained glass by John La Farge, the church was built in 1888–93 as a memorial to Adoniram Judson, said to be the first American Baptist missionary in Asia. John D. Rockefeller, Jr. *(see p46)* contributed to the construction. White's novel use of mottled yellow brick and white terra-cotta trim introduced light coloration into American church architecture.

⑩ 75½ Bedford Street

MAP N3 ■ Between Morton & Barrow Sts

New York's narrowest home, just 9.5 ft (3 m) wide, was built in 1873 on a carriageway that led to former stables behind Nos. 75 and 77. Poet Edna St. Vincent Millay lived here, as did actors John Barrymore and, later, Cary Grant. No. 77 is the oldest house in the Village, dating from around 1799, and at No. 103 is "Twin Peaks," an 1830 structure that was remodeled in 1925 by Clifford Reed Daily to house artists and writers, who would presumably be inspired by the quirky architecture.

THE HALLOWEEN PARADE

Anything goes in this wildly gaudy annual parade of cross-dressers, floats, and amazing costumes **(below)**. Drawing more than 60,000 participants and reportedly two million spectators, it is the largest Halloween parade in the world. The parade route goes up 6th Avenue, from Spring Street in the Village to 23rd Street, starting at 7pm.

A VILLAGE STROLL

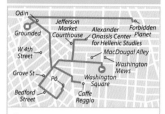

▶ **MORNING**

Begin at **Washington Square** *(p112)* and the elegant town house row where Edith Wharton and Henry James once lived. Find the charming houses of **Washington Mews** and **MacDougal Alley** *(p109)*, then follow 6th Avenue, past the **Jefferson Market Courthouse**, to West 10th Street.

Stroll down the passageway at the front of the **Alexander Onassis Center for Hellenic Studies**. This walkway once led up to the Tile Club, a gathering place for the artists of the Tenth Street Studio, where Augustus Saint-Gaudens, John La Farge, and Winslow Homer lived and worked. Continue along Waverly Place, Grove Street, and Bedford Street, each with its share of prize town house architecture. Have lunch at the lovely, pocket-size Italian bistro, **Pó** *(see p113)*.

AFTERNOON

After lunch, while away a few hours browsing in the local shops. Vintage clothing can be admired at specialty shops such as **Odin** at 106 Greenwich Ave, while at No. 832 Broadway you'll find **Forbidden Planet**, a nirvana for comic book fanatics.

West 8th Street and West 4th Street are also crammed with shops, and there are several coffeehouses, which are great for people-watching. Try **Caffe Reggio**, 119 MacDougal Street, where the literary lights of the Beat Generation used to read their poetry, or **Grounded**, 28 Jane St, for good coffee.

See map on p108

Literary Landmarks

1 Washington Square
MAP N3

Prominent figures who lived here include Edith Wharton, at No. 7 in 1882. Henry James was born nearby at 2 Washington Place in 1843.

2 St. Luke's Place
MAP N3 ■ Between Hudson St & 7th Ave South

Poet Marianne Moore lived here, and Theodore Dreiser wrote *An American Tragedy* at No. 16.

3 Patchin Place
MAP N3 ■ West 10th St

A charming pocket of 19th-century houses that later attracted e. e. cummings, John Masefield, and Eugene O'Neill, among various others.

4 Café Wha?
MAP N3 ■ 115 MacDougal St, between Bleecker & West 3rd Sts

Beat poet Allen Ginsberg was a regular here, a venue that also saw early appearances from Bob Dylan and Jimi Hendrix.

5 White Horse Tavern
MAP N3 ■ 567 Hudson St at 11th St

Favorite hangout of Norman Mailer and Dylan Thomas, who announced one night in 1953, "I've had 18 straight whiskeys," and passed out. He died the next day.

6 Willa Cather Residence
MAP N3 ■ 5 Bank St, between Waverly Pl & Greenwich St ■ Closed to public

Willa Cather penned six novels in this house and her Friday "at homes" were attended by the likes of D. H. Lawrence.

7 Mark Twain Residence
MAP M3 ■ 21 5th Ave at 9th St ■ Closed to public

The former home (1904–8) of Mark Twain, designed by James Renwick, Jr., architect of St. Patrick's Cathedral, was demolished in 1954. Twain received guests while propped up in a carved bed.

Mark Twain

8 William Styron Residence
MAP M3 ■ 43 Greenwich Ave ■ Closed to public

This was William Styron's first "tiny but rather nice" apartment after he wrote *Lie Down in Darkness* at the age of 23.

9 Edward Albee Residence
MAP N3 ■ 238 West 4th St ■ Closed to public

Edward Albee wrote *The Zoo Story* here. He first saw the words "Who's Afraid of Virginia Woolf?" written in soap on the mirror of the bar in a nearby saloon.

10 West 10th Street
MAP M3

This street has had several literary residents. Mark Twain lived at No. 14 from 1900 to 1901, Hart Crane lived at No. 54 in 1917, and Edward Albee lived in the carriage house at No. 50 during the 1960s.

White Horse Tavern

Restaurants

PRICE CATEGORIES

For a three-course meal for one with a glass of house wine, and all unavoidable charges including tax.

$ under $25 $$ $25–$75 $$$ over $75

1 Babbo
MAP N3 ■ 110 Waverly Place ■ 212 777 0303 ■ $$$

An attractive setting and the inventive Italian fare by celebrity chef Mario Batali make this a very popular spot. Reserve in advance.

2 Il Mulino
MAP N3 ■ 86 West 3rd St, between Sullivan & Thompson Sts ■ 212 673 3783 ■ $$$

Another top Italian. Quality is consistent, portions are large, and the brick-walled room is inviting.

3 Blue Hill
MAP N3 ■ 75 Washington Place at MacDougal St ■ 212 539 1776 ■ $$$

Highly praised New American fare that uses local, seasonal ingredients, served in elegant surroundings.

4 Blue Ribbon Bakery
MAP N3 ■ 35 Downing St at Bedford St ■ 212 337 0404 ■ $$$

A Village favorite with an enormous, eclectic menu that includes everything from croissants and caviar to the signature fried chicken.

5 Pó
MAP N4 ■ 31 Cornelia St ■ 212 645 2189 ■ $$$

This tiny spot is beloved on the block and beyond for its beautifully executed Italian cuisine made with the freshest seasonal produce.

6 Minetta Tavern
MAP N3 ■ 113 MacDougal St ■ 212 475 3850 ■ $$$

While this classic tavern dates back to 1937 (Ernest Hemingway and Eugene O'Neill drank here), it's now best known for upscale bistro fare.

7 Da Silvano
MAP N3 ■ 260 6th Ave, between Bleecker & West Houston Sts ■ 212 982 2343 ■ $$$

Watch the celebrities come and go from a table outside. The northern Italian fare here is consistent, and the buzz even better.

8 Morandi
MAP M3 ■ 211 Waverly Place ■ 212 627 7575 ■ $$

Enjoy a slice of rustic Italy at this wildly popular West Village restaurant, with excellent pastas, grilled meats and seafood.

9 The Little Owl
MAP N3 ■ 90 Bedford St ■ 212 741 4695 ■ $$

This tiny but cozy restaurant run by Joey Campanaro has a great Italian-accented American bistro menu, serving everything from grilled scallops to Parmesan risotto with truffles.

10 Sushi Samba
MAP N3 ■ 87 7th Ave South at Bleecker St ■ 212 691 7885 ■ $$$

The Japanese/Brazilian fusion cuisine and cocktails are inspired, but the trendy crowd comes here for the rooftop deck and live music on sunny days.

Sushi Samba

See map on p108

⭑⓾ Union Square, Gramerc Park, and Flatiron

Change is in the air in this flourishing section of Manhattan. Union Square, once a hangout for drug dealers, has been transformed. A Greenmarket fills it with fresh produce four times a week, and the surrounding neighborhood is attracting new apartments, shops, and restaurants. Shops and lively eating places now extend up 5th Avenue into the once-neglected Flatiron District. Opposite the Flatiron Building that gives the area its name, Madison Square is home to some of the city's hottest restaurants and Madison Square Park. No change was needed in Gramercy Park, the most European of the city's neighborhoods.

Union Square Greenmarket

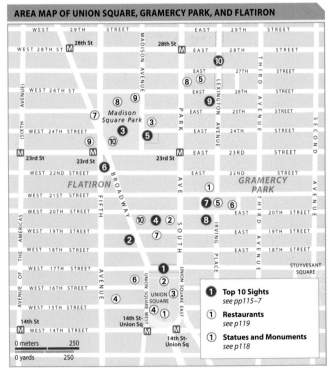

AREA MAP OF UNION SQUARE, GRAMERCY PARK, AND FLATIRON

1 Top 10 Sights
see pp115–7

1 Restaurants
see p119

1 Statues and Monuments
see p118

0 meters 250

0 yards 250

Statue-filled Madison Square Park

① Union Square Greenmarket

MAP M4 ■ At Broadway & 17th St ■ Open 8am–6pm Mon, Wed, Fri, Sat

Herbs, berries, miniature vegetables, fresh flowers, homebaked pastries, newly woven yarns, hams, honey – all of these and more can be found at the bountiful Greenmarket that fills Union Square each Monday, Wednesday, Friday, and Saturday. Over 150 regional farmers take part in the market, each offering only goods that they have grown or made. Not to be missed.

② ABC Carpet & Home

MAP L4 ■ 881 & 888 Broadway at East 19th St

The city's most eclectic emporium, with two landmark buildings that are part flea market, part antiques fair, and part Middle Eastern bazaar. Offerings include fancy French or rugged Mexican furniture, fabrics, accessories, bedding, flowers, and rugs. There are also the notable dining spaces ABC Cocina and ABC Kitchen.

③ Madison Square Park

MAP L3 ■ 23rd to 26th Sts, between Broadway & Madison Ave

The square opened in 1847 at the center of a residential area where politician Theodore Roosevelt and writer Edith Wharton were born. The original Madison Square Garden was here, at Madison Avenue and 26th Street. Development brought distinguished sites such as the Flatiron and Metropolitan Life Buildings. Today the statue-filled park and the area are increasingly buzzy.

④ Theodore Roosevelt Birthplace

MAP L4 ■ 28 East 20th St, between Broadway & Park Ave 5th ■ Open 9am–5pm Tue–Sat ■ Visits are by guided tour only ■ Free ■ www.nps.gov/thrb

The boyhood home where the colorful 26th president of the United States was born in 1858 has been reconstructed. Exhibits trace his political career as well as his explorations, displaying everything from toys to campaign buttons, and emblems of the trademark "Rough Rider" hat Roosevelt wore in the Spanish–American War. The house offers a rare glimpse of a privileged 19th-century New York lifestyle.

Birthplace of Theodore Roosevelt

⑤ Metropolitan Life Tower
MAP L4 ▪ 1 Madison Ave, near 24th St ▪ Open during office hours

This 54-story tower, built along the east side of Madison Square in 1909, was the world's tallest building at that time – an appropriate corporate symbol for the world's largest insurance company. Designed by Napoleon LeBrun & Sons, the tower follows the form of the campanile in Piazza San Marco in Venice. Although it was altered in the 1960s, when the entire structure was renovated, its ornate four-faced clock and crowning cupola remain a familiar landmark on the New York skyline.

⑥ Flatiron Building
MAP L3 ▪ 175 5th Ave at Broadway & 23rd St ▪ Open office hours

Though dwarfed by countless taller structures today, this unusual building – its shape conforming to a triangular plot of land – remains striking, a symbol of the beginning of

Flatiron Building

THE CITY'S SQUARES

Manhattan has only four London-style squares: Union, Madison, Stuyvesant, and Gramercy Park, all formed in the 1800s by real estate speculators hoping to profit by selling surrounding lots to the wealthy. The squares provide welcome breaks among the city's dense, tall buildings, but only Gramercy Park **(below)** has remained residential.

the skyscraper era. Its slim, rounded facade is as proud as a ship's prow sailing up the avenue. Completed in 1902, it anchored the north end of the prestigious Ladies' Mile shopping district, located between Union and Madison Squares. The designer, famous Chicago architect Daniel Burnham, included detailed Italian Renaissance decoration on the building from top to bottom, much of it in terra-cotta.

⑦ Gramercy Park
MAP L4 ▪ Lexington Ave, between 20th & 21st Sts ▪ Closed to public

Samuel Ruggles laid out this neighborhood around a private park in the 1830s. It remains the city's only private park and a desirable place to live. Architect Stanford White remodeled No. 16 in 1888 for Edwin Booth, who founded the Players Club here. Booth's statue (see p118) can be seen standing in the park.

⑧ National Arts Club
MAP L4 ▪ 15 Gramercy Park South ▪ Open 10am–5pm Mon–Fri

Originally the home of Samuel Tilden, a governor of New York and opponent of the notorious "Boss" Tweed (see p46), this Gothic Revival brownstone was designed by Calvert Vaux, of Central Park fame. The National Arts Club, whose members have included leading American artists since the 1800s, bought the building in 1906. Each member is asked to donate a work to the club. Though it is a private club, its galleries are open to the public.

The National Arts Club brownstone

(9) 69th Regiment Armory
MAP L4 ■ Lexington Ave, between 25th & 26th Sts
■ **Closed to public**

This Beaux Arts building was used as the drill hall and offices of a military unit privately formed in 1848. In 1913, the controversial exhibition of modern art known as the Armory Show was held here, including works by Van Gogh, Duchamp, and Brancusi. The show was widely panned in the press, but it brought modern art to New York on a large scale and had a profound and lasting effect on American art.

(10) "Curry Hill"
MAP L4 ■ Lexington Ave, between 26th & 29th Sts

Despite changes around it, this three-block corridor just south of Murray Hill remains filled with Indian shops selling saris and gifts, and is lined with restaurants that are a boon for diners (particularly vegetarians) in search of interesting food at reasonable prices. Kalustyan's, 123 Lexington Avenue, is a treasure trove of spices and grains, with some 31 different kinds of rice.

EXPLORING GRAMERCY PARK AND FLATIRON

▶ MORNING

Book-lovers should start on 12th Street, where the city's biggest used bookstore, the **Strand**, is located at No. 828. From here, head north up Broadway to Union Square, visiting the **Union Square Greenmarket** *(see p115)*. Continue walking up Broadway to get to the **Paragon Sports** superstore, 867 Broadway at 18th Street, and **Fishs Eddy**, 889 Broadway at 19th, which sells both vintage and new china and glassware. The fascinating **ABC Carpet & Home** awaits at No. 888 *(see p115)*.

At the **Flatiron Building**, turn east to **Madison Square** *(p115)*, then stop to have lunch at the gourmet **11 Madison Park** *(p119)*. Several restaurants on "Curry Hill" also offer inexpensive lunches – these include Pongal at No. 110, and the popular Saravanaa Bhavan at 81 Lexington Avenue.

AFTERNOON

While in the neighborhood, check out the range of intriguing spices at **Kalustyan's**, located at 123 Lexington Avenue.

More shops can be found on **Fifth Avenue** between 14th and 23rd Streets, including Anthropologie at No. 85, Zara at No. 101, Paul Smith at No.108, and H&M at No. 111.

End your day in the oasis of the **Gramercy Park** neighborhood. Stroll up East 19th Street, known as the "Block Beautiful," for its handsome 1920s houses.

See map on p114 ←

Statues and Monuments

1 George Washington

MAP M4 ▪ Union Square facing 14th St

The city's first major outdoor statue was created in 1856 by Henry Kirke Brown. The statue is a 14-ft- (4-m-) tall equestrian figure on a granite pedestal.

2 Abraham Lincoln

MAP M4 ▪ North end of Union Square near 16th St

This pensive figure by Henry Kirke Brown was commissioned shortly after the assassination of the president in 1865.

George Washington,
Union Square

3 Marquis de Lafayette

MAP L3–4 ▪ Madison Square

A larger-than-life 1873 statue of Lafayette pledging his heart to the American Revolution by Frédéric-Auguste Bartholdi, creator of the Statue of Liberty.

4 Mohandas K. Mahatma Gandhi

MAP M4 ▪ Union Square

The site for this 1986 statue of the hero of Indian independence was chosen because the park was the frequent site of protest gatherings.

5 Edwin Booth as Hamlet

MAP L4 ▪ Gramercy Park

The founder of the Players Club is shown in his most famous role, about to give Hamlet's soliloquy. The 1917 statue faces his former house.

6 Fantasy Fountain

MAP L4 ▪ Southeast corner of Gramercy Park

Greg Wyatt's 1983 smiling sun and moon are flanked by dancing giraffes, from whose mouths water flows in warm weather.

7 Worth Monument

MAP L3 ▪ Traffic Island, 23rd St & Broadway

An 1850s obelisk marks the grave of General Worth, hero of the Mexican Wars and the only public figure to be buried underneath the streets of Manhattan.

8 Farragut Monument

MAP L3–4 ▪ Madison Square

This 1880 memorial to a naval hero established Augustus Saint-Gaudens as the nation's foremost sculptor. The architect Stanford White designed the base.

9 Chester Alan Arthur

MAP L3–4 ▪ Madison Square

Arthur became the 21st President when James Garfield was assassinated. George Edwin Bissell created this bronze sculpture of him standing in front of an elaborate chair in 1898.

10 William Seward

MAP L3–4 ▪ Madison Square

In 1876 Randolph Rogers immortalized the secretary of state under Lincoln with this imposing statue. Seward is best remembered for his much-criticized purchase of Alaska in 1867.

William Seward, **Madison Square**

Restaurants

1 Maialino
MAP L4 ■ 2 Lexington Ave
■ 212 777 2410 ■ $$$
In celebration of its name – *maialino* means "little pig" in Italian – this trattoria serves superb pork dishes, along with equally excellent pasta, like the creamy and peppery spaghetti carbonara.

2 Gramercy Tavern
MAP L4 ■ 42 East 20th St
■ 212 477 0777 ■ $$$
Unpretentious fine dining where the inventive American cuisine is universally praised. The desserts are great too *(see p67)*.

3 11 Madison Park
MAP L4 ■ 11 Madison Ave at East 24th St ■ 212 889 0905 ■ $$$
Restaurateur Danny Meyer has made 11 Madison Park a chic spot with his imaginative New American cuisine, which is served up in elegant Art Deco surroundings.

4 Tocqueville
MAP M4 ■ 1 East 15th St, between Union Square West & 5th Ave ■ 212 647 1515 ■ $$$
French cuisine is prepared with Japanese touches in this hidden gem, which also has an award-winning wine list.

5 Blue Smoke
MAP L4 ■ 116 East 27th St, between Park & Lexington Aves
■ 212 447 7733 ■ $$
Another Danny Meyer success, this time with an authentic Southern pit barbecue. Downstairs, at Jazz Standard, the live music sizzles too *(see p65)*.

6 Blue Water Grill
MAP M4 ■ 31 Union Square West at 16th St ■ 212 675 9500 ■ $$
The ultra fresh seafood (plus sashimi and sushi rolls) isn't the only draw; there's also the bustling sidewalk café and downstairs jazz bar.

PRICE CATEGORIES
For a three-course meal for one with a glass of house wine, and all unavoidable charges including tax.

$ under $25 $$ $25–$75 $$$ over $75

7 ABC Cocina
MAP L4 ■ 38 East 19th St
■ 212 677 2233 ■ $$
Farm-to-table fresh fine dining with a Latin-American fusion feel is on offer here. Great seasonal menu and creative tapas.

8 Bread and Tulips
MAP L4 ■ 365 Park Ave South
■ 212 532 9100 ■ $$
Cozy homestyle Italian restaurant, sleek but welcoming. Fantastic wine selection. Great value in the area.

Italian food emporium Eataly

9 Eataly
MAP L3 ■ 200 5th Ave
■ 212 229 2560 ■ $$
At this sprawling emporium of all things edible and Italian there are multiple dining options, from quick takeaway counters to sit-down gourmet eateries.

10 Craftbar
MAP M4 ■ 900 Broadway at East 20th St ■ 212 461 4300 ■ $$
Tom Colicchio's scaled-down version of Craft next door gives diners the chance to experience the chef's take on flavor, but at cheaper prices.

See map on p114

🔟 Chelsea and Herald Square

A neighborhood that has seen a great deal of change, Chelsea was a quiet enclave of 19th-century brownstones that never made it as a fashionable address. Now it is a hub for gay New Yorkers and a center for avant-garde art galleries and nightclubs. Superstores and discount outlets now occupy 6th Avenue, and Chelsea Piers has transformed the waterfront. Uptown, the Garment District begins around 27th Street, with Herald Square and Macy's at the heart of the city's busiest shopping area.

Chelsea Flea Market

AREA MAP OF CHELSEA AND HERALD SQUARE

1 Top 10 Sights
see pp121–23

1 Places to Eat
see p125

1 Chelsea Galleries
see p124

Shops along 6th Avenue

1 6th Avenue Shopping

MAP L3 ▪ 6th Ave, West 18th to 23rd Sts

This was once a popular district known as "Fashion Row." The 1876 cast-iron facade of the Hugh O'Neill

Dry Goods Store at Nos. 655–71 exemplifies the era, when the arrival of the elevated line provided easy access to the district. As Manhattan's commercial center moved north, these cast-iron palaces were left deserted until the 1990s, when they found new life as bargain fashion outlets and superstores.

2 Chelsea Flea Market

MAP L3 ▪ West 25th St, between Broadway & 6th Ave ▪ Open 9am–6pm Sat & Sun ▪ Adm

On weekends, year-round, in the shadow of the Cathedral of St. Sava, sprouts one of the city's most popular markets, a tradition since 1976. More than 135 vendors set up booths selling clothing, silver, jewelry, furniture, art, and "junktiques." Many prize antiques can be discovered at The Showplace (open 10am–6pm Mon–Fri, 8:30am–5:30pm Sat & Sun), 40 West 25th Street, with more than 250 galleries spread over four floors.

3 The High Line

MAP L2–M2 ▪ Gansevoort to 30th Sts ▪ Open 7am–10pm daily ▪ www.thehighline.org

What was once a disused elevated railroad track, overgrown with weeds, is now a city park, planted with native grasses, trees and shrubs. The High Line attracts more than five million visitors annually, and has transformed a formerly run-down neighborhood. The second section, which runs between West 20th and West 30th streets, opened in 2011. The final section, to 34th Street, opened in September 2014.

The High Line

Chelsea Market

4 Chelsea Market

MAP M2 ■ 75 9th Ave, between 15th and 16th Sts ■ Open 7am–9pm Mon–Sat, 8am–8pm Sun

Near the High Line and several high profile restaurants, foodies of all types flock to the mouth-watering Chelsea Market, located in a complex that fills an entire city block. From organic soups and farm-fresh dairy products to spicy Thai curries, treats from Morocco, and freshly-caught seafood, almost anything edible and delicious can be found here. Explore the small stores and kiosks selling artisanal products and visit the colorful shops nearby.

5 Chelsea Historic District

MAP L2 ■ Between 9th & 10th Aves, 20th & 21st Sts

Clement Moore, author of *A Visit from St. Nicholas*, developed this land during the 1830s. The finest of the townhouses built here are the seven known as "Cushman Row," Nos. 406–18 West 20th Street, which are among the city's best examples of Greek Revival architecture. Houses at Nos. 446–50 West 20th are in the Italianate style, for which Chelsea is also known.

6 General Theological Seminary

MAP L2 ■ 20th to 21st Sts ■ Open 10am–3pm Mon–Sat

America's oldest Episcopal seminary was founded in 1819. This campus was built around two quadrangles in the 1830s, on a site donated by Professor Clement Clarke Moore, who taught at the seminary. The main building, which was added in 1960, includes a library with the largest collection of Latin Bibles in the world. There are lovely inner gardens (9th Avenue entrance).

7 Chelsea Piers

MAP L2 ■ 23rd St at Hudson River ■ Open 5:30am–11pm Mon–Fri (to 10pm Fri), 8am–9pm Sat & Sun ■ Adm ■ www.chelseapiers.com

Four neglected piers have been turned into a 30-acre (12-ha) sports and recreation complex, and Manhattan's largest venue for film and TV production. Sports facilities include ice skating, inline skating and skateboarding, batting cages, playing fields, a basketball court, bowling alley, golf driving ranges, and a marina offering harbor cruises and sailing instruction. Pier Park is a place to relax with a river view.

Chelsea Historic District

⑧ Fashion Institute of Technology (F.I.T.)

MAP L3 ▪ 7th Ave at West 27th St ▪ Museum open noon–8pm Tue–Fri, 10am–5pm Sat ▪ www.fitnyc.edu

Founded in 1944, the Fashion Institute of Technology is a prestigious school teaching art, fashion design, and marketing. The institute boasts many famous alumni, including Calvin Klein, Norma Kamali, and David Chu. Students benefit from internships with New York's leading stores and designers. Of greatest interest to the public is the museum at F.I.T., which has changing exhibits, often drawn from the school's own textile and clothing collections.

⑨ Herald Square

MAP K3 ▪ Broadway at 6th Ave

This was center of a rowdy theater district known as the Tenderloin in the 1870s and '80s, until it was reformed. The Manhattan Opera House was razed in 1901 to make way for Macy's, and other stores soon followed. The clock on the island where Broadway meets 6th Avenue is all that is left of the building that was occupied by the *New York Herald* until 1921.

Herald Square clock

⑩ Macy's

MAP K3 ▪ 151 West 34th St, between Broadway & 7th Ave ▪ www.macys.com

Former whaler Rowland Hussey Macy founded the store in 1858 on 6th Avenue and 14th Street; the red star logo was inspired by Macy's tattoo, a souvenir of his sailing days. Innovations to the retail industry included pricing goods a few cents below a full dollar and offering a money-back guarantee. The original store was sold in 1888 and moved to the present building *(see p70).*

A DAY AROUND CHELSEA

▶ MORNING

Wind your way through Chelsea, starting with the megastores now occupying former "Fashion Row," on **6th Avenue** *(p121)* between 18th and 23rd streets. Walk west on 16th Street to 9th Avenue and **Chelsea Market**, a one-time Nabisco factory where the first Oreo cookies were made, now a block-long line of stalls offering all manner of food. The Food Network tapes its TV shows in a street-level studio here.

Continue up 9th Avenue to 20th Street, for the **Chelsea Historic District, General Theological Seminary,** and **The High Line** *(p121).* Browse the art on "Gallery Row," from 21st to 27th streets, 10th to 11th Avenues. A good lunch bet is **The Red Cat**, which offers Mediterranean-inspired American fare *(see p125).*

AFTERNOON

Walk east on 23rd Street to view the wrought-iron balconies of the Chelsea Hotel, and when you get to 6th Avenue, turn uptown for the antiques market and colorful Flower District around 27th Street. A stroll for one block further west on 27th brings you to the **Fashion Institute of Technology**, where the gallery usually has interesting displays.

There is a great hidden treasure in this area, **St. John the Baptist Church**, at 210 West 31st Street, whose dingy facade belies a glowing Gothic interior. Continue to 34th Street for **Herald Square** and **Macy's**.

See map on pp120–21 ←

Chelsea Galleries

Gagosian gallery

1 Gagosian
MAP L2 ▪ 555 West 24th St & 522 West 21st St ▪ Open 10am–6pm Tue–Sat

Gagosian is one of the premier names in the gallery scene (see p50).

2 Matthew Marks
MAP L2 ▪ 523 West 24th St between 10th & 11th Aves; 523 West 24th St between 10th & 11th Aves ▪ Open 10am–6pm Tue–Sat

The Matthew Marks Gallery maintains a huge exhibition space in Chelsea, showing large-scale works and contemporary art (see p51).

3 Paula Cooper
MAP L2 ▪ 534 West 21st St between 10th & 11th Aves ▪ Open 10am–6pm Tue–Sat

The lofty setting itself is worth a visit. Many of Cooper's shows are controversial (see p51).

4 Paul Kasmin
MAP M2 ▪ 293 10th Ave at 27th St ▪ Open 10am–6pm Tue–Sat

Son of a British art dealer, Kasmin has nurtured many newcomers (see p51). Exhibitions have featured Kenny Scharf, Robert Indiana, Deborah Kass, and Barry Flanagan.

5 Barbara Gladstone
MAP L2 ▪ 515 West 24th St between 10th & 11th Aves ▪ Open 10am–6pm Tue–Sat

A dramatic backdrop for large-scale video and photography pioneers.

6 Andrea Rosen
MAP L2 ▪ 525 West 24th St between 10th & 11th Aves ▪ Open 10am–6pm Tue–Sat

Since moving from SoHo to Chelsea, the eclectic exhibitions at both of Andrea Rosen's galleries have made them two of the most visited art galleries in the area.

7 Marlborough Chelsea
MAP L3 ▪ 545 West 25th St between 10th & 11th Aves ▪ Open 10am–5:30pm Tue–Sat

The 57th Street branch of Marlborough Gallery shows established luminaries, while this downtown satellite has modern sculpture and painting (see p50).

8 Robert Miller
MAP L2 ▪ 524 West 26th St between 10th & 11th Aves ▪ Open Sep–Jun: 10am–6pm Tue–Sat; Jul: 10am–6pm Mon–Fri

This gallery shows big names like Diane Arbus, Walker Evans, Andy Warhol, and Alex Katz.

9 Lehmann Maupin
MAP L2 ▪ 536 West 22nd St between 10th & 11th Aves ▪ Open 10am–6pm Tue–Sat

Representing early pop artists, and still on the lookout for new trends, this gallery is a powerful presence in the art world.

Visitors at Lehmann Maupin

10 Pace
MAP L2 ▪ 510 West 25th St ▪ Open 10am–6pm Tue–Sat

World-class gallery of established and emerging artists' work (see p50).

Places to Eat

1 Da Umberto
MAP M3 ▪ 107 West 17th St, between 6th & 7th Aves ▪ 212 989 0303 ▪ $$$
Popular over the years thanks to the sophisticated Tuscan fare and the long list of daily specials on offer.

2 Cookshop
MAP L2 ▪ 156 10th Ave ▪ 212 924 4440 ▪ $$
Countrified restaurant with a menu rooted in local farmers' markets, from grilled squid with capers to organic buckwheat pasta with brussels sprouts and sage.

The warm interior of The Red Cat

3 The Red Cat
MAP L2 ▪ 227 10th Ave, between 23rd & 24th Sts ▪ 212 242 1122 ▪ $$
This warm neighborhood place serves first-rate American fare; don't miss the cheddar grits (creamy polenta) with sautéed shrimp.

4 East of Eighth
MAP L3 ▪ 254 West 23rd St, between 7th & 8th Aves ▪ 212 352 0075 ▪ $$
Many locals frequent this spot, which has an eclectic international menu. The prix-fixe brunch is particularly good value.

5 Buddakan
MAP M2 ▪ 75 9th Ave at 16th St ▪ 212 989 6699 ▪ $$$
The star of this trendy spot is not the good Asian fusion food, but the decor.

6 Rocking Horse Café
MAP L2 ▪ 182 8th Ave, between 19th & 20th Sts ▪ 212 463 9511 ▪ $$
Always packed; serves great margaritas and authentic Mexican food at reasonable prices.

7 Hill Country
MAP L3 ▪ 30 West 26th St ▪ 212 255 4544 ▪ $$
Known on the barbecue scene for its brisket and sausages. Live music Thursday–Saturday evenings.

8 NoMad
MAP L3 ▪ 1170 Broadway ▪ 212 796 1500 ▪ $$
Delight the taste buds at this handsome restaurant where chef Daniel Humm serves elevated American-European fare with a twist, from lobster minestrone to a superlative roast chicken.

9 Morimoto
MAP M2 ▪ 88 10th Ave ▪ 212 989 8883 ▪ $$
At this chic outpost of world-famous chef Masaharu Morimoto's global empire, the lengthy menu of hard-to-find items is a delight for sushi lovers and culinary enthusiasts.

10 Txikito
MAP L2 ▪ 240 9th Ave between 24th & 25th Sts ▪ 212 242 4730 ▪ $$
The line for this place serving Basque-inspired tapas often stretches out the door; book ahead.

See map on p120

🔟 Midtown

Detail, 30 Rockefeller Plaza entrance

The lights of Times Square, the spires of the Empire State and Chrysler buildings, Rockefeller Center, stores on Fifth Avenue, museums, theaters, and grand buildings galore – all are found in New York's midtown. Fifth Avenue, the dividing line between the East and West sides, is in many ways the Main Street of Manhattan, and in itself offers a generous sampling of the city's riches, from architecture to commerce. Midtown also reflects the city's characteristic diversity, with attractions that range from the bustling retail outlets of the Diamond District, to the stately halls of the New York Public Library.

AREA MAP OF MIDTOWN

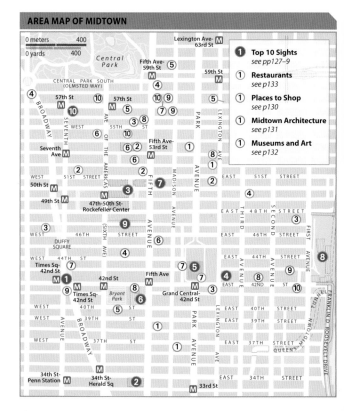

1	**Top 10 Sights** see pp127–9
1	**Restaurants** see p133
1	**Places to Shop** see p130
1	**Midtown Architecture** see p131
1	**Museums and Art** see p132

Bright lights and advertising hoardings of Times Square

① Times Square
The city's most famous intersection, dazzling Times Square is also a symbol of the lively theater district *(see pp28–31)*.

② Empire State Building
New York's best-known skyscraper is an iconic feature of the city's skyline. Since the structure was completed in 1931 more than 120 million visitors have admired the views across the city from its observatories *(see pp12–13)*.

③ Rockefeller Center
Rockefeller Center is the hub of midtown New York, alive with activity day and night, integrating shops, gardens, dining and office space, and its own aerial vantage point *(see pp16–19)*.

④ Chrysler Building
MAP K4 ■ 405 Lexington Ave at 42nd St ■ Open (lobby only) 7am–6pm Mon–Fri
The unmistakable shimmering spire of the Chrysler Building is one of New York's great landmarks. The grand Art Deco lobby, once used as a showroom for Chrysler cars, has been restored to show off its lavish marble and granite, and a vast painted ceiling depicts transportation scenes of the late 1920s *(see p52)*.

⑤ Grand Central Terminal
MAP J–K4 ■ 42nd St, between Park & Lexington Aves ■ Open 5:30am–1:30am daily ■ www.grandcentralterminal.com
One of the world's great rail terminals, the outstanding Beaux Arts building *(see p55)* is New York's most visited, with 500,000 people passing through it daily. Since restoration work was completed, its admirers are no longer limited to travelers. Grand Central has become an attraction in its own right, with shops, close to 50 restaurants and food vendors, and the New York City Transit Museum.

Grand Central Terminal clock

New York Public Library

6 New York Public Library
MAP K3 ▪ 5th Ave at 42nd St ▪ Open 10am–6pm Mon, Thu–Sat, 10am–8pm Tue & Wed, 1–5pm Sun ▪ www.nypl.org

Carrère and Hastings won a competition for the design of this great Beaux Arts building. Their genius reached its height in the Main Reading Room, a paneled space as majestic as a cathedral, extending almost two city blocks, with enormous arched windows, 18 grand chandeliers, and an elaborately decorated, vaulted ceiling *(see p55)*.

7 St. Patrick's Cathedral
MAP J3 ▪ 5th Ave, between 50th & 51st Sts ▪ Open 6:30am–8:45pm daily

America's largest Roman Catholic cathedral is a place where up to 3,000 people worship every Sunday. When Archbishop John Hughes decided to build a cathedral here in 1850, many criticized the choice of a site so far from the city's center at the time. Today the archbishop's foresight has given James Renwick's magnificent church one of the best locations in Manhattan *(see p54)*.

TIME FOR TEA

Taking tea is an increasingly popular custom in New York. Among the top places are the elegant Four Seasons Hotel, 57 East 57th Street near Madison; Lady Mendl's, at the Inn at Irving Place *(see p174)*; the tea room at the St. Regis Hotel *(see p173)*; and Tea & Sympathy at 108 Greenwich Ave.

---

8 United Nations Headquarters
MAP J5 ▪ 1st Ave at 46th St ▪ Open (for tours) 9am–4:30pm Mon–Fri, 10am–4:30pm ▪ Adm ▪ www.un.org

John D. Rockefeller, Jr. donated $8.5 million to purchase the 18-acre East River site, and American Wallace Harrison worked with international consultants to create this striking headquarters. The United Nations was formed in 1945 to work for global peace and economic and social well-being. Currently, 193 members meet in the General Assembly, the closest thing to a world parliament. Guided tours allow visitors to see the various council chambers, the General Assembly Hall, and many of the works by prominent artists, includ-ing Marc Chagall and Henry Moore.

United Nations Headquarters

9 Diamond District

MAP J3 ■ 47th St, between 5th & 6th Aves

Jewels glisten in every window of this block, the center of the city's retail and wholesale trade, handling 80 percent of the diamonds coming

Diamond necklace

into the US. Developed largely by Orthodox Jews, the district grew in importance during World War II when thousands fled the diamond centers of Europe to settle here. Above the shops are the workshops where the stones are cut and set.

Carnegie Hall

10 Carnegie Hall

MAP H3 ■ West 57th St at 7th Ave ■ Museum open Nov–Jun: 11am–4:30pm daily ■ www. carnegiehall.org

New York almost lost its most famous concert hall when the New York Philharmonic moved to the newly built Lincoln Center in the 1950s. However, a coalition, led by violinist Isaac Stern, saved the building from demolition. It was bought by the city in 1960 and became a National Historic Landmark in 1964. A major 1986 renovation restored much of the original appearance while updating technical facilities and preserving the hall's famous acoustics. Musical memorabilia fills the halls and the Rose Museum (see p54). Tours are available for a fee.

A DAY EXPLORING MIDTOWN

▶ MORNING

Start at the **Morgan Library & Museum** (see p49) and see Morgan's opulent study, then proceed to 42nd Street and turn east for a tour through **Grand Central Terminal** (see p127). Continue east on 42nd Street, stopping to look at the outstanding lobbies of the **Chrysler Building** (see p127), the **Daily News Building**, and the **Ford Foundation**, and climbing the stairs to see the **Tudor City** complex (see p131).

End the morning with a tour of the **United Nations HQ**. If you reserve ahead, you can lunch in the special U.N. delegate's dining room (212 963 7626).

AFTERNOON

Take the 42nd Street crosstown bus back to 5th Avenue and visit the **New York Public Library**. Walk uptown to 47th Street and turn west for the **Diamond District**, then pay a quick visit to the **Paley Center For Media** (see p132) on 52nd Street, between 5th and 6th avenues. Head to the **Museum of Modern Art** (see p48), stop for a coffee in the museum's second-floor café, and take in some of the splendid exhibits.

Return to 5th Avenue where the uptown shops include **Tiffany and Company**'s (see p14) windows of jewels and **Bergdorf Goodman**'s (see p14) stylish displays. Round the day off at **Salon de Ning** in the Peninsula Hotel (see p69), with stunning views over Central Park.

See map on p126 ←

Places to Shop

1 Department Stores
MAP K3–H3 ■ 5th Ave, between 38th & 58th Sts
Bountiful stocks of beautiful clothing and jewelry await at Bergdorf Goodman, Saks Fifth Avenue, Lord & Taylor, and Bloomingdale's.

2 H&M
MAP J3 ■ 5th Ave at 51st St
Flagship store of the Swedish retailer known for great young fashion with small price tags (see p71).

Henri Bendel

3 Henri Bendel
MAP H3 ■ 712 5th Ave at 55th St
This is one of the most attractive stores in the city, featuring designer fashions and a notable selection of cosmetics (see p70).

4 Apple Store
MAP H3 ■ 767 5th Ave at 59th St
This 32-ft- (9.75-m-) tall glass cube is worth a visit for the aesthetics alone. The below-ground sales floor is always busy – but it's also open 24 hours a day.

5 Barneys
MAP G4 ■ 660 Madison Ave at 61st St
This gleaming department store has long been New York's paragon of high-end and elegant style. Peruse clothing, shoes, and bags by both big-name and up-and-coming designers.

6 Museum of Modern Art Design Shop
MAP J3 ■ 44 West 53rd St, between 5th Ave & 6th Aves
Lamps, furniture, toys, jewelry, posters, books – whatever the item, you can be sure it will be the epitome of good design.

7 Designer Boutiques
MAP H4 ■ 57th St, between 5th & Madison Aves
57th Street is lined with impressive designer boutiques, including Burberry, Hermès, Tiffany & Co., Chanel, and Dior. Prada is at No. 724 5th Avenue.

8 Harry Winston
MAP H4 ■ 718 5th Ave
You will likely only be window shopping here; the diamonds and gems, many of which Harry Winston supplies to the rich and famous, are very expensive.

9 Niketown
MAP H4 ■ 6 East 57th St, between 5th & Madison Aves
Commercial, high-tech shopping fun, all to entice you to buy sneakers and sportswear.

10 Louis Vuitton
MAP H4 ■ 1 East 57th St
Perhaps the flashiest of the high-end stores from the outside, LV's windows are imprinted with the same pattern as is on the handbags.

Apple Store entrance

Midtown Architecture

1 Lever House
MAP H4 ■ 390 Park Ave ■ Lobby open during office hours
This 24-story glass-and-steel building built by Gordon Bunshaft was New York's first "glass box" (see p53).

Lever House

2 General Electric Building
MAP H4 ■ 570 Lexington Ave ■ Closed to public
This 1931 Art Deco building has a clock crowned by disembodied arms grasping at lightning bolts.

3 Chanin Building
MAP K4 ■ 122 East 42nd St ■ Lobby open during office hours
One of the great early Art Deco skyscrapers (c.1929) notable for its terra-cotta frieze and bronze band illustrating the theory of evolution.

4 NY Yacht Club
MAP J3 ■ 37 West 44th St ■ Closed to public
The window bays of this 1899 private club are the carved sterns of ships, sailing on a sea of sculpted waves.

5 American Standard Building
MAP K3 ■ 40 West 40th St ■ Lobby open during office hours
Raymond Hood's first New York skyscraper is an ornate black tower built in 1924. It is now a hotel.

6 Fred F. French Building
MAP J3 ■ 551 5th Ave ■ Lobby open during office hours
Built in 1927 for the best-known real estate firm of its day, this opulent building has a stunning lobby.

7 Condé Nast Building
MAP J3 ■ 4 Times Square ■ Lobby open during office hours
The 48-story tower, built in 1999 for the global magazine publisher, is striking and environmentally friendly, with photovoltaic cells on the facade and integrated recycling chutes.

8 Daily News Building
MAP K4 ■ 220 East 42nd St at 2nd Ave ■ Lobby open during office hours
The *Daily News* has moved on, but this fine 1930 building is still an Art Deco classic. Step inside and marvel at the revolving globe.

9 Ford Foundation
MAP J4 ■ 320 East 43rd St at 1st Ave ■ Lobby open during office hours
Headquarters of Ford's philanthropic arm, this is considered one of the city's best modern designs (1967). Every office opens onto a sky-lit, 12-story atrium with lush land-scaping and a pond.

10 Tudor City
MAP J4–K4 ■ 1st to 2nd Aves, 40th to 43rd Sts ■ Lobby open during office hours
Fred F. French created this mock-Tudor enclave in the 1920s, designed to prove that middle-class housing could succeed in Midtown.

Tudor City apartment building

See map on p126

Museums and Art

Morgan Library

1 Morgan Library and Museum

MAP K4 ■ 225 Madison Ave at 36th St ■ Open 10:30am–5pm Tue–Thu, 10:30am–9pm Fri, 10am–6pm Sat, 11am–6pm Sun ■ www.themorgan. org ■ Adm

The library holds a private collection of rare books, prints, and manuscripts (see p49). The steel-and-glass pavilion houses an impressive performance hall.

2 Museum of Modern Art

MAP J3 ■ 11 West 53rd St at 5th Ave ■ Open 10:30am–5:30pm daily (to 8pm Fri) ■ Adm ■ www.moma.org

A vast collection of paintings, films, and photography housed in a stunning building (see p48).

3 Japan Society

MAP J5 ■ 333 East 47th St ■ Open 11am–6pm Tue–Sun (to 9pm Fri, to 5pm Sat & Sun) ■ www. japansociety.org ■ Adm

Explore Japanese culture, from contemporary art to Kabuki dance, at this esteemed cultural institution.

4 Museum of Arts and Design

MAP H3 ■ 2 Columbus Circle ■ Open 10am–6pm Tue–Sun (to 9pm Thu–Fri) ■ www.madmuseum.org ■ Adm

The permanent collection includes 2,000 craft exhibits.

5 Marian Goodman

MAP H3 ■ 24 West 57th St ■ Open 10am–6pm Mon–Sat ■ www. mariangoodman.com

Works by Giovanni Anselmo, Thomas Struth, Steve McQueen and others are exhibited in this art space.

6 Paley Center for Media

MAP J3 ■ 25 West 52nd St, between 5th & 6th Aves ■ Open noon–6pm Wed–Sun (to 8pm Thu) ■ Adm ■ www.paleycenter.org

Watch your favorites from over 60,000 radio and TV programs.

7 Transit Museum Gallery Annex

MAP K3 ■ Shuttle Passage, Grand Central Terminal ■ Open 8am–8pm Mon–Fri, 10am–6pm Sat–Sun ■ www.mta.info/mta/museum

Displays images and objects from the Brooklyn museum (see p59).

8 New York Public Library Galleries

MAP K3 ■ 5th Ave at 42nd St ■ Open 11am–6pm Tue–Wed, 10am–6pm Thu–Sat

Rare prints, vintage posters, paintings, and changing exhibitions.

9 Sculpture Garden at 590 Madison

MAP J3 ■ 590 Madison Ave at 57th St

The zen-like atrium of the IBM building houses a rotating cast of sculptures within its glass walls.

10 Pace Gallery

MAP H4 ■ 32 East 57th St ■ Open 10am–6pm Tue–Sat ■ www.thepacegallery.com

Works by leading contemporary American and European artists are on display at this gallery.

Restaurants

PRICE CATEGORIES
For a three-course meal for one with a glass of house wine, and all unavoidable charges including tax.

$ under $25 $$ $25–$75 $$$ over $75

1 Four Seasons
MAP J4 ▪ 99 East 52nd St at Park Ave ▪ 212 754 9494 ▪ $$$

This has been an award-winning New York institution since it opened in 1959. The decor is landmark and the opportunities for celebrity spotting are great *(see p67)*.

2 Le Bernardin
MAP J3 ▪ 155 West 51st St at 6th Ave ▪ 212 554 1515 ▪ $$$

The acclaimed French chef Eric Ripert does wonders here with every kind of fish and seafood – the dining experience is nothing short of perfection *(see p66)*.

3 Blue Fin
MAP J3 ▪ 1567 Broadway at 47th St ▪ 212 918 1400 ▪ $$

One of the trendiest places in the area, this restaurant is dedicated to serving the highest quality seafood dishes, including sushi and raw bar selections.

4 Smith & Wollensky
MAP J4 ▪ 201 East 49th St at 5th Ave ▪ 212 753 0444 ▪ $$$

Fill up on a *Flintstones*-esque sirloin steak and irresistible fries amid masculine surroundings of wooden floors and old black-and-white photographs of New York.

5 Le Colonial
MAP H4 ▪149 East 57th St at Lexington Ave ▪ 212 752 0808 ▪ $$

The sultry decor is straight out of 1930s Saigon and sets the scene nicely for a Vietnamese/French menu that is full of delicate combinations and contrasts. After dinner, relax with a drink in the atmospheric lounge upstairs.

6 Osteria del Circo
MAP H3 ▪ 120 West 55th St at 6th Ave ▪ 212 265 3636 ▪ $$

The sons of Le Cirque's owner have created their own whimsical circus, serving traditional Tuscan fare.

7 Grand Central Oyster Bar and Restaurant
MAP K4 ▪ Grand Central Terminal, lower level, 42nd St at Lexington Ave ▪ 212 490 6650 ▪ $$

A New York classic, this bustling and ever-popular restaurant serves only the freshest seafood.

Grand Central Oyster Bar and Restaurant

8 Brasserie
MAP J4 ▪ 100 East 53rd St at Lexington Ave ▪ 212 751 4840 ▪ $$

Remodeled with sleek, high-tech decor, it features an updated menu of modern French/American Pacific dishes but still with a few classics.

9 Counter Burger
MAP K3 ▪ 7 Times Square at 41st St & Broadway ▪ 212 997 6801 ▪ $

This innovative chain serves delicious, custom-made burgers that are a notch above other fast food outlets.

10 La Bonne Soupe
MAP H3 ▪ 48 West 55th St, between 5th & 6th Aves ▪ 212 586 7650 ▪ $$

This theater district favorite, with French bistro charm, is great for after a show. Most entrées are under $15.

See map on pp126

⊞ Upper East Side

Buddha statue at the Met

New York's upper crust moved uptown to the Upper East Side over a century ago. Most of their Beaux Arts mansions around 5th Avenue are now occupied by embassies or museums; today's elite live in apartment buildings on 5th and Park Avenues, convenient for Madison's exclusive boutiques. Only churches and a few restaurants remain of German Yorkville or the Hungarian and Czech neighborhoods that used to fill the blocks east of Lexington. Young families now occupy the newer buildings in this area. For visitors, the Upper East Side is home to many of the city's best museums.

1 Central Park

Designed in the 19th century, the 843-acre (341-ha) swathe of green in the city center provides recreation and beauty for more than 40 million annual visitors, from rowboat and bicycle rental to flowers and sculptures (see pp32–3).

2 Metropolitan Museum of Art

More a collection of museums than a single one, the Met displays over two million pieces spanning more than 5,000 years of global culture, from Ancient Egypt to 20th-century Afghanistan (see pp34–7).

View of Central Park Lake and Jacqueline Kennedy Onassis Reservoir

Previous pages Aerial view of the Manhattan skyscrapers at night

Guggenheim Museum's spiral design

3 Solomon R. Guggenheim Museum

A notable collection of modern art is located in Frank Lloyd Wright's iconic, spiral-design building, which is the only edifice in New York he designed (see pp38–9).

4 Museum Mile

MAP D4–F4 ■ 5th Ave from 82nd to 104th Sts ■ Opening times vary

Nine museums are situated within one mile. They unite for a free open-house day one Tuesday in June. Participants include the Metropolitan Museum of Art (see pp34–7), National Academy Museum, Cooper-Hewitt, Smithsonian Design Museum, Solomon R. Guggenheim Museum (see pp38–9), Jewish Museum, Neue Galerie, Museum of the City of New York (see p49), and El Museo del Barrio. There is street entertainment and music, and 5th Avenue closes to traffic.

AREA MAP OF UPPER EAST SIDE

1 Top 10 Sights
see pp136–9

1 Restaurants
see p141

1 Madison Boutiques
see p140

5 Neue Galerie
MAP E4 ■ 1048 5th Ave at East 86th St ■ Open 11am–6pm Thu–Mon ■ Adm ■ www.neuegalerie.org

Dedicated to early 20th-century art from Austria and Germany, this enchanting museum is housed in an ornate 1914-mansion. Once the residence of New York socialite Grace Vanderbilt and her millionaire husband Cornelius Vanderbilt III, the building was converted into a museum, largely due to the efforts of art collectors Sabarsky and Ronald S. Lauder. The star attraction of the gallery is Gustav Klimt's *Portrait of Adele Bloch-Bauer I* (1907).

6 Roosevelt Island
MAP H5 ■ Trams every 15 mins from Tram Plaza, 2nd Ave at 59th St

A 4-minute aerial tram ride is the route to this East River enclave. Once known as "Welfare Island," when it was home to a prison, poorhouse, and hospital for the insane, the 147-acre (60-ha) island was renamed and redeveloped in the 1970s according to a master plan drawn up by Philip Johnson and John Burgee, intended to create a quiet, almost traffic-free residential community. The plan was not fully developed, although more than 3,000 apartments were built, and while there is a subway stop from Manhattan, the only access by car is via a bridge in Queens.

Aerial tram to Roosevelt Island

ST. NICHOLAS RUSSIAN ORTHODOX CATHEDRAL

An unexpected slice of Russia at 15 East 97th Street, this building (below) was constructed in 1902 in Muscovite Baroque style with a facade of red brick, white stone, and blue and yellow tiles. The incense-filled interior has marble columns and an altar enclosed by wooden screens trimmed with gold. Mass is still said in Russian.

7 Park Avenue Armory
MAP G4 ■ 643 Park Ave at 66th St ■ 212 616 3930 ■ Open noon–8pm Tue–Fri, noon–6pm Mon, Sat, & Sun

The socially prominent members of the Seventh Regiment, formed in 1806, constructed a remarkable armory in 1877–89, with a drill room 200 by 300 feet (60 by 90 m) and 100 feet (30 m) high, and an administration building in the form of a medieval fortress. Interior decoration was by Louis Comfort Tiffany, Stanford White, and others, and the result is opulent rooms with lavish Victorian furnishings. The drill room is used for the prestigious Winter Antiques Show every January. Following a $150-million renovation project, the space now allows for the development of unconventional performing and visual art.

8 Henderson Place Historic District
MAP F5 ■ East End Ave, between 86th & 87th Sts

Built in 1881 by the developer John C. Henderson for "persons of moderate means," these winning Queen Anne houses made of brick and stone are embellished with towers, bays, gables, dormers, and slate roofs. They were an investment and remained in Henderson's family up until the 20th century. Today they are unique in the city and rank among the most desirable places to live. Each block front was composed as a unit, with small towers at the end and arched entryways. Twenty-four of the original 32 units remain.

⑨ Gracie Mansion and Carl Schurz Park

MAP E5 ■ East End Ave at 88th St ■ 212 639 9675 ■ For information about tours call on 212 570 4773 ■ Adm

The wooden country home built by merchant Archibald Gracie in 1799 was the original home of the Museum of the City of New York and became the official mayoral residence under Fiorello LaGuardia in 1942. It is located at the northern end of a park laid out in 1891, with a wide promenade that stretches along the East River. The park was named for Carl Schurz, a statesman and newspaper editor who lived nearby.

Gracie Mansion

⑩ Mount Vernon Hotel Museum and Gardens

MAP H5 ■ 421 East 61st St, between 1st & York Aves ■ Open 11am–4pm Tue–Sun, closed public holidays ■ Adm ■ www.mvhm.org

This was the stone carriage house of a 1799 estate. When the house burned in 1826, the carriage house was converted into an inn and became a fashionable resort for New Yorkers in what was then still countryside. The building and garden were restored by the Colonial Dames of America in 1939.

A DAY EXPLORING UPPER EAST SIDE

▶ MORNING

Start at the **Guggenheim** (see p137) and admire Frank Lloyd Wright's great architectural achievement before seeing the modern art collection. "Must sees" include Chagall's *Paris Through the Window*, Modigliani's *Nude*, and Picasso's *Woman Ironing*. Stop for coffee at the café.

Head east along 92nd Street to see two rare remaining wooden houses, No. 120, built in 1859, and No. 122, in 1871. Continue east for **Gracie Mansion** and **Henderson Place** and rest on a bench with a river view in **Carl Schurz Park**. Recharge at **Daniel** (see p141), an elegant French restaurant.

AFTERNOON

Take the 57th Street crosstown bus back to Madison Avenue and head uptown, browsing the designer boutiques. Detour down the side streets in the upper 60s and 70s to see the town houses of affluent New Yorkers. Pay a quick visit to the **Frick Collection** (see p49), then stop for coffee at one of the cafés on Madison Avenue. Alternatively, get another dose of fine art at **Neue Galerie**, further along 5th Avenue.

Spend the rest of the afternoon at the **Metropolitan Museum of Art** (see p136), a New York "must," and admire Rembrandt's *Self-Portrait*, *Cypresses* by Van Gogh, and Michelangelo's Sistine Chapel studies. End the day with a meal at **Erminia** (see p141).

See map on p137

Madison Avenue Boutiques

1 Bottega Veneta
MAP G4 ▪ 849 Madison Ave, between 70th & 71st Sts
The first in the Madison Avenue boutique line-up, known for luxury leather goods, shoes, and fashion.

2 Kate Spade
MAP F4 ▪ 789 Madison Ave
Dress up your wardrobe with colorful and innovative bags, shoes, and jewelry from this perennially popular designer.

3 Valentino
MAP G4 ▪ 821 Madison Ave at 69th St
If you can afford it, join the rich and famous; many of his gowns are worn at the Oscars.

4 Giorgio Armani
MAP G4 ▪ 760 Madison Ave at 65th St
The New York flagship of the Italian master, known for his superb tailoring, offers a good range from his collection.

5 Ralph Lauren
MAP G4 ▪ 867 Madison Ave at 72nd St
The 1898 Rhinelander Mansion is the backdrop for the king of preppy fashion, who spent $14 million renovating the old mansion. Ralph Lauren sportswear is in a separate shop across the street.

DKNY store, Madison Avenue

6 DKNY
MAP H4 ▪ 655 Madison Ave at 60th St
Donna Karan is known for designing wearable fashions for every lifestyle and occasion.

7 BCBG Max Azria
MAP G4 ▪ 770 Madison Ave at 66th St
"Bon chic, bon genre" ("good style, good attitude") is the motto of this hot designer. Fans of his sexy fashions include many young Hollywood stars.

8 Tom Ford
MAP B1 ▪ 845 Madison Ave
Off-the-rack options at this dual-level store include three-piece suits, dressing gowns, and dress shirts in 350 colors. The store also offers customized suits and private shopping appointments.

9 Dolce & Gabbana
MAP G4 ▪ 827 Madison Ave, between 67th & 68th Sts
You can spot the celebrities at this chic outpost of the world-famous Italian brand, with its striking all-black decor.

10 Vera Wang
MAP F4 ▪ 991 Madison Ave at 76th St
The flagship store of the esteemed designer of wedding gowns also features ready-to-wear fashion and accessories.

Ralph Lauren store, Madison Avenue

Restaurants

PRICE CATEGORIES
For a three-course meal for one with a glass of house wine, and all unavoidable charges including tax.

$ under $25 $$ $25–$75 $$$ over $75

① Daniel
MAP G4 ▪ 60 East 65th St at Park Ave ▪ 212 288 0033 ▪ $$$

A flower-filled dining room provides the setting for Daniel Boulud's award-winning seasonal French menus *(see p67)*.

② Serendipity 3
MAP H4 ▪ 225 East 60th St ▪ 212 838 3531 ▪ $$

Famous for its sinful concoctions, including massive sundaes, this dessert emporium is an old favorite with celebratory couples and families.

③ Café d'Alsace
MAP F4 ▪ 1695 2nd Ave at 88th St ▪ 212 722 5133 ▪ $$

A charming bistro that blends French regional and contemporary New York cuisines. The highlights include a great lunchtime prix-fixe menu and a huge beer selection.

Dessert at Serendipity 3

④ Café Boulud
MAP G4 ▪ 20 East 76th St at Madison Ave ▪ 212 772 2600 ▪ $$$

This was Daniel Boulud's original restaurant. Since his other venture, called Daniel, opened, this has become more casual, but the menu and tab are serious. In summer, the terrace tables are a fine dining spot, convenient for Museum Mile.

⑤ Toloache
MAP F4 ▪ 166 East 82nd St ▪ 212 861 4505 ▪ $$

This lively restaurant serves terrific Mexican cuisine, from creamy guacamole and tangy ceviches to tacos that are spilling over with fresh shrimp or grilled chicken, and topped with salsa.

⑥ Erminia
MAP F4 ▪ 250 East 83rd St, between 2nd & 3rd Aves ▪ 212 879 4284 ▪ $$

They don't come more romantic than this tiny, candlelit Italian with beamed ceilings and a menu of well-prepared classics. A popular choice on Valentine's Day.

⑦ Uva
MAP F4 ▪ 1486 2nd Ave, between 77th & 78th Sts ▪ 212 472 4552 ▪ $$

An intimate, cozy wine bar serving genuine Italian cuisine at reasonable prices, Uva is *the* go-to spot for the city's wine connoisseurs.

⑧ Orsay
MAP G4 ▪ 1057 Lexington Ave at 75th St ▪ 212 517 6400 ▪ $$

This chic French brasserie is busy and cozy, serving modern and authentic brasserie fare. There is a definite Gallic vibe to the place, with mahogany-paneled walls and Art Nouveau chandeliers.

⑨ The Meatball Shop
MAP F4 ▪ 1462 2nd Ave at 76th St ▪ 212 257 6121 ▪ $

Calling all meatball lovers: this friendly spot serves juicy meatballs every which way, including smothered in tomato sauce, Parmesan cream, mushroom gravy, or pesto.

⑩ E. J.'s Luncheonette
MAP G4 ▪ 1271 3rd Ave at 73rd St ▪ 212 472 0600 ▪ No credit cards ▪ $

A family-friendly diner that serves large portions of well-prepared American breakfasts. Great pancakes are served all day, along with granola and fresh fruit.

See map on p137

TOP10 Upper West Side

Soldiers' & Sailors' Monument

This area did not begin to develop until the 1870s, when the 9th Avenue El went up, making it possible to commute to Midtown. When the Dakota, New York's first luxury apartment building, was completed in 1884, it was followed by others on Central Park West and Broadway, while side streets were filled with handsome brownstones. The West Side remains a desirable neighborhood with much of the city's best residential architecture. The creation of the Lincoln Center in the 1960s was a great boost to the area, and the fantastic American Museum of Natural History is also a draw.

1 American Museum of Natural History

The mammoth museum's holdings include more than 32 million artifacts and specimens (see pp40–43).

2 Lincoln Center for the Performing Arts

MAP G2 ▪ Columbus to Amsterdam Aves, between 62nd & 66th Sts ▪ Tours twice daily ▪ Adm

Built on 15 acres (6 ha) during the 1960s, transforming slums into a giant cultural complex, the Lincoln Center houses an array of venues and organizations: the Metropolitan Opera, the New York City Ballet, the New York Philharmonic, the Vivian Beaumont and Walter Reade theaters, David Geffen and Alice Tully halls, and the Julliard School (see p62).

Lincoln Center for the Performing Arts

In the summer, the popular Mostly Mozart concerts take place, and free concerts are held in the adjacent park. The Jazz at Lincoln Center headquarters is located in the Time Warner building at Columbus Circle.

3 New York Historical Society

MAP G2 ▪ 170 Central Park West at West 77th St ▪ Open 10am–6pm Tue–Sat (to 8pm Fri), 11am–5pm Sun ▪ Adm ▪ www.nyhistory.org

New York's oldest museum, founded in 1804, reopened in 2011 after an extensive renovation that saw $70 million invested over three years. The museum features more than 40,000 objects divided into such areas as paintings, sculpture, furniture, silver, tools, and, notably, Tiffany lamps. Other galleries within the museum are used to display changing exhibits. The New York Historical Society also maintains a children's gallery, as well as a research library.

4 Columbus Circle

MAP H2 ▪ Columbus Circle

One of the largest building projects in New York's history has transformed this neglected urban plaza into an important public site. The

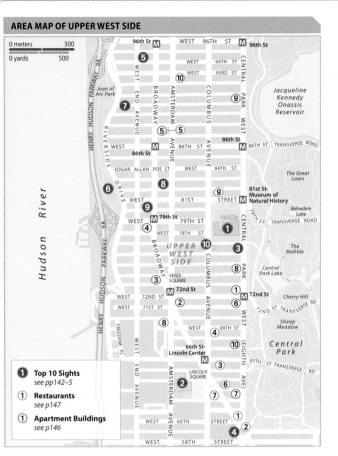

AREA MAP OF UPPER WEST SIDE

0 meters 500
0 yards 500

Hudson River

Henry Hudson Parkway 9A

Joan of Arc Park

Riverside Drive

West End Avenue
Broadway
Amsterdam Avenue
Columbus Avenue
Central Park West
Eighth Avenue
Freedom Pl

Jacqueline Kennedy Onassis Reservoir

96th St Ⓜ WEST 96TH ST Ⓜ 96th St

WEST 94TH ST

WEST 93RD ST

⑤

⑩

⑨

⑤ ⑤

86th St Ⓜ 86TH ST TRANSVERSE ROAD

WEST 86TH AVENUE 86TH AVENUE

EDGAR ALLAN POE ST WEST 84TH ST

The Great Lawn

⑧

81st St–Museum of Natural History

⑨ STREET WEST 81ST ST

⑨

Belvedere Lake

⑥

Ⓜ 79th St 79TH ST 79TH ST TRANSVERSE ROAD

⑨

④ WEST 78TH ST

①

UPPER WEST SIDE

⑩ ③

The Ramble

⑧ Central Park Lake

VERDI SQUARE

③

Ⓜ 72nd St 72ND ST ① Ⓜ 72nd St

② WEST 72ND ST

⑥

WEST 71ST ST

⑧ WEST Cherry Hill

Sheep Meadow

⑩ WEST 69TH ST

66th St–Lincoln Center Ⓜ

③ 65TH ST TRANSVERSE RD

LINCOLN SQUARE

② ⑥

⑦ ⑦

Central Park

① STREET

② WEST 60TH

④ WEST 58TH STREET

① Top 10 Sights
see pp142–5

① Restaurants
see p147

① Apartment Buildings
see p146

redevelopment has attracted national and international business, such as giant media company Time Warner, which has its headquarters in an 80-story skyscraper. The building contains shops, entertainment, restaurants, and the Mandarin Oriental hotel. It is also home to Jazz at Lincoln Center, the world's first performing arts facility dedicated to jazz. Other structures around Columbus Circle include the Museum of Arts and Design, Trump International Hotel, and the USS Maine Monument.

Skyscrapers behind Columbus Circle

Pomander Walk

5 Pomander Walk
MAP E2 ■ 261–7 West 94th St, between Broadway & West End Ave

This double row of small brick and stucco, timbered, Tudoresque townhouses, hidden on a private street, is one of the many delightful surprises to be discovered in Manhattan. The developer, a restaurateur named Thomas Healy, took his inspiration in 1921 from the sets used for a popular play by Louis Parker called *Pomander Walk*, hoping to recreate the village atmosphere depicted in the romantic comedy. Gloria Swanson, Rosalind Russell, and Humphrey Bogart are among the actors who have lived here.

6 Riverside Park
MAP C1 ■ Riverside Drive, 72nd to 155th Sts ■ Open 6am–1am daily ■ Free

Another example of the landscape genius of Frederick Law Olmsted, Riverside Park is a woodsy band of green planned in 1873 that follows Riverside Drive for 70 blocks and hiding the abandoned railroad tracks below. Playgrounds, sports fields, a promenade, and monuments were added later. Dating from 1902, the impressive marble Soldiers' and Sailors' Monument at 89th Street is a memorial to those who died during the American Civil War.

7 Riverside Drive/West End Historic District
MAP E1 ■ Between Riverside Drive & West End Ave, 85th & 95th Sts

A walk through this historic area showcases the late 19th-century townhouses that characterize the Upper West Side. West 88th Street is a good example. The earliest houses, Nos. 267–71, were built in 1884. Nos. 302–38, dating from the early 1890s, have stepped gables and Roman brick, while Nos. 315–23, built around 1896, have bow fronts in brown or white stone. The Yeshiva Ketana School, at 346 West 89th Street, begun in 1901 by Herts and Tallant, occupies one of the few surviving mansions that once lined Riverside Drive.

8 Children's Museum of Manhattan
MAP F2 ■ 212 West 83rd St at Broadway ■ Open 10am–5pm Tue–Sun (to 7pm on Sat) ■ Adm ■ www.cmom.org

Founded in 1973, in a former school building, this museum is dedicated to the principle that children learn best through self-discovery. It uses a variety of participatory activities and fantasy world environments to engage its young visitors in learning that is fun. The museum's range of activities include exhibits to intrigue older children, while Adventures with Dora and Diego provides a distraction for two- to six-year-olds at the same time as educating them about animals and their environments *(see p58)*.

Riverside Park

UPPER WEST SIDE ARCHITECTURE

The Upper West Side's side streets are lined with fine rows of the typical brownstones favored by New York's 19th-century middle classes. Built of inexpensive, local, brown sandstone, the narrow buildings are usually three or four stories high, and have a flight of steps called a "stoop" that leads from street level to the living floors.

9 Zabar's
MAP F2 ■ 2245 Broadway at 80th St

A monument to New York's mania for finding the best foods and a landmark since 1934, this always-crowded store sells smoked salmon, sturgeon, and other Jewish delicacies, along with wonderful bread, desserts, coffee, and cheeses, and big selections of oils, vinegars, olives, and gourmet gift baskets. The second floor is filled with cooking equipment, and the adjacent coffee counter at the 80th Street corner offers delicious baked goods, sandwiches, coffees, and smoothies.

Deli counter at Zabar's

10 Green Flea Market/ 77th Street Flea Market
MAP F2 ■ 100 West 77th St at Columbus Ave

Flea market junkies throng this school yard every Sunday, hoping for finds among the piles of vintage clothing, books, jewelry, prints, and memorabilia. Less glamorous, new merchandise is also sold here. On a good day as many as 300 booths crowd the premises. A weekly green market shares the same space.

WALK ON THE WEST SIDE

▶ MORNING

Begin at **Lincoln Center** (see p142) and admire the plaza, the Chagall windows at the Metropolitan Opera, and the Henry Moore statue in front of Vivian Beaumont Theater. The New York Public Library for the Performing Arts on Amsterdam Avenue, behind the theater, is notable for its enormous collection of books about the performing arts.

Make your way up Broadway, window shopping and noting some of the landmark buildings such as the **Apthorp Apartments** (see p146) and the **Ansonia Hotel** (see p146), and the West Side's gastronomic palaces, such as Fairway at 75th Street and **Zabar's**. Almost any side street will reveal examples of the area's great line-up of brownstone townhouses. Finally, head east to Columbus Avenue and **Calle Ocho** (see p147) for a Cuban lunch.

AFTERNOON

The **American Museum of Natural History** (see p40–43) can easily fill an entire afternoon, and the **New York Historical Society** (see p142) has an amazing collection on show.

Stroll down Central Park West and admire the landmark **apartment buildings** (see p146) that can be seen here, and then head for **Central Park** (see pp32–3), the city's vast "backyard". Take a boat out on the lake, or enjoy a gondola ride around it, followed by drinks at the Loeb Boathouse, the perfect end to an afternoon.

See map on p143 ←

Apartment Buildings

The Dakota, John Lennon's last home

1 The Dakota
MAP G2 ■ 1 West 72nd St at Central Park West ■ Closed to public

Famous as the site of John Lennon's murder, it was thought so far west in 1884, it might as well be in the Dakota.

2 Dorilton
MAP G2 ■ 171 West 71st St at Broadway ■ Closed to public

One of the most flamboyant examples of the Beaux Arts era, this 1902 apartment house has an iron gate fit for a palace.

3 Ansonia
MAP G2 ■ 2109 Broadway, between 73rd & 74th Sts ■ Closed to public

This 1908 apartment-hotel included soundproof partitions, a feature that has attracted many distinguished musicians.

4 Apthorp
MAP F2 ■ Broadway, between 78th & 79th Sts ■ Closed to public

Modeled after an Italian Renaissance palazzo, this 1908 full-block building includes a huge interior courtyard.

5 Belnord
MAP F2 ■ 225 West 86th St, at Amsterdam Ave ■ Closed to public

Even larger than the Apthorp, and also with its own large interior courtyard, this 1908 Renaissance Revival structure is where Nobel Prize-winning author Isaac Bashevis Singer lived and wrote.

6 Majestic
MAP G2 ■ 115 Central Park West, between 71st & 72nd Sts ■ Closed to public

The first of architect Irwin Chanin's two 1931 landmarks, and one of the original four twin towers that dominate the West Side skyline.

7 Century
MAP H2 ■ 25 Central Park West, between 62nd & 63rd Sts ■ Closed to public

Irwin Chanin's second twin tower, consisting of 30 stories, is the tallest on the block, and an Art Deco icon.

8 San Remo
MAP G2 ■ 145–6 Central Park West, between 74th & 75th Sts ■ Closed to public

Architect Emery Roth's 1930 Art Deco masterpiece is an extremely sophisticated adaptation of Renaissance forms. The twin towers hide water tanks.

San Remo's twin towers

9 Eldorado
MAP E2 ■ 300 Central Park West, between 90th & 91st Sts ■ Closed to public

Another Art Deco design by Emery Roth. Past celebrity tenants have included Groucho Marx and Marilyn Monroe.

10 Hotel des Artistes
MAP G2 ■ West 67th St, between Central Park West & Columbus Ave ■ Closed to public

Built in 1918 as artists' studios and apartments, with double-height windows, the spaces are much coveted. Residents have included Noël Coward and Isadora Duncan.

Restaurants

PRICE CATEGORIES
For a three-course meal for one with a glass of house wine, and all unavoidable charges including tax.

$ under $25 $$ $25–$75 $$$ over $75

1 Jean-Georges
MAP H2 ■ 1 Central Park West, Trump International Hotel ■ 212 299 3900 ■ $$$

Jean-Georges Vongerichten's namesake restaurant is among the finest in New York *(see p66)*.

2 Per Se
MAP H2 ■ Time Warner Center, Columbus Circle ■ 212 823 9335 ■ $$$

Book well in advance for this critically acclaimed restaurant owned by well-known restaurateur Thomas Keller *(see p67)*.

3 Shun Lee Café
MAP G2 ■ 43 West 65th St ■ 212 769 3888 ■ $$

This clean-lined, black-and-white dim sum café is arguably the best one to be found north of Chinatown.

Lantern, Shun Lee Café

4 Telepan
MAP G2 ■ 72 West 69th St at Columbus Ave ■ 212 580 4300 ■ $$

Enjoy market-fresh cuisine, from fresh trout with onion cream to hearty root vegetable soups, by New York chef Bill Telepan at this welcoming restaurant.

5 Mermaid Inn
MAP F2 ■ 570 Amsterdam Ave ■ 212 799 7400 ■ $$

Everybody's favorite New England fish shack transplanted to Manhattan is best for simple seafood and fish options. If you are here on a Sunday for "Lobsterpalooza" (a lobster, red bliss potatoes, and grilled corn on the cob), then consider yourself lucky.

6 Boulud Sud
MAP F4 ■ 20 West 64th St ■ 212 595 1313 ■ $$

Daniel Boulud celebrates flavors of the Mediterranean at this elegant restaurant, with dishes like grilled octopus with Marcona almonds.

Rosa Mexicano

7 Rosa Mexicano
MAP H2 ■ 61 Columbus Ave at 62nd St ■ 212 977 7700 ■ $$

This is a branch of one of the city's most popular Mexican restaurants, famous for its excellent guacamole that is made to order and its power-packed margaritas.

8 Café Luxembourg
MAP G2 ■ 200 West 70th St at Amsterdam Ave ■ 212 873 7411 ■ $$

A classic Parisian bistro with a zinc-topped bar and a hip clientele. The steak-frites can't be beaten.

9 Calle Ocho
MAP F2 ■ 45 West 81st St at Columbus Ave ■ 212 873 5025 ■ $$

Every night feels like a Latin party; modern dishes are inspired by cuisine from Puerto Rico to Cuba.

10 Gennaro
MAP E2 ■ 665 Amsterdam Ave, between 92nd & 93rd Sts ■ 212 665 5348 ■ No credit cards ■ $$

Fans say Gennaro serves the best Italian food in the area, at reasonable prices (explains the constant lines).

See map on p143

TOP 10 Morningside Heights and Harlem

The area between Morningside Park and the Hudson River is dominated by Columbia University and two important churches. Extending north is Harlem, America's best-known African-American community. Irish, Italian, and Jewish families occupied large townhouses here in the 1880s, but by the 1920s black families predominated. The Harlem Renaissance, when black artistic and intellectual culture flourished, ended with the Depression. Nevertheless, development is reviving the area, causing some to declare a second Renaissance.

Statue of St. John the Divine

1 Columbia University
MAP C3 ■ West 116th St at Broadway ■ www.columbia.edu
One of America's oldest universities, noted for its law, medicine, and journalism schools, Columbia was founded in 1754 as King's College. It moved in 1897 to its present campus, designed by American Beaux Arts architect Charles McKim. Notable buildings include McKim's 1898 Low Memorial Library and St. Paul's Chapel, which has three stained-glass windows by La Farge.

2 Cathedral Church of St. John the Divine
MAP C3 ■ 1047 Amsterdam Ave at 112th St ■ Open 7:30am–6pm daily ■ www.stjohndivine.org
The mother church of the Episcopal Diocese of New York, begun in 1892 and still incomplete, is one of the world's largest cathedrals. Over 600 ft (180 m) long and 320 ft (96 m) wide, the church is a mix of Romanesque and Gothic styles. Features include the west entrance, the rose window, bay altars, and the Peace Fountain on the south lawn. The medieval stone carving techniques used on the building are taught in workshops for disadvantaged youths (see p54).

St. Paul's Chapel, Columbia University

AREA MAP OF MORNINGSIDE HEIGHTS AND HARLEM

0 meters 500
0 yards 500

HARLEM

MORNINGSIDE HEIGHTS

1	**Top 10 Sights** see pp148–51
1	**Restaurants** see p153
1	**Places for Music** see p152

3 Riverside Church

MAP C1 ■ 490 Riverside Drive, between 120th and 122nd Sts ■ Open 7am–10pm daily ■ www. theriversidechurchny.org

This skyscraper Gothic church financed by John D. Rockefeller Jr. in 1930, has a 21-story tower with wonderful views. The tower houses the world's largest carillon, dedicated to Rockefeller's mother. The stained-glass windows are copies of those at Chartres cathedral with four exceptions – the early 16th-century Flemish windows on the east wall.

Riverside Church

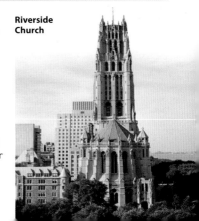

Hamilton Heights Historic District

4 Hamilton Heights Historic District

MAP A2 ■ West 141 St to West 145th St

Once part of the country estates of the wealthy, like Alexander Hamilton whose 1802 home, Hamilton Grange, is here, this location on a hill above Harlem became desirable in the 1880s when an elevated rail line was built. Fine residences went up between 1886 and 1906, and in the 1920s and 1930s they attracted Harlem's elite, when the area was dubbed Sugar Hill. Chief Justice Thurgood Marshall and musicians Count Basie, Duke Ellington, and Cab Calloway were among those who lived here.

5 St. Nicholas Historic District (Strivers' Row)

MAP A3 ■ 202–250 West 138th St, between Powell & Frederick Douglass Blvds

These fine houses, originally known as the King Model Houses, were built in 1891 when Harlem was a neighborhood for the gentry. Three architects, including McKim, Mead, and White, managed to blend Renaissance, Georgian, and Victorian styles to create a harmonious whole. Successful African-Americans, such as congressman Adam Clayton Powell Jr., moved here in the 1920s and 1930s, giving rise to the nickname Strivers' Row.

6 Abyssinian Baptist Church

MAP A3 ■ 132 West 138th St, at Powell Blvd ■ Sunday services at 11am ■ www.abyssinian.org

One of the oldest and most influential African-American churches in the US was organized in 1808 by a group protesting segregation within the Baptist church. The congregation became politically active (starting in 1908) under such leaders as congressman Adam Clayton Powell, Jr. Today the church is popular for its gospel choir.

Abyssinian Baptist Church

7 Marcus Garvey Park

MAP B3 ■ West 120th to West 124th Sts, between Malcolm X Blvd & 5th Ave

A black nationalist who encouraged emigration to Africa, Garvey became a hero of the Black Pride movement, and the park's name was changed from Mount Morris in 1973 to honor him. It adjoins the Mount Morris Historical District of handsome houses and churches from an earlier, German-Jewish era. In the 1920s, as Harlem became mostly African-American, the synagogues became churches, and the houses were divided up.

Studio Museum in Harlem

8 Studio Museum in Harlem

MAP B3 ■ 144 West 125th St ■ Open noon–9pm Thu & Fri, 10am–6pm Sat, noon–6pm Sun ■ Donations ■ www.studiomuseum.org

Opened in 1967 as an artists' studio, the organization has become an important center for work by black artists. The present building, which opened in 1982, has undergone a major expansion to add more gallery space, an enlarged sculpture garden, an auditorium, and a café.

9 Schomburg Center for Research in Black Culture

MAP A3 ■ 515 Malcolm X Blvd at 135th St ■ Open noon–8pm Tue–Thu, 10am–6pm Fri & Sat

This complex, opened in 1991, houses the largest research center for African and African-American culture in the US. The immense collection was assembled by Arthur Schomburg. The original building was the unofficial meeting place for the black literary renaissance of the 1920s; the present building includes a theater and two art galleries.

10 Masjid Malcolm Shabazz/Harlem Market

MAP C3 ■ Mosque: 102 West 116th St ■ Open by appointment ■ MAP C3 ■ Harlem Market: 52–60 West 116th St, between 5th Ave & Malcolm X Blvd ■ Open 10am–9pm daily

The Malcolm Shabazz Mosque was the ministry of the late Malcolm X, and the area around it has become the center of an active Muslim community. Harlem Market nearby sells African art, dolls, and prints.

A DAY IN HARLEM AND MORNINGSIDE HEIGHTS

▶ MORNING

Begin late Sunday morning and take the No. 2 or No. 3 subway uptown to 135th Street and Lenox Avenue. Walk to Odell Clark Place and turn west to hear the fabulous choir at the **Abyssinian Baptist Church**.

Continue west along the street to see the fine 1890s homes of the **St. Nicholas Historic District** and stop on 8th Avenue to enjoy a gospel brunch at **Londel's Supper Club** (see p152).

AFTERNOON

Retrace your steps to Lenox Avenue and head downtown to 125th Street to browse the shops. Turn west for the famous **Apollo Theater** (see p152) and excellent displays of African-American art at the **Studio Museum in Harlem**. Stop for coffee at the Starbucks on Lenox Avenue at 125th Street.

Take the M60 bus from 125th Street and Malcolm X Boulevard to West 120th Street and Broadway. Walk down to **Riverside Church** (see p149) for fine views over the Hudson River. Across the street is the tomb of the 18th US president, Ulysses S. Grant. At 116th Street, head east two blocks to Broadway and the entrance to **Columbia University** (see p148). One block east on Amsterdam Avenue is the **Cathedral Church of St. John the Divine** (see p148) with its immense interior. End the day with some good southern cooking at **Miss Mamie's** (see p153) and return to Broadway for the No. 1 subway back downtown.

See map on p149

Places for Music

Harlem Stage auditorium

1 Harlem Stage
MAP A2 ■ City College campus, 150 Convent Ave at West 135th St

Home to jazz series, as well as ballet, modern dance, opera, and the Harlem Stage on Screen film festival.

2 Paris Blues
MAP C2 ■ 2021 Adam Clayton Powell, Jr. Blvd

Open since 1968, this dive bar is a neighborhood favorite and offers live jazz performances every night with no cover charge.

3 Showman's Jazz Club
MAP B2 ■ 375 West 125th St, between St. Nicholas & Morningside Dr

Live jazz and blues have been the lure since 1942 at this club, where the vibes and the people are as cool as the music.

4 Londel's Supper Club
MAP A3 ■ 2620 Frederick Douglass Blvd (8th Ave), between West 139th & 140th Sts

Part of the new Harlem, with an upscale ambience, waiters in tuxedos, delicious Southern fare, and live jazz on weekends.

5 Bill's Place
MAP B3 ■ 148 West 133rd St

A Harlem hideaway modeled after the speakeasies that once dotted this neighborhood. There are great jazz sets by saxophonist Bill Saxton on Fridays and Saturdays at 8pm and 10pm, but no alcohol is allowed inside.

6 Sylvia's
MAP B3 ■ 328 Malcolm X Blvd, between West 126th & 127th Sts

Sylvia Woods founded this soul food restaurant in 1962. The place is jammed for Saturday and Sunday gospel brunches, and always fun despite the tour groups.

7 Cotton Club
MAP B2 ■ 656 West 125th St at Riverside Dr

Duke Ellington and Cab Calloway are long gone, and the location has changed, but the famous club of the 1920s is making a comeback.

The famous Apollo Theater

8 Apollo Theater
MAP B3 ■ 253 West 125th St, between 7th & 8th Aves

This is Harlem's famous showcase, where Ella Fitzgerald and James Brown launched their careers.

9 Minton's
MAP C4 ■ 206 West 118th St

Bebop was born at this legendary jazz club which has been revitalized and has a nightly lineup of jazz, along with cocktails and Southern cuisine.

10 Smoke
MAP D2 ■ 2751 Broadway at West 106th St

Music lovers congregate here to hear top-notch jazz groups every weekend.

Restaurants

PRICE CATEGORIES
For a three-course meal for one with a glass of house wine, and all unavoidable charges including tax.

$ under $25 $$ $25–$75 $$$ over $75

1 Red Rooster
MAP B3 ▪ 310 Malcolm X Blvd ▪ 212 792 9001 ▪ $$

Celebrity chef Marcus Samuelsson brings Downtown style to Harlem, drawing in an eclectic crowd to enjoy a cutting-edge menu that honors the area's colorful culinary history.

2 BLVD Bistro
MAP C3 ▪ 239 Malcolm X Blvd ▪ 212 678 6200 ▪ $$

Relax into the night at this engaging wine bar and restaurant. Enjoy classic American dishes with a soul food twist, like pan-fried chicken and cornmeal-crusted grouper.

3 Miss Mamie's Spoonbread Too
MAP D2 ▪ 366 Cathedral Pkwy, between Manhattan Ave & Columbus Ave ▪ 212 865 6744 ▪ $$

This cheerful café is run by Norma Jean Darden, who knows her Southern cooking. The excellent food has attracted the likes of former US president Bill Clinton to eat here.

4 Dinosaur Bar-B-Que
MAP B1 ▪ 700 West 125th St at Riverside Dr ▪ 212 694 1777 ▪ $$

The generous portions live up to the name of this roadhouse-style BBQ joint. A wide selection of microbrews along with pit-smoked meats.

5 Tom's Restaurant
MAP C2 ▪ 2880 Broadway ▪ 212 864 6137 ▪ $$

Immortalized as a location in the popular *Seinfeld* TV series, this family-owned eatery is popular for its filling portions of affordable diner classics.

6 Pisticci
MAP B1 ▪ 125 La Salle St, between Broadway & Claremont Ave ▪ 212 932 3500 ▪ $$

A cozy Italian eatery serving up pasta dishes to a mostly local crowd.

7 Amy Ruth's
MAP C3 ▪ 113 West 116th St, between A. C. Powell & Malcolm X Blvds ▪ 212 280 8779 ▪ $$

A cheerful café with an updated slant on Southern classics. Waffles are a house specialty.

8 Le Baobab
MAP C3 ▪ 120 West 116th St at Lenox Ave ▪ 212 864 4700 ▪ No credit cards ▪ $$

The Senegalese cooking and the tab are both agreeable here.

9 Harlem Shake
MAP D2 ▪ 100 West 124th St ▪ 212 222 8300 ▪ $

Fill up on juicy burgers, all-beef hot dogs and creamy milkshakes at this playful restaurant.

10 Jin Ramen
MAP B1 ▪ 3183 Broadway, between Tiemann Pl & 125th St ▪ 646 559 2862 ▪ $$

This Japanese restaurant attracts patrons with its bowls of ramen, tasty pork buns, and other specialties.

Interior of Amy Ruth's

See map on p149

🔟 The Outer Boroughs

Manhattan is just one of New York's five boroughs, each of which has its own unique attractions. Brooklyn alone, with its fine brownstone neighborhoods and numerous top-class sights, would be one of the largest cities in the US. The Bronx, to the north, boasts one of New York's finest zoos, plus the New York Botanical Garden and Yankee Stadium, while Queens, a veritable melting pot of nationalities, is famous for its museums, ethnic dining, and numerous sports events. The ferry to Staten Island leads to New York's only restored historic village.

World Fair Unisphere, Flushing Meadows-Corona Park

AREA MAP OF THE OUTER BOROUGHS

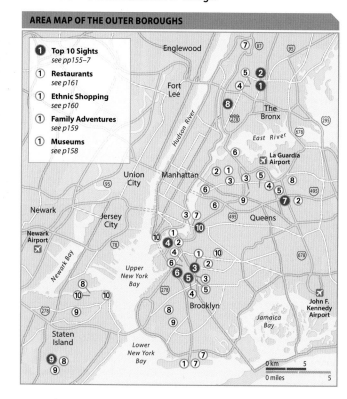

1 Top 10 Sights
see pp155–7

1 Restaurants
see p161

1 Ethnic Shopping
see p160

1 Family Adventures
see p159

1 Museums
see p158

The Zoo Center building at Bronx Zoo

① Bronx Zoo

Bronx River Parkway & Boston Rd, Bronx ■ **Subway (2, 5) West Farms Sq/East Tremont Ave** ■ **Open Apr–Oct: 10am–5pm Mon–Fri, 10am–5:30pm Sat, Sun, & hols; Nov–Mar: 10am–4:30pm daily** ■ **Adm** ■ **www.bronxzoo.com**

Established in 1895, this sprawling zoo on 265 acres (107 ha) gets better all the time. Exhibits include Madagascar!, while Tiger Mountain and the 6.5-acre (2.6-ha) Congo Gorilla Forest, an African rainforest habitat, bring visitors nose to nose with the inhabitants. The Bug Carousel is particularly appealing to young children.

② New York Botanical Garden

Bronx River Parkway & Kazimiroff Blvd, Bronx ■ **Subway (B, D, 4) Bedford Park Blvd** ■ **Open 10am–6pm Tue–Sun (to 5pm in Jan–Feb)** ■ **Adm** ■ **www.nybg.org**

One of the oldest and largest botanical gardens in the world, this National Historic Landmark covers 250 acres (101 ha), which includes 50 gardens and plant collections, and 50 acres (20 ha) of forest, the only remains of woods that once covered New York. The Enid A. Haupt Conservatory, a restored Victorian glass house, is home to tropical rain forest and arid desert plants. A tram makes it easy to see the highlights; guided tours are offered. The Leon Levy Visitor Center has a shop, a visitor orientation area, and a café.

③ Brooklyn Botanic Garden

900 Washington Ave, Brooklyn ■ **Subway (2, 3) Eastern Pkwy** ■ **Open Mar–Oct: 8am–6pm Tue–Fri, 10am–6pm Sat, Sun, & hols; Nov–Feb: 8am–4:30pm Tue–Fri, 10am–4:30pm Sat, Sun, & hols** ■ **Adm (free Tue & Sat am)** ■ **www.bbg.org**

This 52-acre (21-ha) garden designed by the Olmsted brothers in 1910 is home to more than 12,000 plantings. It is best known for the Cranford Rose Gardens, where thousands of roses cascade down arches and climb lattices, and the authentic Japanese Hill-and-Pond Garden, planted in 1915. It is also known for its Cherry Esplanade and Cherry Walk, one of the foremost cherry-blossom sites outside Japan. The Steinhardt Conservatory houses tropical and desert plants, and a large bonsai collection.

New York Botanical Garden, Bronx

④ Brooklyn Heights Historic District

Court St to Furman St, between Fulton & State Sts ■ **Subway (2, 3) Clark St**

Overlooking the East River and lower Manhattan skyline, this district is an enclave of old-world charm. Along its quaint streets are preserved Federal, wooden and brick townhouses of the 1820s and even grander Greek Revival homes of the following decades.

Soldiers' and Sailors' Arch at the main entrance to Prospect Park, Brooklyn

5 Prospect Park
Between Eastern Pkwy & Parkside Ave, Brooklyn ▪ Subway (2, 3) Grand Army Plaza

Frederic Olmsted and Calvert Vaux considered this park, opened in 1867, their masterpiece. The 90-acre (36-ha) Long Meadow is the longest unbroken green space in the city. The pools and weeping willows of the Vale of Cashmere are particularly fine, along with Vaux's Oriental Pavilion and Concert Grove.

THE NO. 7 TRAIN TO QUEENS

This subway route (**below**), dubbed the International Express, serves New York's most varied ethnic communities. Exit at 61st Street for Irish pubs, 46th Street for the Middle East, 69th Street for the Philippines. A guide is available from Queens Council on the Arts, 37–11 35th Ave, Astoria, NY 11101 (www.queenscouncilarts.org).

6 Park Slope Historic District
Prospect Park West to 8th Ave, between 14th St & St. John's Pl, Brooklyn ▪ Subway (F) 7th Ave

These blocks on the western edge of Prospect Park became desirable places to live after the opening of the Brooklyn Bridge in 1883. The Victorian brownstones from the late 19th and early 20th centuries are outstanding US Romanesque Revival and Queen Anne residences.

7 Flushing Meadows-Corona Park
Queens ▪ Subway (7) 111th St, Willets Pt–Shea Stadium

The site of two World Fairs, this is now a spacious park with picnic areas, fields for cricket and soccer, paths for bikers and skaters, boating lakes, and many other attractions. The New York Mets' Citi Field, the U.S. Tennis Center, the New York Hall of Science, and the Queens Museum of Art are also here. The Unisphere, the symbol of the 1964 World Fair, still stands.

8 Yankee Stadium
East 161st St & River Ave, Bronx ▪ Subway (B, D, 4) 161st St Yankee Stadium ▪ Opening times vary ▪ Adm

This sports shrine, completed in 1923 and known as "The House that

Ruth Built" for the legions of fans who came to see superhero Babe Ruth, was retired in 2008. Other legendary heroes of America's most successful baseball team include Joe DiMaggio and Mickey Mantle. The new Yankee stadium across the street incorporates Monument Park and exhibits retired number plaques and statues of the greatest players.

⑨ Historic Richmond Town
441 Clarke Ave, Staten Island ■ Bus S74 from ferry ■ Open 1–5pm Wed–Sun; tours at 2:30pm weekdays, at 2 and 3:30pm weekends ■ Adm ■ www.historicrichmondtown.org

This restored village has 29 buildings from the town of Richmond, Staten Island's seat of government from 1729. Other historic buildings were moved here from other sites. The Dutch-style Voorlezer's House (1695) is the island's oldest home on its original site.

Historic Richmond Town

⑩ Williamsburg
Bedford Ave, Brooklyn ■ Subway L to Bedford Ave; Bus B39 or B61

This was mostly a community of Hasidic Jews, Puerto Ricans, and Italians until the 1990s when artists from Manhattan began to move here. The heart of Williamsburg is Bedford Avenue, which is only one stop from Manhattan on the L subway line. Here you'll find stores promoting local designers, as well as bars and restaurants, where prices are often lower than in Manhattan.

A DAY OUT IN BROOKLYN

▶ MORNING

Take the No. 2 or 3 subway train to Eastern Parkway – Brooklyn Museum, for the world-class **Brooklyn Museum** (see p49). The museum is part of a civic complex that includes the stately Grand Army Plaza, the **Brooklyn Botanic Garden** (see p155), with its well-known Japanese garden, and neighboring **Prospect Park**.

Along the western edge of Prospect Park is the beautiful **Park Slope Historic District**. Stop for coffee at Gorilla Coffee, 97 5th Avenue, before taking in the area's historic residences. Browse the hip lineup of small shops along 7th Avenue, and stop for lunch at one of the area's many cafés.

AFTERNOON

Return by train to Borough Hall and head for the **Brooklyn Heights Historic District**. Walk along Pierrepont, Willow, and Cranberry streets to see some 19th-century houses; Truman Capote wrote *Breakfast at Tiffany's* in the basement of No. 70 Willow, and Arthur Miller once owned the property at No. 155.

A short walk east brings you to **Atlantic Avenue** (see p160). Look in on the spice shops here, and stop for refreshments at the **Long Island Bar**, 110 Atlantic Avenue. Head back to **Brooklyn Bridge**, stopping at the **Brooklyn Heights Promenade** for dramatic vistas of Lower Manhattan's towers. End the day with dinner at the romantic **River Café** (see p161).

See map on p154 ←

Museums

1 Brooklyn Museum
200 Eastern Parkway, Brooklyn ▪ Subway (2, 3) Eastern Pkwy ▪ Open 11am–6pm Wed–Sun (to 10pm Thu); 11am–11pm first Sat of month (except Sep) ▪ Adm

The permanent collection has it all, from ancient Egyptian objects to contemporary art (see p49).

2 Noguchi Museum
9-01 33rd Rd at Vernon Blvd, Queens ▪ Bus 103 to Vernon Blvd ▪ Open 10am–5pm Wed–Fri, 11am–6pm Sat & Sun ▪ Adm

Thirteen galleries and a serene Japanese sculpture garden.

3 Museum of the Moving Image
6-01 35th Ave at 37th St, Queens ▪ Subway (M, R) Steinway St ▪ Open 10:30am–5pm Tue–Thu (to 8pm Fri), 11:30am–7pm Sat & Sun ▪ Adm (free 4–8pm Fri)

Artifacts and screenings show the history and techniques of film and TV.

4 New York Hall of Science
47-01 111th St, Queens ▪ Subway (7) 111th St ▪ Open Apr–Jun: 9:30am–2pm Mon; Sep–Mar: 9:30am–2pm Tue–Thu, 9:30am–5pm Fri, 10am–6pm Sat & Sun ▪ Adm

A science and technology museum with hands-on exhibits on color, light, and physics, and outdoor play area.

Hall of Science

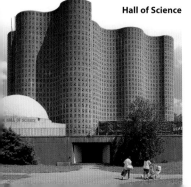

5 Queens Museum
New York City Building, Queens ▪ Subway 111th St ▪ Open Jul–Aug: noon–6pm Wed–Sun (to 8pm Fri); Sep–Jun: noon–6pm Wed–Sun; ▪ Adm

The New York Panorama scale model has over 800,000 buildings.

6 MoMA PS1
22–25 Jackson Ave at 46th Ave, Queens ▪ Subway (E, V) 23rd St-Ely Ave ▪ Open noon–6pm Thu–Mon ▪ Adm

This center displays contemporary art and provides studio space for artists.

7 Van Cortlandt House Museum
Van Cortlandt Park, Broadway and West 246th St, Bronx ▪ Subway (1) 242nd St ▪ Open 10am–4pm Tue–Fri, 11am–4pm Sat & Sun; last tickets 30 mins before closing ▪ Adm ▪ www.vchm.org

This restored 1748 Georgian house is the Bronx's oldest building.

8 Jacques Marchais Museum of Tibetan Art
338 Lighthouse Ave, Staten Island ▪ Bus S74 from ferry ▪ Open 1–5pm Wed–Sun (closed Thu in winter) ▪ Adm

A collection of Tibetan art in a Himalayan-style building.

9 Historic Richmond Town
441 Clarke St, Staten Island ▪ Bus S74 from ferry ▪ Opening times vary ▪ Adm

The museum housed in the County Clerk's office, built in 1848, is just one of 27 buildings in the museum village.

10 Snug Harbor Cultural Center
1000 Richmond Terrace, Staten Island ▪ Bus S40 from ferry ▪ Opening times vary ▪ Adm

Chinese garden, performance spaces, art center, children's museum, and a maritime collection.

Family Adventures

1 New York Aquarium
Surf Ave & West 8th St, Brooklyn ▪ Subway (F, Q) W 8th St ▪ Open Apr–May, Sep–Oct: 10am–5pm Mon–Fri (to 5:30pm Sat, Sun, & hols); Jun–Aug: 10am–6pm Mon–Fri (to 7pm Sat, Sun, & hols); Nov–Mar: 10am–4:30pm daily ▪ Adm

Walk through a swamp, stay dry beneath a waterfall, and admire the more than 350 species.

Brooklyn Children's Museum

2 Brooklyn Children's Museum
145 Brooklyn Ave at St. Marks Pl, Brooklyn ▪ Subway (3) Kingston ▪ Open 10am–5pm Tue–Sun (to 6pm Thu); free 2–6pm every Thu ▪ Adm

Founded in 1899, this is said to be the first children's museum in the United States. The interactive, hands-on exhibits have informed and entertained countless children.

3 Prospect Park Zoo
450 Flatbush Ave, Brooklyn ▪ Subway (B, Q) Prospect Park ▪ Open Apr–Oct: 10am–5pm daily (to 5:30pm Sat & Sun); Nov–Mar: 10am–4:30pm daily ▪ Adm

Tunnel through a prairie-dog town, master baboon language, and leapfrog across lily pads.

4 Prospect Park Carousel
Prospect Park, Brooklyn ▪ Subway (B, Q) Prospect Park ▪ Open Apr–Oct: noon–5pm Sat, Sun, & hols (to 6pm Jul–Aug) ▪ Rides $2

This 1912 carousel came here from Coney Island in 1950.

5 Lefferts Historic House
Prospect Park, Brooklyn ▪ Subway (B, Q) Prospect Park ▪ Open Feb–Mar: noon–4pm Sat & Sun; Apr–early Sep: noon–5pm Thu–Sun

This rare 18th-century Dutch Colonial farmhouse shows early farm life.

6 Puppetworks
338 6th Ave at 4th St, Brooklyn ▪ Subway (F) 7th Ave (Brooklyn) ▪ Performance times vary ▪ Adm, reservations required

Hand-carved marionettes are used to present children's classics.

7 Sheepshead Bay Fishing Boats
Emmons Ave, Brooklyn ▪ Subway (B, Q) to Sheepshead Bay ▪ Boats leave 6:30–9am, 1, & 7pm, or can be chartered ▪ Adm

A fishing fleet takes passengers for day and evening trips.

8 Staten Island Children's Museum
1000 Richmond Terrace, Staten Island ▪ Bus S40 from ferry ▪ Open 11am–5pm Tue–Fri (10am–6pm school hols), 10am–5pm Sat & Sun ▪ Adm

A 6-ft (2-m) kinetic porpoise welcomes you to this interactive playground exploring water, insects, and visual and performing arts.

9 Staten Island Zoo
614 Broadway, Staten Island ▪ Bus S48 from ferry ▪ Open 10am–4:45pm daily ▪ Adm

The Amur Leopard Habitat and Tropical Forest are highlights.

10 Staten Island Ferry
Bus to St. George Terminal, Staten Island ▪ Boats every 15 mins–1 hr, 24 hours daily from Whitehall and South Sts

A free ride with fabulous views (see p72). St. George Terminal buses go to Staten Island's sights.

See map on p154

Ethnic Shopping

1 ### Broadway, Astoria
Broadway, Astoria, Queens
■ Subway (N, Q) Broadway

Astoria has the largest Greek community outside Greece, with restaurants, coffee shops, and bakeries on Broadway.

2 ### Main Street, Flushing
Main St, Flushing, Queens
■ Subway (7) Main St

Flushing's Chinatown offers bakeries, gifts, restaurants, herbal remedies, and acupuncture. Queensborough Library has material in 40 languages.

3 ### 74th Street, Jackson Heights
74th St, Jackson Heights, Queens
■ Subway (E, F, R) Roosevelt Ave

The shop windows of New York's Indian community are filled with ornate gold jewelry and rich saris. The food stores are redolent with delicious spices.

4 ### Arthur Avenue, Bronx
Arthur Ave, Bronx ■ Subway (4) Fordham Rd

In this Italian neighborhood, dozens of small, family-run stores sell everything from Italian wines, handmade pastas, and sausages to rosaries and votive candles.

Italian food stall, Arthur Avenue

5 ### Roosevelt Avenue, Jackson Heights
Jackson Heights, Queens ■ Subway (E, F, R) Roosevelt Ave

Around the corner from Indian 74th Street, loudspeakers play Latin American rhythms, street vendors sell hot churros (fried dough), and shops offer music, hats, and piñatas.

6 ### Nassau Avenue, Greenpoint
Nassau Ave, Greenpoint, Brooklyn
■ Subway (G) Nassau

Shops in America's largest Polish community are full of home-made *kielbasas* (sausages), *babkas* (cakes), statues of saints, books, and music.

7 ### Brighton Beach Avenue, Brooklyn
Brighton Beach Ave, Brooklyn
■ Subway (B, Q) Brighton Beach

Everything from fish to *matryoshka* dolls are sold in "Little Odessa", where Russian is the first language.

8 ### 13th Avenue, Borough Park
13th Ave, Borough Park, Brooklyn
■ Subway (D) 55th St

The main street of America's largest Orthodox Jewish community bustles with shops filled with religious articles, baked goods, and linens.

9 ### 18th Avenue, Bensonhurst
18th Ave, Bensonhurst, Brooklyn
■ Subway (D) 18th Ave

Though the old-world Italian community is slowly giving way to other nationalities, the street still offers generous samplings of traditional Italian foods.

10 ### Atlantic Avenue, Brooklyn
Atlantic Ave, Brooklyn ■ Subway (R) Court St

This Middle-Eastern shopping center offers baklava and many varieties of olives, dried fruits, and spices.

Restaurants

River Café, with the Brooklyn Bridge

① River Café
1 Water St, Brooklyn ■ Subway (A, C) High St ■ 718 522 5200 ■ Men require jackets after 5pm ■ $$$

Lobster, duck, and seafood are among the many specialties served here. Dessert choices include a mini chocolate Brooklyn Bridge.

② Chef's Table at Brooklyn Fare
200 Schermerhorn St, Brooklyn ■ Subway (A, C) Hoyt St–Schermerhorn ■ 718 243 0050 ■ Men require jackets ■ $$$

This 18-seat counter, adjacent to a grocery, has three Michelin stars due to Cesar Ramirez's stunning small-plate dishes (20 courses in all). Book at least six weeks in advance.

③ Peter Luger Steak House
178 Broadway, Brooklyn ■ Subway (J, M, Z) Marcy Ave ■ 718 387 7400 ■ No credit cards ■ $$$

Beef lovers flock to Peter Luger's beer hall-style location for what have long been considered New York's best steaks. It is necessary to book ahead.

④ al di la Trattoria
248 5th Ave, Brooklyn ■ Subway (R) Union St ■ 718 636 8888 ■ $$

This cozy, northern Italian trattoria serves regional dishes like hanger steak, clams in a white wine sauce, and wonderful pastas.

⑤ Dominick's Restaurant
2335 Arthur Ave, Bronx ■ Subway (D) Fordham Road ■ 718 733 2807 ■ No credit cards ■ $$

Stand in line, join a table, and feast on home-made southern Italian food. There's no menu; order your favorite or trust the waiter's choice.

⑥ Agnanti
19-06 Ditmars Blvd, Queens ■ Subway (N, Q) Ditmars Blvd–Astoria ■ 718 545 4554 ■ $$

Greek favorites, perfectly cooked, in a charming location with a shady terrace in the summer.

⑦ Marlow & Sons
81 Broadway, Brooklyn ■ Subway (7) Main St ■ 718 384 1441 ■ $$

This whimsical restaurant with sturdy communal tables serves a Mediterranean-accented menu.

⑧ Joe's Shanghai
136–21 37th Ave, Queens ■ Subway (7) Main St ■ 718 539 3838 ■ No credit cards ■ $$

The original of this Chinese café chain is popular for its pork or crab soup dumplings, or "steamed buns."

⑨ Jackson Diner
37–47 74th St, Queens ■ Subway (E, F, G, R, V) Roosevelt Ave ■ 718 672 1232 ■ No credit cards ■ $$

No ambience, but one of New York's best Indian restaurants, with an all-you-can eat buffet lunch.

⑩ Enoteca Maria
27 Hyatt St, Staten Island ■ 5-min walk from ferry ■ 718 447 2777 ■ No credit cards ■ $$

Authentic Italian *enoteca*; everything on the daily menu is freshly made.

See map on p154

Streetsmart

Yellow New York cabs on 8th Avenue

Getting To and Around New York

Arriving by Air

New York can be reached by air direct from most major cities. Allow extra time at the airport, both at arrival and departure, for the careful passport and security checks in the US. The two main international airports in the New York City area are **John F. Kennedy International** (JFK) and **Newark Liberty International** (EWR). Both also handle some domestic flights. The third major airport is **LaGuardia** (LGA), which handles mostly domestic flights. All three airports offer connecting flights to most US cities.

Cab fares to the city from JFK are fixed at $52, plus any tolls and a New York State Tax Surcharge of $0.50 on each trip. From Newark, the fare ranges between $55 and $75, and from LaGuardia, it ranges between $29 and $40.

SuperShuttle vans operate door-to-door and cost less than taxis. They pick up several passengers, so allow plenty of time for the journey. Prices are between $16 and $25, depending on the zip code. Coaches, like **NYC Airporter** ($14–20), offer transport from the airports to central Midtown points.

The subway and buses are other options. From JFK, take the **AirTrain** to the A, E, J, and Z subway trains into Manhattan. From Newark, take the AirTrain to **New Jersey Transit** or **Amtrak** into Manhattan. Take the M60

SBS bus from LaGuardia, to 125th St, where you can catch many subway lines, including the 4, 5, and 6 lines or the A, B, C, and D lines. Alternatively, the Q70 Limited bus runs directly from LaGuardia to Jackson Heights/ Roosevelt Ave EFMR and 74th St/Broadway 7.

Arriving by Bus

Greyhound is the main bus company in the US, and all its long-distance and intercity buses, as well as commuter lines, arrive at the **Port Authority Bus Terminal**. Cabs wait at the 8th Ave entrance. Discount buses, including **Megabus** and **Bolt**, usually depart and arrive near Penn Station.

Arriving by Train

Amtrak, the national rail system, pulls in to **Penn Station** at 7th Ave and 33rd St. Long Island Rail Road, operated by the **Metropolitan Transit Authority (MTA)**, and New Jersey Transit commuter trains also use Penn station. Metro-North regional trains (also run by the MTA) use Grand Central Terminal, at Park Avenue and 42nd Street. Cabs wait outside station entrances.

Arriving by Sea

Numerous cruise ships arrive in New York at the NYCruise terminals in Manhattan and Brooklyn. Customs and immigration officials are on duty at both

to process passengers arriving on international cruises. Cabs wait outside both terminals.

Getting Around by Subway

The 24-hour subway, run by the MTA, is the fastest way to get around, with over 450 stations across all five boroughs, and routes that fan out to the farthest reaches of New York City. Subways run north and south (uptown and downtown) along Lexington Ave, 6th Ave, 7th Ave, Broadway, and 8th Ave. The E, F, L, N, Q, R, and 7 trains to Queens run east to west, crossing Manhattan. The A, B, C, D, J, L, M, N, Q, R, Z, 2, 3, 4, and 5 lines all run as far as Brooklyn.

MetroCards, sold in subways and some shops, are good for both buses and subways. There are pay-per-ride cards, where each ride automatically deducts one $2.75 fare from the card, and transfers are free between buses, two interconnected subways, and subways and buses. There are also weekly and monthly travel cards. The $31 weekly pass is a great option.

Getting Around by Bus

You can see more of the city from a bus, but they run much slower, particularly during rush hour (morning and late afternoon). Manhattan buses run on every north–south artery except on Park Ave and West End Ave. The most useful crosstown buses run on 96th, 86th, 79th, 66th, 57th, 49/50th, 42nd, 34th, 23rd, and 14th Sts. Route indicators (M for Manhattan, Q for Queens, B for Brooklyn) are displayed above the front windshield. Without a MetroCard, the exact change for the $2.75 fare is required in coins; bills are not accepted.

Getting Around by Taxi

Manhattan yellow taxis can be hailed anywhere. The light atop the cab goes on when it is available. Good places to look for a cab are near the big hotels and main stations. Taxis accept cash and credit cards. For any **taxi complaints**, you can call 311.

The green **Boro taxis** operate in areas of New York not commonly served by yellow cabs – north of West 110th St and East 96th St in Manhattan, the Bronx, Queens (excluding the airports), Brooklyn and Staten Island.They can drop you off anywhere in the city, but can not pick up passengers in Manhattan below 96/110th Sts.

Getting Around by Car

Perhaps the biggest challenge for driving in New York is the cost and availability of parking – this is the priciest city to park in the US. Check in advance with your hotel to see if they offer parking. Otherwise, there are parking meters across the city, where you can park from 1 to 12 hours, starting at $1 per hour (meters do not have to be paid on Sundays). New York also has numerous parking lots, but these can be expensive, starting from an average of $40 per day. For more details about driving and parking, check the Department of Transportation (DOT) website. Major US car rental companies, such as **Hertz** and **Avis**, are dotted throughout the city. Drivers must be over 25, and have a valid license as well as a major credit card.

Ferries and Boats

New York Waterway ferries connect New Jersey and Manhattan, providing handy transportation to New York Yankee and Mets baseball games. **Water Taxi** operates from East 90th Street Pier to Pier 84. The 24-hour **Staten Island Ferry** is free and offers views of Lower Manhattan and the Statue of Liberty.

DIRECTORY

AIRPORTS

John F. Kennedy (JFK)
718 244 4444
paynynj.gov

LaGuardia (LGA)
718 533 3400
panynj.gov

Newark (EWR)
973 961 6000
panynj.gov

BUSES AND COACHES

Bolt Bus
1 877 265 8287
boltbus.com

Greyhound
1 800 231 2222
greyhound.com

Megabus
1 877 462 6342
us.megabus.com

NYC Airporter
855 269 2247
nycairporter.com

Port Authority Bus Terminal
MAP K2 ■ 625 8th Ave
212 564 8484
panynj.gov

SuperShuttle
1 800 258 3826
supershuttle.com

TRAINS AND SUBWAY

AirTrain
718 244 4444
panynj.gov/airtrain

Amtrak
1 800 872 7245
amtrak.com

Metropolitan Transport Authority (MTA)
511
mta.info

New Jersey Transit
973 275 5555
njtransit.com

Penn Station
MAP K3 ■ 234 W 31st St
1 800 872 7245
amtrak.com

TAXIS AND CAR HIRE

Avis
800 331 1212
avis.com

Hertz
800 654 3131
hertz.com

Taxi Complaints
311

FERRIES AND BOATS

New York Waterway
800 533 3779
nywaterway.com

Staten Island Ferry
718 876 8441
siferry.com

Water Taxi
212 742 1969
nywatertaxi.com

Practical Information

Passports and Visas

Before traveling, always make sure to check with your embassy that you have the proper documents and meet the latest requirements. Most UK and Canadian passport holders do not need visas if staying in the US for 90 days or less; however, those planning to visit under the Visa Waiver Scheme must register in advance online and pay a charge. Visit the US Customs and Border Protection **Electronic System for Travel Authorization** (ESTA) for details. Note that all necessary landing cards and customs forms are usually distributed on the plane.

Customs Regulations and Immigration

It is possible to bring the following into the US without customs fees: $100 worth of gifts ($400 for US citizens), 200 cigarettes, 100 cigars, and 35 fl oz (1 litre) of liquor. No meat, seeds, growing plants, or fruit may be brought in. Check the **US Customs** website.

Prescription drugs should be clearly marked. When flying within the US, liquids can only be carried in bottles of 3 fl oz (100 ml), meaning you can carry duty-free alcohol only to your first port of call. If you have a connecting flight, the liquids will be confiscated if you can't move them to your checked luggage.

Travel Insurance

Travel insurance is imperative in helping protect you from the cost and challenges of air travel delays, lost luggage, and, most importantly, the high fees for medical care in the US. Most US insurance is effective throughout the country, but those with foreign insurance coverage should take out comprehensive medical travel insurance before arriving. Check with your home insurance company and/or doctor for travel insurance that best fits your needs.

Travel Safety Advice

Visitors can get up-to-date travel safety information from the Foreign and Commonwealth Office in the UK, the State Department in the US, and the Department of Foreign Affairs and Trade in Australia.

Tourist Information

NYC & Company, the official tourist office for the city, has a variety of visitor centers around the city, from Herald Square to City Hall. NYC & Company also has travel apps, including apps for cabs and the subway.

Health

New York City has walk-in medical clinics and emergency rooms throughout the city. Note that your hotel will also be able to assist with connecting you to doctors on call. **Mount Sinai Beth Israel** offers convenient walk-in or by-appointment services for adults and children at locations around the city, from the West Village to Midtown. Other good hospitals include **Mount Sinai Roosevelt Hospital** and **Bellevue Hospital Center**. For dental issues, Beth Israel also has walk-in clinics, or you can contact **NYU Dental Care**. Hospital emergency treatment is available 24 hours a day. If you are able, call the number on your policy first, and check which hospitals your insurance company deals with. There are also numerous 24-hour pharmacies across the city, including **Duane Reade** and **Rite Aid**. If you need an **ambulance**, call 911.

Personal Security

Despite its historical infamy as a dangerous city, New York is one of the safest urban centers in the US. That said, it is imperative always to be on the alert and aware of your surroundings. Most city parks are perfectly safe during the day, but it's usually best to avoid them after dark. If you plan to venture further afield, to the edges of Manhattan or the other boroughs, inquire at your hotel about safety concerns – and again, after dark, take caution. Deposit passports in the hotel safe and keep one credit card and some cash there. When you are out on the streets, don't advertize your tourist status by wearing a waistpack and sporting a camera around your neck. A local grocery store bag is a good, inconspicuous place for your camera. Beware of distractions when boarding buses or subways; a pickpocket behind you may be after your wallet. If you leave property on a bus, subway or taxi, call 311 to report the loss to the taxi commission or transit authority. The best way to keep track of the taxis you have traveled in is to ask for receipts, which contain identifying numbers.

Currency and Banking

Most New York banks open 9am–5pm Monday–Friday, although individual branches may have longer opening hours, including weekends. Larger banks are able to exchange foreign currency. Be prepared to show a passport or other photo identification when changing currency.

ATMs (Automated Teller Machines) are available at nearly every bank. Most ATMs are part of the worldwide Plus or Cirrus networks. They accept almost all bank cards and credit cards, although a small service fee is usually charged. ATMs also generally give the best exchange rates. Cash advances can be obtained from ATMs using Visa and MasterCard cards. Make sure you have the relevant PIN numbers when leaving home. **American Express** members can also withdraw cash with their credit card at American Express offices.

Major credit and debit cards are accepted throughout the US, in hotels, restaurants, grocery stores, sights, and for transport. While declining in use, travelers' checks in dollars issued by well-known organizations

such as American Express or **Travelex** are still accepted in the US, although personal checks from a foreign bank are not. Currency exchanges/bureaux de change are generally the most expensive ways to change money – and are slowly being rendered obsolete, thanks to the accessibility of ATMs – but you will still find these options around the city, including those run by Travelex.

Driving License

If you plan on any trips out of New York City in a rented car, be sure to bring a valid driving license with you. You will also need to show official identification with a photograph and signature, such as a passport. A credit card will also be required when renting a car.

DIRECTORY

VISAS

ESTA
📞 800 697 3662
🌐 esta.cbp.dhs.gov

CUSTOMS

US Customs
🌐 cbp.gov

TRAVEL SAFETY ADVICE

Australia
🌐 dfat.gov.au
🌐 smartraveller.gov.au

UK
🌐 www.gov.uk/
foreign-travel-advice

US
🌐 travel.state.gov

EMBASSIES

Australia
MAP K4 ▪ 150 E 42nd St
📞 212 351 6500
🌐 dfat.gov.au

Canada
MAP J3 ▪ 1251 6th Ave
📞 212 596 1628
🌐 can-am.gc.ca

New Zealand
MAP K4 ▪ 295 Madison Ave
📞 212 832 4038
🌐 nzembassy.com

UK
MAP J4 ▪ 845 3rd Ave
📞 212 745 0200
🌐 gov.uk

TOURIST INFORMATION

NYC & Company
📞 212 484 1200
🌐 www.nycgo.com

HEALTH

Ambulance
📞 911

Bellevue Hospital Center
MAP L5 ▪ 550 1st Ave
📞 212 263 7300
🌐 med.nyu.edu

Duane Reade
🌐 duanereade.com

Mount Sinai Beth Israel
📞 1 800 420 4004
🌐 bethisraelny.org

Mount Sinai Roosevelt Hospital
MAP H2 ▪ 428 W 59th St
📞 212 523 4000
🌐 www.roosevelt
hospitalnyc.org

NYU Dental Care
MAP L5 ▪ 345 E 24th St
📞 212 998 9800
🌐 dental.nyu.edu/
patientcare

Rite Aid
🌐 www.riteaid.com

CURRENCY AND BANKING

American Express
🌐 americanexpress.com

Travelex
🌐 travelex.com

Disabled Travelers

Healing Arts Initiative is a valuable resource, providing information on access to New York's cultural institutions and art centers. The **Mayor's Office for People with Disabilities** provides services to residents and also has information on city facilities. New York City law requires that all facilities built after 1987 provide entrances and accessible restroom facilities for the disabled. All city buses now have steps that can be lowered to allow wheelchair access, and most street corners also have curb cuts for wheelchairs.

The **Theater Development Fund** offers the superb Theater Access Project, which aims to increase access to theater for those who are hearing- and sight-impaired, as well as for those with other disabilities. **Lighthouse Guild** is an organization devoted to enabling the vision-impaired through rehabilitation and education. Check its website for tips on exploring New York.

Time Difference

New York is on Eastern Standard Time (EST), 5 hours behind GMT (UK time) and 3 hours ahead of PST (California time). Australia is 15 hours ahead of EST and New Zealand is 17 hours ahead.

Weather

New York has distinct seasons, with average temperatures ranging from 26° to 38° F (−3° to 3° C) in the winter and from 67° to 84° F (19° to 29° C) in the summer. Despite the averages, New York weather is predictably unpredictable. Layers are the solution – a short-sleeved knitted shirt, long-sleeved cotton shirt, and sweater will see you through most changes, plus a warm coat for winter. The months of March and August have the heaviest rainfall, but an umbrella and raincoat are useful all year round.

Metric Conversion Chart

Unlike most of the world, the US does not use the metric system. A conversion chart or electronic pocket converter makes it simple to convert miles into kilometers for distance, ounces into litres for capacity, kilograms to pounds for weight, and Fahrenheit into Celsius for temperature.

Electric Current Adapter

The US uses a 115–120V electrical current, rather than the 220V current used in Europe and other countries. Some hair dryers are equipped with an automatic conversion switch, but most 220V appliances will need adapters, which are available in airport shops and some department stores. The US also uses two-prong plugs, so travelers from countries using three-prong plugs will need a plug adapter.

Cell Phones

Most cell phones are compatible with US services, though it is key that you confirm roaming charges with your home service provider, as these can be sky-high. Many mobile phone networks have special offers to help mitigate international charges, so make sure to inquire before traveling. Another economical option is to use a US SIM card, which works with some phones. Public telephones, which take coins or telephone cards, are no longer common in New York; if you do need to use one, look for them in department stores or larger hotel lobbies.

Dialing Codes

You need to dial 1 before making any phone call in New York, even a local one. For example, to make a call to a New York number, dial 1-212, followed by the number. To call an overseas number, dial 011, plus country code, city area code, and number.

Internet Access

Most hotels offer Internet access, some free and others for a fee; ask when you book, as fees can be as high as $10–$15 a day. Free Wi-Fi is available at all public libraries, Starbucks, McDonald's, Bryant Park, Battery Park, and a number of bookstores.

Postal Service

Post offices are open from 9am to 5pm Monday

to Friday. Some are open on Saturday. The **General Post Office** stays open 24 hours a day. Most hotels sell stamps and will mail letters for their guests. Postage for letters sent within the US costs $0.49 for the first ounce (28 g), and $0.22 for additional ounces; stamps for postcards cost $0.35. To send mail internationally, postcards cost $1.20, and letters start at $1.20 for the first half-ounce (14 g).

Media

New York is a media capital, and is the East Coast headquarters of numerous outlets, from TV to magazines and newspapers. The *New York Times* is the daily newspaper in the city, covering local, national, and international news. It has extensive entertainment listings, as well as more in-depth coverage of local performances, art exhibits, and the like. The weekly *Time Out New York* has top-notch coverage of events around the city, as well as restaurant openings, as does the *Village Voice* and *New York Magazine*. The major TV networks include CBS, NBC, ABC, CNN and Fox.

Shopping

New York is one of the premiere shopping cities in the world. And while the city is widely known for its high fashion (and high prices), there is also a huge array of discount options. MasterCard and Visa are accepted everywhere; American Express and Discover in most places.

For clothes, department stores have the widest selections (see p70), Madison Avenue has the designer names (see p140) and SoHo has the trendiest fashions (see p71). For discounts, try Orchard Street (see p97) and the perennially popular Century 21 (see p70). For men's designer fashion, head to Barneys (see p70) or the traditional **Brooks Brothers**. For hipper designs, try **Thomas Pink** and for sporty outfits, **John Varvatos**. New York also has a wealth of children's clothing stores, including **My Little Sunshine** and the national chain **Children's Place**.

For books, **Barnes & Noble** carries a huge range; **Rizzoli** specializes in photography and art; **Books of Wonder** is the place to go for children's books; and the **Strand Book Store** has a wide range of used books.

Opening Hours

Business hours are usually weekdays 9am–5pm. Shops in the city open at 9 or 10am Monday to Saturday; smaller shops may close at 6 or 7pm, but department stores often stay open until 8 to 10pm, often with extended hours during the holidays. Sunday shop hours are generally from 10am to 6 or 7pm. Banks are usually open 8am–5pm on weekdays and 9am to 3pm Saturdays. Many museums close on Mondays and major holidays – check with individual venues for their specific times.

DIRECTORY

DISABLED TRAVELERS

Healing Arts Initiative
W hainyc.org

Lighthouse Guild
W lighthouseguild.org

Mayor's Office for People with Disabilities
W nyc.gov/mopd

Theater Development Fund
W tdf.org

POSTAL SERVICE

General Post Office
MAP K2 ▪ 421 8th Ave
☎ 800 ASK USPS
W usps.com

MEDIA

New York Magazine
W www.nymag.com

New York Times
W nytimes.com

Time Out New York
W timeout.com

Village Voice
W villagevoice.com

SHOPPING

Barnes & Noble
MAP J3 ▪ 555 5th Ave

Books of Wonder
MAP M3 ▪ 18 W 18th St

Brooks Brothers
MAP J4 ▪ 346 Madison Ave

Children's Place
MAP M4 ▪ 36 Union Square East

John Varvatos
MAP N3 ▪ 122 Spring St

My Little Sunshine
MAP L2 ▪ 177 9th Ave

Rizzoli
MAP L3 ▪ 1133 Broadway

Strand Book Store
MAP M4 ▪ 828 Broadway

Thomas Pink
MAP H4 ▪ 520 Madison Ave

Dining

Few US cities equal the world-class and marvelously diverse culinary offerings of New York City. Here in the foodie capital of America, you will find restaurants of all stripes throughout the five boroughs.

Different neighborhoods have their specialties: The Upper East Side features the finest French restaurants. The no-nonsense Korean eateries clustered on and around West 32nd Street dole out superb food. Fans of Chinese need look no farther than the thronged eateries of Chinatown. For hearty soul food, head up to Harlem. Italian food is served throughout New York, from Little Italy to the West Village and from Chelsea to Brooklyn. You will also find old-world delis across town, but particularly on the Lower East Side, with places like Katz's Delicatessen (see p101). When it comes to dessert, don't miss a creamy wedge of New York-style cheesecake, which makes for a sweet finale to any meal.

Although New York is pricier than other cities, you will find many discount options too, including diners where you can fill up on comfort food like juicy burgers for under $10. Note that many restaurants, like Balthazar (see p107), offer more casual bar menus, where you can sample from the chef's repertoire, usually at lower prices than are offered in the dining room. Many of the more expensive restaurants offer a set-price menu at lunch and dinner – in the early evening it may often be called the pre-theater menu. Set-price lunch buffets are popular in Indian restaurants. New York celebrates Restaurant Week (see p73) twice a year, usually in January and June, during which discount lunch and dinner menus are available at top restaurants throughout the city.

It is wise to make reservations at any restaurant above the diner/fast-food level, especially on weekends. A few of the trendiest restaurants won't even accept reservations less than two months in advance. You should be sure to make reservations for lunch at a Midtown restaurant. Note that you may still have to wait at the bar, even if you have booked ahead. Waits of an hour at the most popular spots are not unusual.

A New York city sales tax of 8.875% will be added to your bill. Service is not usually included. Tipping can run from 10% at a coffee shop to 20% at the fanciest places, with 15% an average fair tip.

New York has a wide variety of gourmet groceries and specialty food stores that are tourist attactions in themselves, where you can pick up everything from silky salmon to local produce. At **Dean & DeLuca**, a chic delicatessen on Broadway, food has been elevated to an art form – don't miss the huge selection of take-out food. The **Gourmet Garage** on Broome Street sells all kinds of delicious fresh food, in particular organic produce. Zabar's (see p145) is perhaps the finest food store in the world, with huge crowds jostling for the excellent smoked salmon, bagels, caviar, nuts and candies, cheese, and coffee.

Tours

At **Big Apple Greeter**, a volunteer guide takes small groups or couples on a free 2- to 4-hour tour of New York neighborhoods. New York has numerous other companies that offer similar tours but for a fee, and often pegged to certain themes, such as **Big Onion Walking Tours** (history) and **Urban Oyster** (history and culture). The **Municipal Art Society**, which is dedicated to preservation and excellence in urban design, offers enlightening "Discover New York" tours highlighting the buildings and neighborhoods of the city. The tours are led by architectural historians.

For boat tours, **Circle Line** offers 2- or 3-hour sightseeing cruises around Manhattan, as well as Harbor Lights evening cruises, 1-hour sails from South Street Seaport, and exciting speedboat rides. **New York Waterways** has 90-minute harbor trips.

Gray Line operates 2- to 10-hour Manhattan sightseeing trips with multilingual guides on double-decker and motor coach, plus Brooklyn tours and Harlem gospel tours. Their all-day "Classic New York" tour includes a 1-hour Statue of Liberty boat cruise and Top of the Rock ticket.

There are various backstage tours available at famous New York locations. Among the offerings are Lincoln Center (see p142), the Metropolitan Opera, Radio City Music Hall (see p63), NBC Studios (see p17), Carnegie Hall (see p129), Madison Square Garden (see p63), Grand Central Terminal (see p127), Gracie Mansion (see p139), and the New York Public Library (see p128).

See the glories and splendor of Central Park (see pp32–3) under the expert guidance of **Urban Park Rangers** or volunteer guides from the **Park Conservancy**. Free programs are held on most weekends and on some Wednesdays. A leisurely, 2-hour spin on a bicycle around the park takes in all the important sights, with a break for refreshments. Costs vary. Some include the bike rental fee. Horse-drawn

carriage tours take passengers on a short, old-fashioned ride through the park. Rides cost between $50 and $150. The **New York Botanical Garden** also holds various tours through its green space.

The Metropolitan Museum of Art (see pp34–7) offers 20 different guided tours daily in several languages, covering the highlights of the museum as well as specific galleries. Tours are included with the price of admission. The Guggenheim Museum (see pp38–9) offers family tours of the museum highlights. These are also free with the price of admission.

Accommodation

It's said that New York is the city that never sleeps, yet it offers plenty of places to do so. There are more than 90,000 hotel rooms in the city, from luxury places with a butler for every floor to

budget pads with bunk beds. Prices vary accordingly. The sky is the limit for upscale hotels, mid-range accommodation hovers around $250 to $400 per night, and budget hotels start at $100. The good news is that every neighborhood, from Midtown to Downtown, has a good mix of hotels, so you can generally find one to suit your budget. **Hotels.com**, **KAYAK** and **NYC Go** are all useful websites for booking hotels.

Beyond hotels, another hugely popular alternative is **Airbnb**, which offers accommodation in apartments and homes throughout the five boroughs. Prices are very competitive, ranging from $50 for a room in an apartment to $200 and up for a full apartment, which can be a big cost-saver for families and groups of friends. Regardless of where you stay, book early – hotels fill up quickly, no matter what the season.

DIRECTORY

DINING
Dean & Deluca
MAP N4 ▪ 560 Broadway
ⓦ deandeluca.com

Gourmet Garage
MAP P3 ▪ 489 Broome St
ⓦ gourmetgarage.com

TOURS
Big Apple Greeter
ⓒ 212 669 8159
ⓦ bigapplegreeter.org

Big Onion Walking Tours
ⓒ 212 439 1090
ⓦ bigonion.com

Carriage Tours
Central Park
ⓦ nycarriages.com

Circle Line
ⓒ 212 563 3200
ⓦ circleline42.com

Gray Line Bus Tours
ⓒ 212 397 2620
ⓦ grayline.com

Municipal Art Society
ⓒ 212 935 3960
ⓦ mas.org

New York Botanical Garden
ⓒ 718 817 8700
ⓦ nybg.org

New York Waterways
ⓒ 212 949 9470
ⓦ nywaterway.com

Park Conservancy
ⓒ 212 310 6600
ⓦ centralparknyc.org

Urban Oyster
ⓒ 347 618 8687
ⓦ urbanoyster.com

Urban Park Rangers
ⓒ 311

ACCOMMODATION
Airbnb
ⓦ airbnb.com

Hotels.com
ⓒ 866 403 9851
ⓦ hotels.com

KAYAK
ⓒ 855 529 2501
ⓦ kayak.com

NYC Go
ⓒ 212 484 1200
ⓦ nycgo.com

Places to Stay

PRICE CATEGORIES

For a standard, double room per night (with breakfast if included), taxes, and extra charges.

$ Under $250 $$ $250–$450 $$$ Over $450

Luxury Hotels

70 Park Avenue

MAP K4 ■ 70 Park Ave, New York, NY 10016 ■ 212 973 2400 ■ www.70parkave.com ■ $$

A small, sophisticated haven, with smart decor of Neo-Classical furnishings and a rich, gold-and-green color scheme. Other features include in-room spa services and a hosted wine hour from 5 to 6pm daily.

Hotel on Rivington

MAP N5 ■ 107 Rivington St, New York, NY 10002 ■ 212 475 2600 ■ www.hotelonrivington.com ■ $$

Somewhat structurally out of place in the low-slung Lower East Side, the high-rise hotel does its best to tap the area's popularity. Rooms (some with balconies) are sensuous and modern, and feature fabulous panoramas of the city.

Lotte New York Palace

MAP J4 ■ 455 Madison Ave at 50th St, New York, NY 10022 ■ 212 888 7000 ■ www.lottenypalace.com ■ $$

This legendary hotel incorporates the opulent 1882 Villard Houses and a 55-story tower, with a choice of traditional or contemporary room decor. The hotel is also home to a French bakery and a cocktail bar.

Mandarin Oriental

MAP H2 ■ 80 Columbus Circle, New York, NY 10023 ■ 212 805 8800 ■ www.mandarinoriental.com ■ $$

If your credit card can take it, there is no better way to spoil yourself than to stay at this luxurious hotel with views over Central Park and the city skyline. Rooms come equipped with flat-screen TVs and high-speed internet access; the spa is world-class.

Le Parker Meridien

MAP H3 ■ 118 West 57th St, New York, NY 10019 ■ 212 245 5000 ■ www.parkermeridien.com ■ $$

The assets of this lively hotel include the soaring public spaces, the fitness facilities, and the rooftop pool with floor-to-ceiling windows overlooking Central Park. The sleek guest rooms offer ergonomic chairs and flat-screen TVs.

Renaissance New York

MAP J3 ■ 714 7th Ave, New York, NY 10026 ■ 212 765 7676 ■ www.marriott.com ■ $$

An upscale oasis located in the Theater District, with an elegant lobby, handsome traditional furnishings, and deep tubs in the bathrooms. The hotel's restaurant offers a dazzling view of Times Square.

Roxy Hotel

MAP P3 ■ 2 6th Ave, New York, NY 10013 ■ 212 519 6600 ■ www.roxyhotelnyc.com ■ $$

TriBeCa's first hotel is still a hit. All the neighborhood gathers at the Roxy Lounge, the dramatic lobby bar with 70 translucent columns of light. Rooms are a calm counterpoint, and come with high-tech toys.

Waldorf Astoria

MAP J4 ■ 301 Park Ave, New York, NY 10017 ■ 212 355 3000 ■ www.waldorfnewyork.com ■ $$

An Art Deco landmark with luxuriously appointed guestrooms of elegant design. Visitors can experience the Guerlain Spa, a steakhouse and a sumptuous brunch.

Carlyle

MAP G4 ■ 35 East 76th St, New York, NY 10021 ■ 212 744 1600 ■ www.rosewoodhotels.com/en/the-carlyle-new-york ■ $$$

Antiques set the stage for this luxury lair that has long attracted the rich and famous with its hushed European ambience and spacious quarters decorated in understated taste. Café Carlyle is the poshest cabaret in New York City.

Four Seasons

MAP H4 ■ 57 East 57th St, New York, NY 10022 ■ 212 758 5700 ■ www.fourseasons.com ■ $$$

For luxury in a modern mode, this dramatic, pale-hued tower by I. M. Pei is the ultimate offering. The rooms are among the city's largest, and every amenity is available. The hotel bar and restaurant draw the city's elite.

Hotel Plaza Athénée
MAP H4 ▪ 37 East 64th St, New York, NY 10021 ▪ 212 734 9100 ▪ www. plaza-athenee.com ▪ $$$
Although it has 152 rooms, this Parisian outpost located on a quiet Upper East Side street retains a sense of intimacy. Facilities include a fitness center and attentive staff.

Loews Regency Hotel
MAP H4 ▪ 540 Park Ave, New York, NY 10021 ▪ 212 759 4100 ▪ www. loewshotels.com/ regency-hotel ▪ $$$
A gilt and mirrored sanctuary favored by show-business moguls, the hotel has Regency decor, which inspired the name, and oversize suites. The restaurant is a power breakfast favorite.

The Mark
MAP F3 ▪ 25 East 77th St, New York, NY 10021 ▪ 212 744 4300 ▪ www. themarkhotel.com ▪ $$$
Discreetly elegant, this member of the Mandarin group is a contemporary sanctuary. The clientele are appreciative of the hotel's Biedermeier furnishings, the antique prints, and the luxury linens.

Mercer Hotel
MAP N4 ▪ 147 Mercer St, New York, NY 10012 ▪ 212 966 6060 ▪ www. mercerhotel.com ▪ $$$
A hit with Hollywood luminaries, the Mercer is housed in an 1890 structure built for John Jacob Astor II, and makes good use of lofty spaces and a voguish, shabby-chic look.

Michelangelo
MAP J3 ▪ 152 West 51st St, New York, NY 10019 ▪ 212 765 0505 ▪ www. michelangelohotel.com ▪ $$$
A handsome New York outpost of an Italian hotel, with unusually spacious rooms in a choice of Art Deco, French Country, or Neo-Classical styles.

Park Hyatt
MAP H3 ▪ 157 West 57th St, New York, NY 10019 ▪ 646 774 1234 ▪ www. newyork.park.hyatt.com ▪ $$$
This superlative hotel, opened in 2014, is the first Park Hyatt in New York City and the first five-star hotel to have opened in the city for more than a decade. Fittingly, every-thing within its walls is top of the line, from the massive, light rooms to the swimming pool that has music piped into it via underwater speakers from nearby Carnegie Hall.

Peninsula
MAP H3 ▪ 700 5th Ave, New York, NY 10019 ▪ 212 956 2888 ▪ www.newyork. peninsula.com ▪ $$$
The Hong Kong hotel group has done itself proud, turning a 1905 classic into state-of-the-art luxury lodging. Rooms are contemporary with Art Nouveau accents and bedside controls for the many gadgets. The health club with pool is superb.

Pierre
MAP H3 ▪ 2 East 61st St, New York, NY 10021 ▪ 212 838 8000 ▪ www. tajhotels.com/pierre ▪ $$$
A landmark opposite Central Park since the 1930s, the Pierre is a bastion of old-world elegance. With staff outnumbering guests by a ratio of three to one, the first-class service is a hall-mark that draws the elite.

The Plaza
MAP H3 ▪ 5th Ave at Central Park South, New York, NY 1001 ▪ 212 759 3000 ▪ www.fairmont. com/the-plaza-new-york ▪ $$$
The grande dame of New York City hotels, this 19-story French Renaissance building opened in 1907 as a residence for the wealthy and is now a National Historic Landmark. The hotel also boasts a champagne bar and tranquil gardens.

St. Regis
MAP H4 ▪ 2 East 55th St, New York, NY 10022 ▪ 212 753 4500 ▪ www.stregis newyork.com ▪ $$$
The elegant guest rooms and suites at this Beaux Arts beauty come complete with Louis XVI furnishings, silk wall coverings, chandeliers, and a butler tending to your every need. The famed King Cole Bar, which serves food as well as its renowned cocktails, is attached to the hotel.

Sherry Netherland
MAP H3 ▪ 781 5th Ave, New York, NY 10022 ▪ 212 355 2800 ▪ www.sherry netherland.com ▪ $$$
Dating from 1927, this ornate hotel features a spectacular marble-and-bronze lobby and a signature clock that marks the 5th Avenue entrance. The rooms are spacious, and most of them have glorious views over Central Park.

Sofitel
MAP J3 ■ 45 West 44th St, New York, NY 10036 ■ 212 354 8844 ■ www.sofitel-new-york.com ■ $$$

Although it only opened its doors in 2000, this hotel boasts a distinct feeling of old-world elegance and charm. Rooms are comfortable, adorned with tasteful art, and sound-proofed. The gift shop stocks exclusive, hard-to-find French products.

Trump International Hotel and Tower
MAP H2 ■ 1 Central Park West, New York, NY 10023 ■ 212 299 1000 ■ www.trumphotel collection.com ■ $$$

High ceilings and tall windows result in fabulous views of New York city and Central Park. Room amenities are equally bountiful – Jacuzzis, room service from the three-Michelin-starred Jean-Georges *(see p66)*, and even laptops are available upon request.

W New York – Union Square
MAP M4 ■ Park Ave South, New York, NY 10003 ■ 212 253 9119 ■ www.wnewyorkunion square.com ■ $$$

Designer David Rockwell has transformed this charming Beaux Arts building into a contemporary showstopper, complete with a beautiful floating staircase. Trademark W features include books and chess sets in the lobby, a well-equipped fitness area, and a lively glamorous bar.

Boutique Hotels

Inn at Irving Place
MAP M4 ■ 56 Irving Place, New York, NY 10002 ■ 212 533 4600 ■ www.innatirving.com ■ $

Two Greek Revival town houses form an elegant, 12-room inn that could have come straight out of a Jane Austen novel. Rooms are antique-filled and come with fireplaces; only the modern TVs bring them up to date.

The Jane
MAP M2 ■ 113 Jane St, New York, NY 10014 ■ 212 924 6700 ■ www.thejanenyc.com ■ $

This Bohemian-inspired hotel in the West Village has rooms modeled after vintage ship cabins, ranging from "bunk bed cabins" to "captain's cabins." There are also complimentary bicycles.

The Archer
MAP K3 ■ 45 West 38th St, New York, NY 10018 ■ 212 719 4100 ■ www.archerhotel.com ■ $$

This 21-story hotel pays homage to the surrounding Garment District by incorporating fabric-inspired design palettes, along with floor-to-ceiling windows, wood floors, and exposed brick. The rooftop bar has views of the Empire State and Chrysler Buildings.

Franklin
MAP F4 ■ 164 East 87th St, New York, NY 10128 ■ 212 369 1000 ■ www.franklinhotel.com ■ $$

An affordable lodging on the Upper East Side, the Franklin offers style rather than size, with sleek furnishings and compact rooms. Breakfast is complimentary, and hot drinks are served all day.

Hotel Giraffe
MAP L4 ■ 365 Park Ave South, New York, NY 10016 ■ 212 685 7700 ■ www.hotelgiraffe.com ■ $$

A glass-walled lobby leads to this award-winning hotel with stylish Retro decor and a delightful roof terrace. Indulgent rooms feature bedside controls for the window shades. Light breakfast and snacks are complimentary, and the Italian restaurant downstairs serves homestyle fare.

Iroquois
MAP J3 ■ 49 West 44th St, New York, NY 10036 ■ 212 840 3080 ■ www.iroquoisny.com ■ $$

One of the suites in this elegant hotel is named for James Dean, who lived here from 1951 to 1953; other Hollywood guests over the years have included Sandra Bullock and Johnny Depp. Rooms are modestly sized but deluxe, with classic French decor and floor-to-ceiling marble in the bathrooms. Packages offer excellent rates.

The James
MAP P3 ■ 227 Grand St, New York, NY 10013 ■ 212 465 2000 ■ www.jameshotels.com ■ $$

Gaze out on the lights of Manhattan from the rooftop bar and seasonal pool of this trendy hotel. Later, cozy up in the handsome rooms, waking to a complimentary breakfast by the well-known chef David Burke.

Library Hotel

MAP K4 ▪ 299 Madison Ave, New York, NY 10017 ▪ 212 983 4500 ▪ www. libraryhotel.com ▪ $$

This themed hotel is filled with books. Each of the 10 floors is devoted to a Dewey Decimal System category, such as Philosophy or the Arts, with appropriate volumes in each room. It includes a rooftop sitting room and terrace, and a complimentary wine and cheese reception every evening.

Morgans Hotel

MAP K4 ▪ 237 Madison Ave, New York, NY 10016 ▪ 212 686 0300 ▪ www. morganshotelgroup.com ▪ $$

Ian Schrager's understated first New York hotel still has loyal fans for its uncluttered, clean look and clever, functional built-ins in the small but trendy rooms. Celebrity favorite restaurant Asia de Cuba adjoins the lobby.

The Muse

MAP J3 ▪ 130 West 46th St, New York, NY 10036 ▪ 212 485 2400 ▪ www. themusehotel.com ▪ $$

A boutique hotel, the Muse inspires with a smart lobby decorated with Matisse-like murals, and good-size rooms, some of which come with their own balcony. Occasionally, the staff host a happy hour with complimentary wine for guests.

SIXTY SoHo

MAP N3 ▪ 60 Thompson St, New York, NY 10012 ▪ 877 431 0400 ▪ www. sixtyhotels.com/hotel/soho ▪ $$

SoHo's 12-story luxurious hotel offers 97 rooms and suites, each elegantly decked out with custom furnishings and marble bathrooms. Guests can enjoy the view from the roof garden lounge or watch the neighborhood scene from the sidewalk café. Sessanta, by restaurateur John McDonald, serves up coastal Italian fare in a casual setting.

Bryant Park

MAP K3 ▪ 40 West 40th St, New York, NY 10018 ▪ 212 869 0100 ▪ www. bryantparkhotel.com ▪ $$$

Raymond Hood's 1924 American Radiator Building has become an ultra-contemporary hotel, with giant windows, bold, red-lacquered lobby desks, and lavishly equipped, pale-hued rooms that are the last word in minimalist decor. Koi restaurant serves Japanese food with a Californian influence.

Casablanca

MAP J3 ▪ 147 West 43rd St, New York, NY 10036 ▪ 212 869 1212 ▪ www. casablancahotel.com ▪ $$$

A Moroccan theme, complete with tiles and arches, sets this Theater District hotel apart. Rooms are small but well furnished. Continental breakfast is served in – where else? – Rick's Café.

Crosby Street Hotel

MAP N4 ▪ 79 Crosby St, New York, NY 10012 ▪ 212 226 6400 ▪ www. firmdalehotels.com ▪ $$$

SoHo's favorite British import offers plush rooms (upper rooms have views of lower Manhattan), a daily service of proper English tea, and a lively bar and restaurant. There is even a screening room featuring weekly films.

Lowell

MAP H4 ▪ 28 East 63rd St, New York, NY 10021 ▪ 212 838 1400 ▪ www. lowellhotel.com ▪ $$$

Luxurious and intimate, the Lowell exudes an old-world charm. Its rooms feature wood-burning fireplaces, libraries, flowers, and marble baths. The decor is an eclectic and appealing mix of French, Art Deco, and Oriental.

NoMad

MAP L3 ▪ 1170 Broadway, New York, NY 10001 ▪ 212 796 1500 ▪ www. thenomadhotel.com ▪ $$$

Relive old-world Paris at this elegant hotel that features rooms with high ceilings, custom-designed furnishings, clawfoot tubs, and minibars disguised by leather steamer trunks.

Refinery Hotel

MAP K3 ▪ 63 West 38th St, New York, NY 10018 ▪ 646 664 0310 ▪ www. refineryhotelnewyork. com ▪ $$$

Celebrate the history of the Garment District at this former hat factory in the 20th-century Colony Arcade building that has been transformed into a sophisticated hotel. The neighborhood's past is revealed throughout the building, from sewing-machine desks in the airy rooms to carpets emblazoned with a design of interlocking scissors.

For a key to hotel price categories see p172

Viceroy

MAP H3 ▪ 120 West 57th St, New York, NY 10019 ▪ 212 830 8000 ▪ www. viceroyhotelsandresorts. com ▪ $$$

For some Downtown edge in Uptown, head to this stylish hotel with a distinctive black brick-and-steel facade, a sexy rooftop lounge and spot-on vistas of leafy Central Park. Rooms are equipped with portable sound systems and espresso makers.

Business Hotels

Hotel Metro

MAP K3 ▪ 45 West 35th St, New York, NY 10001 ▪ 212 947 2500 ▪ www. hotelmetronyc.com ▪ $

Popular with the fashion industry, but also good value, the Metro has a sophisticated Art Deco feel and offers good-sized rooms. Public spaces include a library, a rooftop terrace, and a spacious dining room.

Benjamin

MAP J4 ▪ 125 East 50th St, New York, NY 10022 ▪ 212 715 2500 ▪ www. thebenjamin.com ▪ $$

This 1927 building designed by Emery Roth has been converted to an all-suite hotel designed for executives, with all the requisite high-tech gadgetry and a chic restaurant, the National, which serves bistro dishes with a Modern American influence by chef Geoffrey Zakarian.

Fifty NYC

MAP J4 ▪ 155 East 50th St, New York, NY 10022 ▪ 212 751 5710 ▪ www. affinia.com/fifty ▪ $$

This stylish residential hotel situated in the heart of Midtown boasts large suites with full kitchens and separate living areas that are outfitted with comfy sofa beds, making this an ideal choice for families and groups.

Gild Hall

MAP Q4 ▪ 15 Gold St, New York, NY 10038 ▪ 212 232 7700 ▪ www. thompsonhotels.com/ hotels/gild-hall ▪ $$

Combining luxury with business in the heart of the Financial District, the Gild Hall is a venture from the Thompson Hotels Group. The sleek rooms are well equipped and the hotel features a library, champagne bar, and a warm, wood-paneled restaurant serving authentic Italian food.

Hilton New York

MAP J3 ▪ 1335 6th Ave, New York, NY 10019 ▪ 212 586 7000 ▪ www. hilton.com ▪ $$

The quintessential business hotel, the 2,040-room Hilton boasts a central location, huge ballroom, and extensive meeting facilities. A redesign transformed the lobby, upgraded the guest rooms, and added a large fitness club and spa.

Hotel 48LEX

MAP J4 ▪ 517 Lexington Ave at 48th, New York, NY 10017 ▪ 212 838 1234 ▪ www.hotel48lex newyork.com ▪ $$

This glossy, contemporary hotel is located within walking distance of Grand Central Terminal and Central Park. All rooms and suites are spacious and sleek, styled in the manner of a luxury pied-à-terre.

The Manhattan at Times Square

MAP J3 ▪ 790 7th Ave, New York, NY 10019 ▪ 212 581 3300 ▪ www. manhattanhoteltimes square.com ▪ $$

An indoor pool, sauna, and free continental breakfast are among the features of this 22-story hotel, a quieter neighbor of the Sheraton New York, which serves as a major convention venue. The Theater District is just steps away.

Millennium Broadway

MAP J3 ▪ 145 West 44th St, New York, NY 10036 ▪ 212 768 4400 ▪ www. millenniumhotels.com ▪ $$

A postmodern skyscraper, encompassing a theater, the Millennium is sleek and streamlined. The compact rooms have cityscape views and are well appointed, with high-tech features that include voicemail in a range of different languages.

ONE UN New York

MAP J5 ▪ U.N. Plaza, 44th St between 1st & 2nd Ave, New York, NY 10017 ▪ 212 758 1234 ▪ www. millenniumhotels.com ▪ $$

Kevin Roche's soaring tower close to the UN Headquarters attracts an international clientele. There are panoramic views from the rooms beginning on the 28th floor, a glass-enclosed swimming pool, and New York City's only indoor hotel tennis court.

Ritz Carlton Battery Park

MAP Q3 ▪ 2 Watt St, New York, NY ▪ 212 344 0800 ▪ www.ritzcarlton.com ▪ $$

This luxury hotel has stunning views of the harbor and impressive attention to detail. Special touches include telescopes in rooms, feather beds, and a "bath butler." Children will enjoy the Skyscraper Museum close by.

Mid-Range Hotels

Belleclaire Hotel

MAP F2 ▪ 250 West 77th St, New York, NY 10024 ▪ 212 362 7700 ▪ www.hotelbelleclaire.com ▪ $

The rooms in this property are sparse, but well-designed and stylish. Bathrooms are small, and some rooms have a shared bath. Ask for a family suite if kids are in tow. Right in the heart of the Upper West Side, it is a great base for exploring.

Blakely New York

MAP H3 ▪ 136 West 55th St, New York, NY 10019 ▪ 212 245 1800 ▪ www.blakelynewyork.com ▪ $

The cosmopolitan mood of this hotel begins in the Art Deco lobby with clocks showing the time around the world. The contemporary rooms have cherrywood furnishings, and come equipped with kitchenettes.

Chelsea Savoy

MAP L2 ▪ 204 West 23rd St, New York, NY 10011 ▪ 212 929 9353 ▪ www.chelseasavoy nyc.com ▪ $

This is an excellent neighborhood lodging, close to the shops, cafés, and galleries of Chelsea. Pleasantly furnished rooms are of a decent size, with all the necessary amenities. Choose rooms that face away from 23rd Street.

Excelsior

MAP F2 ▪ 45 West 81st St, New York, NY 10024 ▪ 212 362 9200 ▪ www.excelsiorhotelny.com ▪ $

A lavish, old-world lobby fronts a refurbished, well-appointed hotel with traditional decor, many suites, in-room computers, and Wi-Fi. A breakfast room, a library, outdoor decks, and a media room are among other features.

Hudson Hotel

MAP H2 ▪ 356 West 58th St, New York, NY 10019 ▪ 212 554 6000 ▪ www.morganshotelgroup.com ▪ $

Ian Schrager and Philippe Starck designed this contemporary, 1,000-room extravaganza, a melting pot of styles described as "organized chaos." The rooms were originally low-budget, but rates went up when the hotel became a hit.

Salisbury Hotel

MAP H3 ▪ 123 West 57th St, New York, NY 10019 ▪ 212 246 1300 ▪ www.nycsalisbury.com ▪ $

Well-placed for visits to Carnegie Hall, shops, and theaters, the Salisbury was once an apartment-hotel and still retains a certain quiet, low-key ambience. It features traditional American decor, good-sized accommodations, and a pleasant breakfast room.

Doubletree Guest Suites

MAP J3 ▪ 1568 Broadway, New York, NY 10036 ▪ 212 719 1600 ▪ www.doubletreehotels.com ▪ $$

The price of an ordinary hotel room will buy you two comfortable rooms (one with a sofa bed), two TVs, and a kitchenette at this modern Theater District hotel.

Hotel Roger

MAP L4 ▪ 131 Madison Ave, New York, NY 10016 ▪ 212 448 7000 ▪ www.therogernewyork.com ▪ $$

An atrium with floor-to-ceiling windows and a mezzanine lounge where complimentary breakfast is served are among the modern features of this hotel, but the rooms are styled more cozily.

Lucerne

MAP F2 ▪ 201 West 79th St, New York, NY 10024 ▪ 212 875 1000 ▪ www.thelucernehotel.com ▪ $$

Housed in a terra-cotta-trimmed 1903 building, this is the best of the Upper West Side's excellent-value hotels. It has a comfortable lobby, business and fitness centers, a rooftop terrace, and tasteful rooms.

Mansfield Hotel

MAP J4 ▪ 12 West 44th St, New York, NY 10036 ▪ 212 277 8700 ▪ www.mansfieldhotel.com ▪ $$

This distinctive Theater District hotel features a copper-domed salon, soaring lobby, and free continental breakfast and afternoon tea. The rooms all have the feel of private apartments.

For a key to hotel price categories see p172

San Carlos Hotel

MAP J4 ■ 50 East 50th St, New York, NY 10022 ■ 800 722 2012 ■ www.sancarloshotel.com ■ $$
All the extra touches – from the morning paper and the nighttime chocolates on your pillow, to the flat-screen TVs – make the San Carlos seem like a four-star hotel. The decor is modern, and it also offers a fitness center.

Shoreham

MAP H3 ■ 33 West 55th St, New York, NY 10019 ■ 212 247 6700 ■ www.shorehamhotel.com ■ $$
A thoroughly modern makeover has included creative use of light and textures. Guest rooms are decorated in pale tones. The breakfast is complimentary, and cappuccinos and espressos are also free to guests between 6am and 11am.

Warwick Hotel

MAP J3 ■ 65 West 54th St, New York, NY 10019 ■ 212 247 2700 ■ www.warwickhotelny.com ■ $$
William Randolph Hearst built the Warwick Hotel in 1927, with large, elegant rooms, and celebrities have been staying here ever since. Room rates have gone up since renovation added stylish decor and bathrooms of Italian marble.

Washington Square Hotel

MAP N3 ■ 103 Waverly Place, New York, NY 10011 ■ 212 777 9515 ■ www.washingtonsquarehotel.com ■ $$
A haven in the heart of Greenwich Village. Rooms are tiny and the hallways are painfully narrow, but the decor is pleasant. A continental breakfast is included, and you can say you stayed where Bob Dylan and Joan Baez once hung out.

Algonquin Hotel

MAP J3 ■ 59 West 44th St, New York, NY 10019 ■ 212 840 6800 ■ www.algonquinhotel.com ■ $$$
A literary landmark, famous for the clique of writers known as the "Round Table," which met for regular luncheons here in the early 20th century. The Algonquin remains an oasis of civility, with antique lighting fixtures and *New Yorker* cartoon wallpaper in the halls. Rooms are small and charming.

Hotel Elysée

MAP J4 ■ 60 East 54th St, New York, NY 10022 ■ 212 753 1066 ■ www.elyseehotel.com ■ $$$
The Elysée manages to convey the warmth of a small inn, serving not only breakfast, but also wine and *hors d'oeuvres* in the evening. Room service is from the Monkey Bar & Restaurant.

The Standard

MAP M2 ■ 848 Washington St, New York, NY 10014 ■ 212 645 4646 ■ www.standardhotels.com ■ $$$
This outpost of LA's hip crash pad has its own style. Set just off the Meatpacking District, the Standard has a happening 18th-floor bar. The 337 rooms, with floor-to-ceiling windows and fantastic views, are airy and open. The glass-enclosed showers are not for the modest.

Budget Accommodations

Best Western Seaport Inn

MAP Q4 ■ 33 Peck Slip, New York, NY 10038 ■ 212 766 6600 ■ www.seaportinn.com ■ $
Situated close to South Street Seaport, this restored 19th-century building has the predictable rooms of a chain hotel, but the lobby is cozy and breakfast is included in the price.

Carlton Arms

MAP L4 ■ 160 East 25th St, New York, NY 10010 ■ 212 679 0680 ■ www.carltonarms.com ■ $
There may not be a TV or a phone, but this budget haven is popular with young visitors for its hip spirit and funky halls, with walls painted by young artists. Private bathrooms are available in just under half of the hotel's 54 colorful rooms.

Cosmopolitan Hotel

MAP Q3 ■ 95 West Broadway, New York, NY 10007 ■ 212 566 1900 ■ www.cosmohotel.com ■ $
This budget gem in the heart of trendy TriBeCa has small but well-maintained rooms with equally tiny but clean bathrooms. There is also easy access to public transport.

Harlem Flophouse

MAP C3 ■ 242 West 123rd St, New York, NY 10027 ■ 212 662 0678 ■ www.harlemflophouse.com ■ $
This restored, 19th-century brownstone features four charming guest rooms each with sinks, and two

shared bathrooms with antique clawfoot tubs. The decor and furnishings evoke an old-world vibe.

Herald Square Hotel
MAP K3 ▪ 19 West 31st St, New York, NY 10001 ▪ 212 279 4017 ▪ www.herald squarehotel.com ▪ $
The cherub over the front door remains from the days when this Beaux Arts building was the first home of *LIFE* magazine. This tiny, budget hideaway has been tastefully renovated. The rooms are small but nicely decorated, and the bathrooms are modern.

Hostelling International
MAP D2 ▪ 891 Amsterdam Ave, New York, NY 10025 ▪ 212 932 2300 ▪ hinewyork.org ▪ Most without en-suite bathrooms ▪ $
Although run by American Youth Hostels, all ages are welcome to share the clean, safe rooms here. There are 4 to 12 beds per dormitory, available at budget prices. This 624-bed facility offers a coffee bar, cafeteria, and self-service kitchen.

Hotel Edison
MAP J3 ▪ 228 West 47th St, New York, NY 10036 ▪ 212 840 5000 ▪ www.edisonhotelnyc.com ▪ $
This has long been one of the best-value hotels in the city's Theater District. Built in 1931, it features a stunning Art Deco lobby and small, well-decorated rooms with updated bathrooms. The hotel's café and restaurant are favorite, inexpensive pre-theater dining choices.

Pod 51
MAP J4 ▪ 230 East 51st St, New York, NY 10022 ▪ 212 355 0300 ▪ www.thepodhotel.com ▪ $
Space is tight but the location is prime. High-tech features include free Wi-Fi and iPod connections. Rooms range from queens to bunk beds. Singles with shared baths start at $89.

La Quinta Manhattan
MAP K3 ▪ 17 West 32nd St, New York, NY 10001 ▪ 212 736 1600 ▪ www.laquintamanhattanny.com ▪ $
On a Midtown block known for its Korean restaurants, this renovated building offers comfortable and well-furnished rooms, modern bathrooms, and first-class services at reasonable rates.

Union Square Inn
MAP M4 ▪ 209 East 14th Street, New York, NY 10003 ▪ 212 614 0512 ▪ www.unionsquareinn.com ▪ $
All the standard comforts at reasonable prices. Rooms have no views and are nothing to write home about, but the bathrooms are clean and the beds comfortable. European breakfast is on offer at the in-house café (limited hours). Those who wish to shop will find Union Square is a good spot for some retail therapy.

Yotel
MAP K2 ▪ 570 10th Ave, New York, NY 10035 ▪ 646 449 7700 ▪ www.yotel.com ▪ $
The sleek, playful Yotel, the largest hotel to open in New York City in 2011,

was inspired by the trendy capsule hotels of Asia. The rooms may be snug but they are ergonomically designed, with comfortable beds that electronically fold into couches, and come with flat-screen TVs.

citizenM
MAP J3 ▪ 218 West 50th St, New York, NY 10019 ▪ 212 461 3638 ▪ www.citizenm.com ▪ $$
"Affordable luxury for the people" is the slogan at this Dutch hotel chain, which has lots of high-tech amenities such as 24-hour self-check-in via touch-screen kiosks and grab-and-go communal kitchens. There are also comfortable shared "living room" spaces.

The Evelyn
MAP L3 ▪ 7 East 27th St, New York, NY 10016 ▪ 855 468 3051 ▪ www.theevelyn.com ▪ $$
This historic New York hotel underwent a total revamp in 2014. Its rooms are now decked out in Art Nouveau style with a subtle music theme throughout and come equipped with a full set of sleek amenities, including iPhone docks and stylish Frette linens.

Hotel Beacon
MAP G2 ▪ 2130 Broadway, New York, NY 10023 ▪ 212 787 1100 ▪ www.beaconhotel.com ▪ $$
Named for the famous theater next door *(see p64)*, the Beacon is a relaxed, comfortable hotel, with generous rooms with standard decor, and, a big plus, kitchenettes with refrigerators and microwaves.

For a key to hotel price categories see p172

General Index

Page numbers in **bold**
refer to Top 10 highlights.